TERRORIZING LATINA/O IMMIGRANTS

ANNA SAMPAIO

TERRORIZING LATINA/O IMMIGRANTS

Race, Gender, and Immigration Politics in the Age of Security

TEMPLE UNIVERSITY PRESS
Philadelphia • *Rome* • *Tokyo*

TEMPLE UNIVERSITY PRESS
Philadelphia, Pennsylvania 19122
www.temple.edu/tempress

Library of Congress Cataloging-in-Publication Data

Sampaio, Anna, 1969–
   Terrorizing Latina/o immigrants : race, gender, and immigration politics in the
age of security / Anna Sampaio.
      pages cm
   Includes bibliographical references and index.
   ISBN 978-1-4399-1285-0 (hardback : alk. paper) — ISBN 978-1-4399-1286-7
(paper : alk. paper) — ISBN 978-1-4399-1287-4 (e-book)   1. Latin America—
Emigration and immigration—History—21st century.   2. United States—
Emigration and immigration—Government policy—History—21st century.
3. War on Terrorism, 2001–2009.   4. Hispanic Americans—Social conditions.
I. Title.
   JV7398.S36 2015
   325.73—dc23

                                                              2015005942

∞ The paper used in this publication meets the requirements of the American
National Standard for Information Sciences—Permanence of Paper for Printed
Library Materials, ANSI Z39.48-1992

Printed in the United States of America

9 8 7 6 5 4

Contents

Preface and Acknowledgments

My interests, like those of many academics engaged in the study of race, gender, immigration, and politics, are personal, professional, and political. As a first-generation Latina, I have long pursued the study of Latina/o politics and women's and gender studies as a means of making sense of my everyday life and explaining the relationships, interactions, tensions, changes, and events that affect the communities in which I have lived. My work has been informed by a line of feminist theory and critical race scholarship dedicated to producing "theory in the flesh" as a means of understanding the particular configurations of race, class, and gender in our own lives.[1] My grounding in U.S.-based racial/ethnic and gender studies intersects with the politics of immigration from Latin America, particularly the changing discourse surrounding Latin American immigrants, its impact on public law and policy, and the changes among U.S. Latina/o and Latin American communities as a consequence of globalization. Eventually, this intersection of Latina/o and Latin American studies evolved into its own field of transnational Latina/o studies—namely, those policies, practices, organizations, and everyday occurrences that cross political borders, alter the configuration of U.S. Latina/o communities, and enter the boundaries of Latina/o scholarship.[2]

The assemblage of personal, professional, and political interests between Latina/o and Latin American communities led me to work in Chiapas, Mexico, where I studied and organized with "communities in resistance" in the formation of cross-border networks of Chicanas, Latinas, indigenous and Latin American women in the late 1990s.[3] Like many people whose research involves participant observation and direct engagement, I became increasingly concerned with the obstacles to transnational organizing in the wake of events surrounding September 11, 2001, especially the unwarranted escalation of spying and scrutiny of everyday activities. The rapid changes to federal, state, and local policies and the resurgence of the state as a domestic and international security regime triggered both fear and anger. Having a history of family members who lived under authoritarian dictators in Latin America, I knew what it looked like when people feared their own government. I had seen the faces of people whose own governments turned on them, scrutinized them without cause, and turned them into enemy outsiders. I knew how those circumstances weighed on people, how those who migrated carried for decades the imprimatur of a government's terrorizing effect, and I was horrified to see the same signs in the faces of women, men, and children I met in Chiapas—and, increasingly, among Latina/o immigrants in the United States.

Witnessing these changes and finding a way to make sense of and write about them was an enormous challenge. Determining how to document, catalogue, and analyze the daily abuses that Latinas/os experienced at the hands of not only immigration authorities but also nativists who felt unleashed and legitimized by their own government was a constant struggle. Like many, I cringed when I read newspaper articles and felt a pit in my stomach as I poured over court records, taking in transcripts, testimonies, interviews, and personal accounts from detainees. My despair was eclipsed only by my anger—which turned out to be a healthy response that kept me writing even when it seemed like a hopeless venture.

The enormity of the task at hand and the many challenges I encountered created a fury of writing and research (in addition to the construction of two separate databases, the first containing all the restrictive immigration legislation passed by Congress between 2001 and 2009, and the second listing the raids and roundups carried out across the country between 2001 and 2010 based on reporting by local, regional, and national news outlets) and generated long moments of pause as I tried to absorb and make sense of it all. Thankfully, my periods of inertia were interrupted by the advice, cajoling, and inspiration of colleagues, friends, and family across the country.

My most heartfelt appreciation goes to Mary Hawkesworth in the Department of Women's and Gender Studies at Rutgers University. So much of my thinking and writing on intersectionality has been shaped by her groundbreaking work bridging feminist theory, critical race scholarship, and political science and by her modeling of social justice in everyday life. I am deeply grateful for her willingness and capacity to provide thoughtful feedback, for her advice and support on countless professional issues, and for her mentoring of not only me and other women of color but also the field of intersectional scholarship.

I also owe a significant debt of gratitude to Ange-Marie Hancock, Ron Schmidt, Cristina Beltran, and Edwina Barvosa, whose work on questions of race, gender, immigration, Latinas/os, and intersectionality has unraveled numerous dilemmas in my own head, introduced new directions to the field, and inspired me to write. Collectively, they have done more to grow the field of intersectional scholarship through panels, workshops, articles, books, blogs, series, organized sections, new journals, and editorships than seems humanly possible.

Rutgers University provided me with the funding, resources, and support to research, write, and edit during a critical juncture in the book's development. The Institute for Women's Leadership Consortium in New Brunswick, and particularly the Department of Women's, and Gender Studies, the Institute for Research on Women, and the Center for American Women and Politics stand as the premier producers of interdisciplinary and intersectional feminist research. I am indebted to the Department of Women's and Gender Studies at Rutgers for providing me with a visiting appointment in 2008 and a full appointment to the faculty between 2009 and 2011. The opportunity to work with such an exceptional consortium of academics and activists expanded my own abilities while enriching the research with new methods and approaches to immigration and intersectionality. The semester I spent in the Institute for Research on Women as part of the Interdisciplinary Research Seminar was a truly remarkable experience, and I owe a special note of appreciation to the colleagues who provided feedback on early drafts of Chapter 6, including Sara Angevine, Jessica Birkenholtz, Darcie Fontaine, Dorothy Hodgson, Allan Isaac, Rocio Magana, Bahia Munem, Julie Rajan, Nancy Rao, Arlene Stein, Alex Warner, and Deborah Gray White.

Nothing serves as a stronger motivation to write than the support of friends and peers. I drew endless inspiration from colleagues who continually shared thoughtful insights and encouraging words, who invited me to join their writing groups and faculty support networks, or who simply offered compassionate shoulders when writing was especially tough. I am thankful for the support of colleagues in multiple institutions, but I am especially grateful to Ramon Chacon, Juliana Chang, Marilyn Edelstein, Laura Ellingson, Eileen Elrod, Linda Garber, Alma Garcia, Anthony Hazard, Kristen Heyer, Francisco Jimenez, James Lai, Sharmila Lodhia, Courtney Mohler, Christine Montgomery, Laura Nichols, Ana Maria Pineda, and Juan Velasco, at Santa Clara University (SCU); Nikol Alexander-Floyd, Radhika Balakrishnan, Barbara Balliet, Ethel Brooks, Abena Busia, Susan J. Carroll, Cynthia Daniels, Carlos Decena, Marissa Fuentes, Judy Gerson, Nancy Hewitt, and

Mary Trigg at Rutgers University; and Jana Everett, Lucy McGuffey, Glenn Morris, Christoph Stefes, and Steve Thomas at the University of Colorado, Denver. I am also grateful to the Provost Office at Santa Clara University for a generous grant to complete final details on the manuscript. Colleagues in the Race, Ethnicity, and Politics section of the American Political Science Association; in the Latina/o caucus; and in the Women and Gender Justice caucus provided me with an intellectual home that was supportive and generative, particularly Christina Bejarano, Susan Burgess, Adrian Felix, Daniel HoSang, Celeste Montoya Kirk, Pei-te Lien, Ray Rocco, Peri Schwartz-Shea, Christine Sierra, and Dvora Yanow. A special note of thanks goes to Janni Aragon and Wendi Walker for the many hours spent over e-mail, on the phone, and in person talking, eating, *chismeando,* and sharing our lives and children (both human and canine) and to Badia Ahad for equipping me with the best possible writing and coping skills during the difficult phase of editing and revisions.

My sincerest appreciation also goes to Alex Holzman and Aaron Javsicas at Temple University Press for their sage advice and artful shepherding of the book. Joan Vidal and Heather Wilcox ensured a seamless and timely production along with masterful editing. I am equally grateful for the thoughtful and critical feedback from anonymous reviewers, whose questions and comments helped strengthen the theoretical linkages throughout the book and made the end product so much clearer and cogent.

Key to the substance of the book is the research on legislative changes since 2001 and enforcement practices. Cataloging and analyzing these issues required the construction of two new databases, countless hours of logging data, and even longer hours of analysis. None of that painstaking work would have been possible without the superb skills of research assistants at the University of Colorado, Denver, and Rutgers University. I am especially grateful to Janna Ferguson, Tara King, Kathryn Miller, and Bahia Munem for their detailed reading, coding, and analysis and their thoughtful feedback. These students exceeded every expectation: They not only efficiently hunted down the sources and data I requested; they also took the initiative to find additional sources, including material that was not yet published, and even went so far as to speak with multiple research teams personally to cull information and insights on reports and gain access to material that was not yet available to the public. Their work made substantive contributions to the quality of my own research, and I would not have been able to complete the project without them. In addition to contributing excellent research skills, they inspired me with their insight, energy, and hunger for new knowledge.

I am also grateful to undergraduate and graduate students in both the Department of Women's and Gender Studies and the Program in Women and Politics at Rutgers University and to students at SCU, who read drafts of the manuscript as it was being developed and provided valuable insights that helped make the book accessible for students at every level. The list includes Gaby Alvarado, Denise Castillo Chavez, Genevieve Cato, Carolyn Craig, Jenny Daniel-Bucay, McKenzie Darr, Debotri Dhar, Kelly Dittmar, Bobak Esfandiari, Lizette Estrada-Valencia, Ashley Falzetti, Libby Furrow, Mayra Garcia-Hernandez, Dulce Guzman, Adriana Hernandez, Feliz Moreno, Monica Noriega, Laura Ornelas, Nancy Orocio, Nataly Quintero, Natali Rodriguez, Gladis Romero, Ariella Rotramel, Anahi Russo, Galilea Silva, Veronica Solorio, and Angela Valadez.

Of course, the functioning and well-being of all academic units hinges on the quality of staff members who serve as the backbone of those programs. I have had the good fortune to work with the finest staff, who ensured not only that the programs were productive and students were well provided for but also that faculty always had the resources and support they needed to excel. This support included making me part of their extended families wherever I went. I am especially grateful for the care provided by Joanne Givand, Cory Gruebele, Mary Suzy Kiefer, and Pauline Nguyen. I also thank Gloria Hofer in SCU Media Services for providing technical help when I needed it most.

My most significant debt of gratitude goes to my husband, co-conspirator, dance partner, and best friend, Manolo Gonzalez-Estay, and my beloved daughter, Eva Justicia. I thank them for never asking whether I was done writing yet, whether I could hurry up, or why it all took so long. I thank Manolo for the many nights he cooked dinner without asking, fed the dogs and walked them when I was busy, sat through lectures when he knew the material, provided perspective when I was stuck, or simply slept in our daughter's tiny twin bed so she would not wake up in the middle of the night and I would have more time to write. Both to him and to my daughter, whose boundless joy and infectious happiness brought such light when I was exhausted and took me out of my head when the work became too much, I offer my love forever and with all my heart.

Portions of the text that appears in Chapters 2, 4, and 5 is based on my article "Racing and Gendering Immigration Politics: Analyzing Contemporary Immigration Enforcement Using Intersectional Analysis," *Politics, Groups, and Identities* 2, no. 2 (2014): 202–221 (www.tandfonline.com / http://www.tandfonline.com/doi/full/10.1080/21565503.2014.909319). I am grateful to the publisher for granting me permission to use this material.

TERRORIZING LATINA/O IMMIGRANTS

1

Reconfiguring Race and Gender
in the War on Terrorism

In 2002, the American Civil Liberties Union (ACLU) filed suit against the
Denver Police Department (DPD) in federal court on behalf of several hundred political activists who had been forging transnational ties with impov-
erished people around the world. Among these activists were members of the
Chiapas Coalition, a nonprofit group that promotes peaceful resolution of
ongoing conflicts in the Mexican state by facilitating fair trade networks and
educational exchanges. According to the DPD, these activists warranted surveillance as "criminal extremists" who posed "threats to the state." To safeguard the American homeland against this perceived threat, U.S. citizens
were subjected to heightened police scrutiny and sustained monitoring of
political activities that are supposed to be protected under First Amendment
guarantees of freedom of assembly and expression. DPD dossiers prepared
on these citizens—including more than ten thousand individuals and three
thousand organizations—were classified as intelligence files and shared with
more than two dozen local and federal law-enforcement agencies.

In March 2002, I was contacted by an attorney with the ACLU of Colorado and informed that my name appeared in criminal intelligence records
maintained by the DPD in association with the Chiapas Coalition. The intelligence file that included my name (and listed other members of this organization) officially (and erroneously) designated us as "Criminal Extremists"
who were part of an organization dedicated to "the violent overthrow of the
Mexican government" (see Figure 1.1).

Person File Report

Anna Sampaio

Description(s)

Date	Gender	Nationality	Race	Religion	Sexual Orientation	Disability	Deceased Date
• 02/02/2000			· White				

Date	Ht	Wt	Eye Color	Hair Color	Hair Type	Hair Length	Facial Hair	Complexion	Teeth	Build
• 02/02/2000	0	0								

Date	Notes
• 02/02/2000	

Scars, Marks, Tattoos, Oddities

Note(s)
• Listed as contact for Chiapas Coalition.

Business Associations

Case Associations

Group Associations

Chiapas Coalition (Member) - Direct Relationship   02/02/2000
Type: Criminal Extremist G
Notes: Group dedicated to overthrow of Mexican government, claiming government abuse of workers. Has hel ...

Incident Associations

Location Associations

1522 Lafayette   Denver (Resides) - Direct Relationship   02/02/2000
Type: Residence
Description:
Comments: Phone subscribe to ███████ Listed phone number fo ███████ and contact for Chiapas Co ...

1052 S High   Denver (Resides) - Direct Relationship   02/02/2000
Type: Residence
Description:
Comments:

Person Associations

 - Direct Relationship   02/02/2000

- Direct Relationship   02/02/2000

Figure 1.1

The gross misrepresentation of the group, whose actual mission was "working towards a peaceful resolution to ongoing conflict in Chiapas, Mexico," included the perverse targeting of a seventy-two-year-old Franciscan nun, among other individuals.

While the Chiapas Coalition had participated in forms of civil disobedience, we were a motley compilation of students, academics, faith-based workers, and local activists—resembling thousands of other peaceful community-based organizations across the country. Our work typically took the form of lectures, workshops, fair trade symposia, press conferences, rallies, and occasional protests (typically at either the local branch of the Mexican consulate or the state capital). In short, the activities of the group were neither "criminal" nor "extreme" but rather peaceful and executed with the most diligent planning to ensure that no harm to individuals or property occurred. In fact, in years of working with the organization, I witnessed only one occasion in which members were arrested when they interrupted a luncheon hosted by the governor of Colorado on September 17, 1999, to challenge the promotion of a new trade office and the expansion of free trade between Colorado and Mexico.[1]

The ACLU's initial investigation into these "spy files" revealed that the Denver Police Department had produced and stored more than 3,500 similar criminal intelligence files in a newly formed electronic database. Included in this compilation were files on the American Friends Service Committee, a Nobel Peace Prize–winning Quaker service organization, as well as Amnesty International and the American Indian Movement; individual files targeted Winona LaDuke, George Carlin, Russell Means, Bishop Desmond Tutu, and many others.[2] The files documented a wide array of information, including membership in organizations, attendance at events, "opinions" of groups and individuals (in many cases characterized inaccurately), physical descriptions, home addresses, license-plate numbers, credit information, and photographs and video recordings of targeted individuals and their "associates" at organizational meetings, protests, workshops, and similar events.

The discovery of these files and the concerns raised regarding violations of civil liberties and unwarranted scrutiny were accompanied by vehement assurances from local law enforcement that no other files existed, that these files were a "mistake," that they had never been shared with other law-enforcement agencies outside Denver, and that they would be quickly purged.[3] However, months of additional investigation uncovered six full-length filing cabinets filled with more hard-copy files, bringing the total number of criminal intelligence files to approximately thirteen thousand (ten thousand files on individuals and three thousand files on organizations). More importantly, the content of the files revealed that the spying was largely directed at ethnic and racial minority activists and organizations working within Latina/o, American Indian, and African American communities. As such, the files were invasive, comprehensive, and gathered without reasonable suspicion of an actual threat, and they brought together an expansive security apparatus with a systematic program of racial and ethnic profiling.[4]

Shortly after the discovery of the files, the ACLU of Colorado filed a federal suit against the city and county of Denver that was settled in 2003.[5] The case uncovered the DPD's extensive use of intelligence officers, undercover operatives, and informants to collect information without the standards of "reasonable suspicion," "probable cause," or any other legitimate law-enforcement purpose. In a glaring attempt to subvert the case, one DPD intelligence officer composed a memo suggesting that bureau personnel destroy or take home files to prevent "the inevitable lawsuits" by "radicals."[6] Even more alarming were revelations that, far from being confined to the local police department, the files were regularly shared with agencies across the country, including the Federal Bureau of Investigation (FBI), the Immigration and Naturalization Service (INS), the Transportation Security Administration (TSA), and more than two dozen local and regional law-enforcement units. Moreover, the files were shared without ensuring that these agencies would guard against the further disclosure of the information or that the promulgation of the information would not result in harm to the people profiled.[7]

For me and other individuals targeted in the files, the revelation and the news that those files had been shared so widely created a number of obstacles. In addition to dramatically chilling our free expression and criminalizing our protected expressive activities, the label of "Criminal Extremist" placed unwarranted scrutiny on our daily activities and cast suspicion on our personal and professional contacts. In my own work with documented and undocumented immigrants and in my travels to parts of Mexico, already heavily scrutinized by state and local law enforcement, this kind of branding was politically dangerous and professionally obstructive. Whatever trust and confidence I had worked to build over the years, whatever "insider status" I had gained through careful cultivations of mutually respectful relationships—relationships central to my ethnographic work and to my own location within these communities—were suddenly subverted.[8]

On a broader scale, these actions foregrounded a troubling surge in securitization efforts across the country that were deeply racialized and coded in the language of "protecting the homeland." Although the ACLU discovered the files in 2002, the preponderance of these files were created and disseminated by local law enforcement *prior* to the events of September 11, 2001—prior to the massive expansion of law-enforcement powers enabled via the USA PATRIOT Act, the creation of the U.S. Department of Homeland Security (DHS), or amendments to the Foreign Intelligence Surveillance Act that paved the way for domestic spying operations. These actions demonstrate a rapid ascension in state authority, even before 9/11, and how shifts in law enforcement, and especially immigration enforcement, occurred before those attacks. The case also demonstrates the shifting relationships between local, state, and federal law enforcement and the rise of regional associations, such as Joint Terrorism Task Forces (JTTFs) and local "fusion centers," which figured centrally in the collection and dissemination of information. Finally, the case illustrates the change in public discourse and the logic of security that increasingly cast immigrants, activists, and those engaged in transnational politics as potential enemies of the state, thereby fueling law enforcement's ability to target political and racial minorities for scrutiny, harassment, apprehension, and imprisonment with virtual impunity.[9]

This ascension in state authority and racial targeting by law enforcement was dramatically accelerated with the onset of the war on terrorism after 9/11. A 2010 report from Glenn Fine, the inspector general of the U.S. Department of Justice (DOJ), documents abuses between 2001 and 2006 within the FBI as it targeted activist organizations engaged in peaceful, nonviolent work for investigation and scrutiny, resulting in several innocent people being placed on the domestic terror watch list for years and former FBI Director Robert S. Mueller lying to Congress about the nature of the investigations. The unwarranted scrutiny of such groups as Greenpeace, People for the Ethical Treatment of Animals (PETA), the Thomas Merton Center, the Catholic Worker Movement, and other peace organizations began prior to 9/11 but mushroomed into a wide-ranging probe that continued for years under the guise of national security.[10]

Surveillance programs begun under the George W. Bush administration were embraced and expanded under President Barack Obama's administration, enabling the federal government to collect and scrutinize telephone calls, e-mails, chat messages, videos, photos, stored data, file transfers, videoconferences, and log-ins of foreigners and Americans.[11] Moreover, local law enforcement extended these domestic spying initiatives through the collection of "suspicious activity reports" that were regularly shared with federal agencies (including the FBI and the JTTF) through information clearinghouses, such as seventy-two "fusion centers" established around the country.[12]

Few actions underscored the intensification of state scrutiny after 9/11 more poignantly than the series of domestic operations intended to identify and remove terrorist threats from within the country. Specifically, in 2002—the same year the DPD spy files were uncovered—under the direction of the newly created DHS, a host of operations were announced that united federal agencies with state and local law enforcement. Invoking the nomenclature of foreign military operations, these new initiatives included "Operation Tarmac," "Operation Community Shield," and "Operation Wagon Train" and relied upon existing federal and state statutes in coordinating a massive effort to root out terrorist threats to the country and secure the nation.

"Operation Tarmac" was one of the earliest coordinated operations after 9/11 and provided a model for the structure and impacts of subsequent undertakings. This operation was a joint effort between the DHS, the DOJ (including the U.S. Attorneys Offices), the Department of Transportation, U.S. Customs, the Social Security Administration, the Federal Aviation Administration, and other agencies, targeting "persons of unknown origin" working at airports and other federally secured facilities around the country.[13] These investigations often extended to the thousands of service workers employed in hotels, restaurants, and other industries adjacent to these buildings.[14] By January 2003, more than 750,000 employment records at more than 1,900 airports, businesses, and federal facilities had been scrutinized, resulting in the detention and arrest of several thousand individuals. Most of these people were janitors, members of cleaning crews, and food-service workers, the vast majority of whom were Latina/o immigrants (including Mexican, Central American, and South American immigrants) arrested for using false identification. While U.S. attorneys referred to the operation as "a highly effective weapon in the domestic war against terrorism," the DHS and the U.S. Attorneys Offices have since confirmed that *not one* of the immigrants detained or deported as part of Operation Tarmac had any relationship to terrorist activity.[15]

These federal initiatives continued to proliferate, with the most high-profile operations targeting employers suspected of hiring large concentrations of unauthorized workers. In accordance with his belief that "illegal documents are not only used by illegal migrants, but they are used by terrorists who want to get on airplanes, or criminals who want to prey on our citizens," DHS Secretary Michael Chertoff launched "Operation Wagon Train" in 2005 to protect the United States by verifying the nationality and immigration status of employees.[16] A coordinated operation involving multiple federal agencies and local law-enforcement departments, Operation Wagon Train investigated persons suspected of using fraudulent identification for employment. This new operation, which targeted thousands of employees in various manufacturing plants throughout the country, including pallet plants in California, meat-packing plants across the Midwest, and fisheries on the East Coast, resulted in a disproportionate level of detentions, arrests, incarcerations, and deportations of Latina/o immigrants who were working in these industries. In the largest raid executed under Operation Wagon Train, which targeted Swift and Company meat-packing plants in six states throughout the Midwest, 1,282 individuals were apprehended, all of whom were unauthorized Latina/o immigrants.[17] As with Operation Tarmac, Operation Wagon Train yielded no actual evidence of terrorist activity or persons with links to terrorist organizations.

Collectively, each of these cases—from the DPD spy files to the Operation Wagon Train raids—rests upon a process of racialization produced in relationship to the surge of state authority that blurs the boundaries of citizenship, immigration, and national security concerns. In the case of Operations Tarmac and Wagon Train, this increased state authority disproportionately affected Latina/o immigrants. Moreover, justifications for the raids regularly conflated apprehended immigrants with terrorists, despite the absence of any evidence to that effect. However, the extent to which Latinas/os have been targeted by the state as potential terrorists is not restricted to these operations. Immigration legislation passed since 2001 reflects an increasingly restrictive agenda aimed at curtailing the resources, rights, and mobility of immigrants, more than half of whom are from Mexico, Central America, South America, and the Caribbean.[18] This legislation and the aforementioned domestic raids trade on racialized depictions of Latina/o immigrants as foreign and threatening, while these same populations are subjected to terrifying forms of ethnic intimidation, harassment, abuse, and discrimination. In short, through the war on terrorism, Latinas/os have increasingly become "potential terrorists" even as they are being terrorized by the state.[19]

Understanding this process and its specific impacts on Latina/o immigrants requires more than a singular attention to patterns of discrimination based on forms of ethnic or racial identity. Borrowing from work in feminist theory, critical race studies, and intersectional analysis, my argument in this book rests upon an understanding of race as a process constructed and executed in relationship to the state and civil society and affected by its operation in relationship with other forms of marginalization. In other words, racialization entails

> a configuration of social, cultural, and political processes by which specific perceived visible differences are imbued with racial significance and meaning that then are incorporated as racial hierarchy both within macro level economic, state, and cultural institutional structures and within the interstitial nodes of quotidian experiences and relations taking place in the sites of civil society.[20]

As discussed in Chapter 3, Latinas/os have been historically constructed as "perpetual foreigners" through a process of racialization, thereby legitimating their political marginalization, excluding them from institutions of public life, and making them vulnerable to restrictive immigration policy and enforcement.[21] Moreover, this enduring construction as "aliens," regardless of nativity or immigration status, has evolved since the mid-1990s, shifting with the intervention of new discourses and technologies of power surrounding "security" and especially with the emergence of a national security regime such that Latinas/os are increasingly positioned by the state as not just foreigners but potential terrorists.

As with other processes of domination, the particular manifestations of racialized marginalization are mediated, altered, negotiated, reconfigured, and informed by intersecting modes of subordination and require an analysis attuned to these simultaneous forms of difference to thoroughly explore changes in immigration politics. While others, including Leo Chavez, Alfonso Gonzales, Joseph Nevins, and Raymond Rocco, highlight the important intersections of racialized immigration policy and practices in the United States and the way these conflations have helped neoliberalism and globalization expand material inequality within Latina/o immigrant communities, their research leaves unexamined the way that racialization and gendering processes have operated in tandem to construct Latina/o immigrants as potential terrorists and to legitimize their terrorization via restrictive state practices.[22] Nor has there been detailed examination of the experiences of Latinas and Latinos within the war on terror and a national security regime that calibrates the degree of threat posed in relation to the racialized and gendered positions of particular "foreigners."

Thus, for example, while the domestic operations described above were deeply racialized, frequently overlooked are the ways in which men's *and* women's bodies also became an important site of enforcement. A 2011 report from the Warren Institute found that 93 percent of immigrants detained in conjunction with the initial phase of large-scale military-style raids and roundups intended to identify and remove potential terrorists were Latinos.[23] However, as the raids shifted from secured and sensitive facilities to commercial employment and residential locations, Latinas became increasing targets, and the number of Latina immigrants detained and imprisoned or deported proliferated. These apprehensions were not isolated incidents: More women and parents with children were detained as the scale of immigration raids expanded, particularly after the launch of Operation Return to Sender and the Secured Communities Program.[24] As the number of apprehensions and detentions escalated, and particularly as more women were held in detention facilities for processing and deportation, reports of gendered violence in the forms of sexual harassment and abuse also increased. The ACLU documented close to two hundred allegations of sexual abuse of immigrants between 2007 and 2010, including sexual assaults by officers working in the detention facilities. In 2014, tens of thousands of mothers with young children and unaccompanied minors fleeing violence from their home countries in Central America and seeking refuge in the United States faced prolonged detention and even deportation, despite the presence of a credible threat to substantiate their fears. As such, both men's *and* women's bodies became the locus upon which shifts in immigration legislation and national security initiatives were executed. Understanding the full extent of their marginalization means understanding how their racialized subordination intersected with the particular vulnerabilities of women and children within Latina/o communities, redefining their lives and their futures in the United States.[25]

Another important way that gender and race intersected in the context of these enforcement initiatives was through the creation of new legislation weaving together expansions of gender-based rights, particularly protections, access, and opportunities for immigrant women and children, with increased scrutiny of immigrants. Here the analysis of race and gender shifts from *subjects* to the racialization and gendering of *legislation* and to a process of unmasking and denaturalizing language in legislation that intensifies the proliferation of raids and roundups. The Violence Against Women and Department of Justice Reauthorization Act of 2005 provides the best example of this intersection of racializing and gendering in legislation tied to the raids. The act extends protections, rights of admission, and legalization to immigrant women and children who have been victims of sexual assault or trafficking in the United States, yet it simultaneously extends the ability of local law enforcement to act as immigration agents, a key feature of the surge in raids and roundups.

Yet another important intersection occurs in the production of new knowledge and discourse animating the federal government's rapid expansion of security. In particular, the national security regime has relied heavily on the production of security discourse founded upon racialized fears and gendered logic of protection to legitimate aggressive military mobilizations abroad and restrictions at home. This particular discourse of masculine protection and racialized demonization not only appears in public declarations, proclamations, and press releases from the DHS to the executive branch but has equally foregrounded shifts in legislation, executions of large-scale raids, surges in immigrant scrutiny and detention, and systematic abridgements of civil liberties for immigrants and citizens alike. In short, framing the war on terror and particularly the production of "securitization" as a knowledge project, race and gender figure prominently in the production of meaning and especially in "truths" proffered by the state to legitimate and expand its authority. Here gender and race are taken as elements of interpretation as opposed to as descriptors of particular subjects, attitudes, or identities.

In this way, racialization not only signifies embodied subjects but equally serves as an important heuristic tool that opens the door to new questions and analyses in immigration politics and policy.

In short, the rise of the security state and the attendant war on terrorism has been deeply racialized, but this process of racial construction, articulation, and execution has been intricately woven together with multiple configurations of gender and subordination that necessitate a more nuanced intersectional analysis. Of particular significance to this study is the expansion of race and gender scholarship, which has developed conceptual tools emphasizing *racialization and gendering processes*. Drawing upon this recent scholarship, I view race and gender as important forms of organization and identity but equally as ways in which difference is constructed, expressed, negotiated, and embodied through complex interactions with political institutions and processes. As new knowledge about immigration and securitization policies and practices in the twenty-first century is produced, discourses and articulations of race and gender play a central analytical role.

This book examines the rise of the national security state as a powerful discursive regime. It illuminates significant legislative and policy shifts pertaining to immigration since 9/11, giving particular attention to the way these processes are racialized and gendered. It investigates how Latinas/os have been affected by these changes. This book probes the inequitable burdens imposed on Latina/o immigrants by recent securitization measures that appear to be racially neutral but in reality work to rearticulate and reinscribe forms of racial and gender hierarchy. Moreover, this book demonstrates how the ascendance of this security state has served as a template to scrutinize, harass, and encumber immigrants while also reconfiguring citizenship. Overall, my aim in this book is conceptual (focusing on developing a framework for analyzing current immigration politics informed by race and gender) and empirical (using this framework to document particular impacts of securitization and the war on terror on Latina/o immigrants and citizens, demonstrating powerful effects on fundamental aspects of citizenship as well). Each of the individual chapters addresses key theoretical, conceptual, and empirical issues essential to immigration and securitization studies.

In Chapter 2, I present a theoretical framework that treats the war on terror and the surge of securitization as a knowledge project. My goal is to make visible the tacit presuppositions of the national security state through the use of intersectional analysis. Rather than accepting the state's construction of the terrorist threat at face value, this chapter situates homeland-security measures in relation to long-standing processes of racialization and gendering that create and legitimize hierarchies among citizens. Drawing upon critical race and gender theory, I analyze shifts in securitization and immigration politics since 9/11 in terms of competing logics of protectionism and demonization that mobilize fear to legitimate heightened modes of surveillance and control. I show how new domestic-security measures construct internal enemies predicated on ethnic and racial profiling to justify the rapid expansion of state authority. Posing as protectors of the nation, local, state, and federal agencies develop a paternalistic relationship with certain residents even as they demonize others as illegitimate predators. These two dynamics—protection and demonization—are neither incongruent nor diametrically opposed. On the contrary, they are intertwined, simultaneously feminizing the legitimate citizenry (rendering them silent, docile, and subservient) while racializing Arab, South Asian, and Latina/o citizens and noncitizens as terrorists.

Although the state's response to 9/11—specifically, the war on terrorism—has profoundly reconfigured immigration politics as well as the rights and opportunities of immigrants in the United States, these shifts have not occurred in a vacuum. To contextualize the war on terror and the shifts in immigration policies and practices, Chapter 3 examines the history of constitutional provisions and federal and state statutes that have circumscribed the lives of Latinas/os throughout the twentieth century. While much of the book focuses on the contemporary national security regime, this chapter focuses on the past—namely, the racialization of Latinas/os within U.S. immigration politics, demonstrating key continuities over the course of the twentieth century. In particular, I trace significant political and economic changes that opened, closed, or reconfigured borders while expanding or contracting immigrants' rights and ultimately redefining Latina/o immigrants as burdens and threats to the country. Rather than treating the aftermath of 9/11 as an exception, this chapter ties the war on terror and the shifts in immigration under the national security regime to a longer trajectory of racialization, paying particular attention in the last section to the escalation of border enforcement, the passage of federal anti-terrorism legislation, and renewed restrictions on immigrants' rights at the state and national levels. By paying close attention to similarities and differences, this chapter assesses exactly what is new in recent immigration policies and what is tied to a much longer tradition of racialization in the construction of citizenship and national identity.

Chapter 4 focuses on the public laws passed by Congress in the seven years after 9/11, closely examining manifestations of racialization, securitization, and restriction within immigration legislation passed during the 107th, 108th, 109th, and 110th sessions of Congress. A comprehensive review of all immigration-related legislation passed by Congress in this period reveals particularly disturbing patterns in the framing of immigration policy. Restrictions abound, with the most common types of legislation coalescing around five central themes: increasing the scrutiny of immigrants (including policing and scrutiny related to immigrants' work authorization); expanding the possibilities for detentions, arrest, and/or deportation; militarizing the southern border between the United States and Mexico; increasing restrictions and/or constraints on federal services and benefits to immigrants; and empowering or extending the capacity of local law enforcement to execute greater levels of investigation, review, apprehension, and/or cooperation with federal immigration authorities. Moving beyond the discursive intersections of race and gender that foreground the legislative shifts, this chapter also examines complicated weavings of race and gender rights, resources, opportunities, and constraints occurring through specific legislation, particularly the passage of the Violence Against Women and Department of Justice Reauthorization Act of 2005 and the Trafficking Victims Protection Reauthorization Act of 2003.

The final portion of Chapter 4 examines in detail those laws that have simultaneously expanded state authority while having the most negative impact on Latina/o immigrants—specifically, the USA PATRIOT Act of 2001, the Homeland Security Act of 2002, and the Emergency Supplemental Appropriations Act for Defense, the Global War on Terror, and Tsunami Relief, 2005. It provides a comprehensive and systematic review of immigration legislation, documenting shifts in immigration law and policy leading to the construction of Latin/o immigrants as security threats as well as new layers of restriction aimed at this population.

Congressional legislation may extend the reach of the state, but the full effects of legislative initiatives turn on implementation. Chapter 5 examines the execution of recent immigration laws that link multiple federal and local agencies in cooperative ventures. In particular, through archival review of newspaper reporting from 2001 to 2010, I examine the proliferation of immigration raids and roundups. While the use of raids for large-scale immigrant removal is not new, efforts since 9/11 have been concentrated in three areas: airports and federally secured facilities, employment sites, and residential raids targeting fugitive absconders. I examine each of these areas, how they are linked to previous raids, and their impacts on Latina/o immigrants.

Although these new initiatives use language that is often race-neutral, they trade upon fear of potential terrorism to legitimate the formation of a masculinized protector embodied in the national security state that overrides long-standing separations of power and jurisdiction between federal, state, and local governments as well as constitutional guarantees of citizens and permanent residents. In tracing how the logic of racialized fear and masculinized protection plays out in particular implementation efforts, I show these policies' disproportionate racial effects, as Latinas/os have been detained, apprehended, deported, arrested, fined, and otherwise encumbered through these operations. Chapter 5 contributes to research that documents how state action that appears to be race-neutral can, in fact, contribute to the production and institutionalization of troubling racial and gendered hierarchies that negatively affect Latina/o communities.

Terrorizing Latinas/os addresses the effects of securitization and immigration policy on various cohorts within Latina/o communities in the United States—including documented and undocumented migrants—but it equally examines changes in citizenship that have emerged in relationship to shifts in immigration politics. In Chapter 6, I examine the broader shifts in citizenship signified in the cases of three natural-born U.S. citizens: John Walker Lindh, Yaser Hamdi, and José Padilla. As discussed in Chapter 2, securitization constitutes more than just a defensive strategy or bureaucratic organization—it is a politically and socially constructed discursive regime that informs policy and strategy but, more importantly in our current context, is also centrally constitutive of community, political identity, and citizenship. Chapter 6 extends the analysis to consider how fundamental rights, values, and conceptions of citizenship were sacrificed in the context of mounting securitization. With growing frequency, the terrorizing restrictions applied to immigrants in the years after 9/11 were applied to the most protected class of persons in the United States—namely, natural-born citizens. Moreover, this slippage from constructing immigrants as terrorists to terrorizing citizens was not accidental. On the contrary, the national security state engaged in a parallel process of racial demonization and de-Americanization, ultimately stripping detainees of legal protection and political agency while publicly appealing to a masculinized discourse of protection. Highlighting the cases of Lindh, Hamdi, and Padilla, this chapter points to a systematic erosion of due process, representation, and political agency as the efforts to expand the security state increased. I trace shifts in meaning and in the construction of citizenship in the context of the discursive regimes of racialized demonization, masculinized protectionism, and securitization.

Although Chapter 6 focuses on the responses of the national security regime in the specific cases of Lindh, Hamdi, and Padilla, these cases also illuminate shifts in the boundaries of citizenship, as the language associated with the purported dangers posed by immigrants is transferred to discussions of citizens. In short, as the state broadened its definition of "enemies" in its war on terrorism, the boundaries between citizen and immigrant blurred. Just as the structure and administration of immigration politics shifted within the war on terror, generating harm to thousands of immigrants far removed from any actual terrorist activity, so too have the boundaries of citizenship been fundamentally reconfigured, undermining key features of democracy for all Americans.

This book ends with an examination of immigration reform under the Obama administration, contrasting the promise of hope and change articulated in his presidential campaign with the effects of his policies on Latinas/os. Chapter 7 considers how the potential for change stagnated as deadlock in Washington became a hallmark of the Obama era. Despite the tenuousness of immigration politics in this moment, I analyze how the politics of immigration under the Obama administration compares with not only the promises made during the campaign but also the record of the Bush administration. Turning from federal to state politics, I examine the shifting racialization and gendering of discourses on immigrants embedded in restrictive legislation in such states as Arizona, which have reignited racialized fears and traded upon gendered stereotypes. This final chapter revisits changes to immigration politics occurring in the context of securitization and the ascension of the national security regime, analyzing the degree to which these changes have expanded or abated under the Obama administration and exploring the prospects for reform and restructuring in light of these changes.

2

Masculinist Protectionism, Racialized Demonization, and the Formation of the Contemporary Security Regime

On November 17, 2001, shortly after the United States launched a war against the Taliban in retaliation for the bombings of the World Trade Center and the Pentagon on September 11, 2001, Laura Bush made history by becoming the only First Lady to deliver a presidential radio address. Focused on the war in Afghanistan, the speech presented a gendered logic for the war, denouncing the "severe repression against women of Afghanistan" and proclaiming the following:

> Civilized people throughout the world are speaking out in horror—
> not only because our hearts break for the women and children in
> Afghanistan, but also because in Afghanistan, we see the world the
> terrorists would like to impose on the rest of us. . . . *Fighting brutality*
> *against women and children is not the expression of a specific culture;*
> *it is the acceptance of our common humanity*—a commitment shared
> by people of good will on every continent. Because of our recent mili-
> tary gains in much of Afghanistan, women are no longer imprisoned
> in their homes. They can listen to music and teach their daughters
> without fear of punishment. Yet the terrorists who helped rule that
> country now plot and plan in many countries. And they must be
> stopped. *The fight against terrorism is also a fight for the rights and*
> *dignity of women.* (Emphasis added)[1]

At the same time this gendered logic for war was being used to justify military incursions abroad, the U.S. Department of Justice (DOJ) was

engaged in a racialized targeting of immigrants at home, requesting that more than eight thousand Arab and Muslim men submit to voluntary "interviews" with FBI agents.[2] Responding to accusations of racial profiling, the DOJ maintained that each of the men were selected for interviews solely on the basis of their ages, dates of arrival, and countries of origin (specifically, countries supportive of Al Qaeda) and justified the urgency of the process as a national security concern. Nonetheless, as David Cole notes, "The countries singled out . . . did not include Great Britain, France, Spain, or Germany, even though Al Qaeda suspects from each of these countries had already been captured," betraying a racialized process at work even in the absence of race-specific language.[3] Ultimately, more than five thousand of these men were subjected to lengthy detentions without being charged with a crime and without having access to a lawyer, prompting the president of the American Bar Association to describe the situation as being "as close to 'disappearing' individuals as we in this country have ever come."[4]

Both instances demonstrate how war making in Afghanistan and terrorist purging in the United States have been driven by a logic of protectionism, which justifies aggressive action as necessary to defend "American values and way of life" from enemies both foreign and domestic. This protectionist logic has constructed an enemy "other" and demonized this enemy as foreign, threatening, suspicious, and potentially "terrorist." As Bush's justification of the invasion of Afghanistan and the DOJ detentions demonstrate, the mutually reinforcing logics of protectionism and demonization are themselves tethered to complex configurations of race and gender—combining a *masculinist* version of protectionism with a *racialized* mode of demonization. Moreover, these gendered and racial logics have come to represent a national consciousness as claims to "our common humanity" and to protection of "our way of life" have become recurring themes in popular discourse, executive orders, and congressional legislation.

The importance of masculine protectionism and racialized demonization to the political shifts occurring after 9/11 become apparent when we view the expansion of state authority occurring in this period not simply as a new phase of institution building, administrative reorganization, or rhetoric resting exclusively within debates about defense strategies and war but as a series of fundamental shifts in meaning and discursive power relations. Borrowing from Jef Huysmans, security is examined here as a "knowledge project": "It is a political technique of framing policy questions in logics of survival with a capacity to mobilize politics of fear in which social relations are structured on the basis of distrust . . . a particular way of arranging social and political relations . . . [with] a specific capacity for fabricating and sustaining antagonistic relations between groups of people."[5]

Despite its prevalence as a fixture of state formations and international relations, security is neither universal nor objective; instead, it is a "politically and socially constructed phenomenon," constantly being reimagined and literally being "written and talked into existence."[6] This framing deepens our understanding of securitization by dissecting the multiple discourses, logics, technologies, and bureaucratic practices that develop and sustain it. Moreover, this process broadens debates around security, linking the process of securitization to fundamental issues of social and political organization, including immigration, citizenship, race, gender, exclusion, and membership. As Nira Yuval-Davis notes, "With the growing number of migrants, the changing nature of economy and society, and especially after 9/11, technologies for regulating migration have become part of the growing discourse of 'securitization' in which (some) people's belonging to their state of residence and even citizenship has become more and more contingent."[7] Ultimately, the process of securitization and the national obsession with "homeland security" that have become central hallmarks of the war on terror constitute a discursive political regime that has fundamentally influenced the functions of governance and society while reframing and reshaping our reality.

Taking the war on terrorism, and especially the securitization process, as a politically and socially constructed knowledge project, this chapter examines how this discourse has been driven by racialized and gendered processes, and particularly how they have relied upon and made use of raced and gendered logics to support, cultivate, legitimate, and maintain the new security regime. Moreover the chapter examines how immigration was enveloped within homeland security, thereby constituting immigrants as terrorist threats unwelcome within a national community while positioning the legitimate protected community within a constrained paternalistic relationship.

As both immigration law and policy and the concentration of resources and authority in the U.S. Department of Homeland Security (DHS) and the DOJ made clear, the national security state drew upon and intensified unevenly distributed burdens associated with race and gender while also articulating new racial and gendered hierarchies. In this rearticulation of race and gender, immigrants who were already marked by race, ethnicity, or religion as "foreign" were easily positioned as "enemies" or "threats."[8] In direct contrast to notions of integration, acculturation, and "naturalization," in which immigrants could become American citizens, the logics of suspicion and demonization "de-Americanized"[9] immigrants (particularly Arabs, South Asians, and later Latinas/os), casting them beyond the boundaries of citizenship and national belonging. This racialization of immigrants as foreign and threatening took place while selected subjects at home were simultaneously gendered as "feminine" and in dire need of the state's paternal protection—rendering them deserving of the state's protective services as well as silent and subservient.

In combination, masculine protectionism and racialized demonization yielded particularly harsh consequences for immigrants who were unlawfully detained or deported. These discursive shifts also had perilous effects on U.S. citizens, leading to the abrogation of constitutional guarantees of due process, free expression, association, privacy, and a host of other democratic values central to civic engagement. In this way, protectionism and feminization, racialization and demonization rendered immigrants suspect while also redefining citizenship. I explore the effect on citizenship more thoroughly in Chapter 6, but this chapter introduces key elements of the conceptual framework developed in the book and applied in subsequent chapters.

Employing a Racialized and Gendered Framework for Analysis of National Security

Of particular significance to this study are recent developments in race and gender scholarship that focus upon *racialization and gendering processes*. Rather than envisioning race and gender as physical attributes or biological constructs, critical race and feminist theories illuminate racialization and gendering as mechanisms for the construction of hierarchical difference within institutions and organizations with profound effects on individual identities. Far from being "given" at birth, race and gender are constructed, expressed, negotiated, and embodied through complex interactions with political institutions and processes. Borrowing from Michael Omi's and Howard Winant's definition of racial formation, Ray Rocco further refines this concept as

> a configuration of social, cultural, and political processes by which specific perceived visible differences are imbued with racial significance and meaning that then are incorporated as racial hierarchy both within macro level economic, state, and cultural institutional structures and within the interstitial nodes of quotidian experiences and relations taking place in the sites of civil society.[10]

The growing sophistication of accounts of racialization and gendering processes emerged from debates in feminist theory about epistemology and methodology as well as challenges within critical race theory attuned to excavating nuanced forms of racial inequality ensconced in legal formalism and shielded by claims of racial neutrality in politics.[11]

The conceptualization of intersectionality,[12] grounded in the lived experiences of women of color, significantly redefined issues of race and gender identity by linking questions of ethnicity and race to gender, sexual orientation, and forms of difference, generating new tools for analyzing enduring questions of access, equality, and justice. As these challenges evolved, they produced new approaches to classic questions of identity and incorporation and introduced nuanced theoretical and methodological tools to understand overlapping and interceding assemblages of power, privilege, and marginalization. Over the past twenty-five years, intersectionality has emerged as its own theory, method, and political practice.

Collectively, these interventions expanded analyses of race and gender from their locus as "descriptors of particular modes of embodiment" toward their use as methodological guides and heuristic devices that could interrogate previous modes of analysis, while investigating processes that created, maintained, and constructed meaning around raced and gendered subjects.[13] Rita Dhamoon describes this as a "critical politics of meaning-making," entailing examinations of "how meanings of difference are produced, organized, and regulated through power, and the effects of these meanings on socio-political arrangements."[14]

However, while Dhamoon situates this analytical framework within interpretive explanations, Ange-Marie Hancock and Mary Hawkesworth, along with social construction theorists Anne Schneider and Helen Ingram, employ intersectionality as methodology within political science and policy studies, invoking a deliberately gendered, raced, and intersectional lens of analysis attentive to technologies of power that construct, reify, and maintain difference.[15]

One aspect of this work especially pertinent to studies of politics is the process of "denaturalization," which draws attention to language and technical properties of bills that create hierarchies among citizens even as they deploy neutral language. By analyzing the process and politics surrounding the development of legislation as well as the larger effects of a bill's passage, it is possible to demonstrate how "seemingly neutral, objective, or even universal phenomena . . . inscrib[e] race and gender hierarchies."[16] By using an intersectional heuristic, it is possible to penetrate the seemingly neutral language associated with budget bills or national security measures to reveal how ostensible linguistic neutrality inscribes hierarchies of race, gender, ethnicity, and sexuality. In their classic work on public policy, Schneider and Ingram demonstrate how "target populations" are socially constructed through policy discourses:

Social constructions become embedded in policy as messages that are absorbed by citizens and affect their orientations and participa-

tion patterns. Policy sends messages about what government is supposed to do, which citizens are deserving (and which not), and what
kinds of attitudes and participatory patterns are appropriate. . . .
Negatively constructed powerless groups will usually be proximate
targets of punishment policy, and the extent of burdens will be greater (oversubscribed) . . . even when it is illogical from the perspective
of policy effectiveness.[17]

Chapter 3 illuminates the social construction of immigrants through a
historical examination of explicit and coded forms of racialization within
U.S. immigration policy. Chapter 4 deepens the analysis by examining
immigration legislation enacted during the height of the war on terror. This
chapter demonstrates how the war on terror appropriated language associated with racial profiling, transformed its negative valence into a positive
asset, and legitimized state action, aided and abetted by citizens' fear that
undermined long-cherished constitutional rights.

Even in a nation that celebrates formal equality and individual freedom,
raced and gendered bodies are produced in relationship to the state, which
normalizes certain identities through the instruments of law and policy
with profound effects on how individuals understand themselves, perform
their designated identities, and relate to fellow citizens. Following Judith
Butler's reading of gender, this formulation moves race and gender "off the
ground of a substantial model of identity to one that requires a conception
of a constituted social temporarity," emphasizing a process of racial and
gender subjectification.[18] In this analysis, identities are not stable or unified;
instead, subjects embody particular identities that are shaped, constituted,
and constricted via specific discourses and technologies of power. In their
own performance of these identities, citizen subjects, resident "aliens," and
undocumented workers reify, resist, alter, and reproduce new meanings and,
by extension, new racial and gendered identities. In this way, the bodies of
Latinas/os are not merely raced and gendered, but perpetually performing,
shaping, altering, and being informed, shaped, and affected by racializing
and gendering processes. Particular modes of embodiment are made possible through the process of racialization and gendering. Only a methodological lens that draws attention to those processes can provide adequate
insights into complex political processes that underlie changing patterns of
immigration politics. In Chapters 5 and 6, I return to these questions of
embodiment, tracing how the bodies of a select group of natural-born citizens were reconstituted as threats to national security and targeted through
the passage and implementation of recent immigration legislation.

Hawkesworth's study of congresswomen of color in the 103rd and
104th congressional sessions introduces the concept of "race-gendering"

as a means of "foregrounding the intricate interactions of racialization and gendering in the political production of distinctive groups of men and women. . . . [R]acing-gendering involves the production of difference, political asymmetries, and social hierarchies that simultaneously create the dominant and the subordinate."[19] Building on work in the social construction of policy, this approach to political institutions shows how laws, policies, and bureaucratic practices produce determinate subjects, constituted in and through hierarchical relationships to each other. By calling attention to the production of political hierarchies, intersectional analysis advances analytical tools that challenge the neutrality of political institutions, processes, and subjects, while illuminating the politics of knowledge production.

The following sections of this chapter examine race-gendering dynamics in immigration discourses in the aftermath of 9/11 and their specific implications for Latina/o immigrants. I pay particular attention to unique manifestations of racialization and feminization in the discourses of the national security state, which blend protectionism, demonization, and de-Americanization in ways that constitute Latina/o immigrants as foreign and threatening, positioning them as potential terrorists. Specific gendering processes ensconced in the rhetoric of the new security state not only feminize all citizens—male and female—but also constitute racialized immigrants as suspicious and in need of constant state surveillance.

Engendering Subjects: The Logics of Fear, Suspicion, and Protection

In her theorization of the contemporary national security state, Iris Marion Young examines a particular form of masculinity associated with understandings of men as family providers and protectors that are mirrored in national discourses, which posit heads-of-state as providers and protectors of the country.[20] Borrowing from Judith Stiehm's earlier articulation of masculine protection in defense and security sectors as well as Jean Bethke Elshtain's work on women and war,[21] Young contrasts the image of a masculine protector with a more traditional model of masculinity as "self-consciously dominative"—a form of masculinity replete with desires of sexual domination, exclusive male bonding, access to benefits from which women are deliberately excluded, and modes of harassment that secure male superiority. In contrast, the notion of a masculine protector is more closely aligned with romanticized images of male chivalry with no apparent desire for domination, personal gain, or sexual gratification. Instead, the gendered role of protector is characterized as courageous, dignified, loving, responsible, and prepared to make sacrifices, particularly to safeguard women. In Young's words:

> He faces the world's difficulties and dangers in order to shield women from harm and allow them to pursue elevating and decorative arts. . . . The good man is one who keeps vigilant watch over the safety of his family and readily risks himself in the face of threats from the outside order to protect the subordinate members of his household. . . . The protector must therefore take all precautions against threats, remain watchful and suspicious, and be ready to fight and sacrifice for the sake of his loved ones.[22]

For this logic of masculine protection to make sense, other central characters are required on the national scene, most notably an external enemy who stands ready to endanger and corrupt the benign world carefully orchestrated by the protectors and citizens who appear happy to relinquish decision-making autonomy in exchange for security. Following Georg Hegel's insight that war can be a stimulus for the moral unification of a people, the leader *qua* protector constructs an external enemy to bring citizens together as dependents in need of protection. Under the rubric of national security, the protector unilaterally determines which actions must be taken to ensure security for citizens and their property. Formerly autonomous and rights-bearing citizens are feminized as they are subordinated to the power of protection. Rather than protest encroachments on long-established civil liberties, feminized citizens gratefully acknowledge the provider for their safety. In this sense, citizen-subjects replicate a stereotypical gendered dynamic associated with wartime protection of the home—and the women and children ensconced within it. In Young's words, "She looks to him with gratitude for his manliness and admiration for his willingness to face the dangers of the world for her sake. That he finds her worthy of such risks gives substance to herself."[23]

Young ties this logic of masculine protection to Thomas Hobbes's account of the state of nature as a state of war of all against all—a world so vile that to escape unrelenting fear, individuals enter into a covenant in which they abdicate their natural rights in exchange for protection by an absolute sovereign. In this context of abject fear, protection becomes the overriding concern, even at the cost of individual autonomy. This violent and chaotic state of nature justifies the presence of an absolute sovereign—a *Leviathan*—who assumes the mantel of the masculine protector. Although legitimated by voluntary consent, the Hobbesian social contract is predicated on fear and the need for protection. As Susan Rae Peterson has argued, however, the protection afforded under these conditions is more akin to a "protection racket": Refusal to accept this social contract (and to pay the price for this service in the form of fidelity, subservience, and restrictions on liberty) is met with brutal reprisal, demonstrating that the protectee has more to fear from the protector than from an external enemy.[24]

Both the discursive properties and the bureaucratic institutions of the contemporary national security regime that emerged in the context of the war on terror strongly illustrate themes underlying Hobbes's conception of political consent grounded in fear. In the aftermath of the bombings of the Pentagon and the World Trade Center, an omnipresent sense of fear engendered a new attachment to homeland security and a tolerance of the suspension of certain civil liberties. If individuals were regularly subjected to searches, seizures, detentions, and review, with no formal due process and few successful avenues for remedy, it seemed a small price to pay for defense against foreign terrorists. But in contrast to Hobbes's assumption that all subjects are equally subordinate to the sovereign, the contemporary national security regime involves a process of gendered and racial subjectification that positions subjects unequally as the fears and anxieties manipulated by the protectionist state are mapped onto particular bodies of racialized immigrants.

The Rise of the Security State and the Re-articulation of Gendered and Racialized Hierarchies

In the wake of the 9/11 terrorist attacks and the subsequent war on terrorism, the federal government positioned itself as protector and provider, seeking to allay citizens' fears and to legitimate its assertion of authority at home and abroad. In effect, the state enhanced its security apparatus to protect American lives and property in a world replete with actual and potential terrorists. In exchange for security within its borders, the state sought obedience and fidelity. Playing to the sense of fear and vulnerability rampant in the country, and reminding citizens of the possibilities of even greater terror by placing the nation in a state of "heightened alert" at fairly regular intervals, the state cajoled residents to forgo liberties for the sake of enhanced protection. Given that the alleged threats to national security lurked within as well as outside national borders, the DOJ, the DHS, the Department of Defense, and the executive branch consolidated particular regimes of truth, which afforded protection to "legitimate" subjects while placing "suspicious" subjects under heightened scrutiny. Those who received political and economic security were expected to mute any concerns they might have about changes in law and policy, especially when these changes encumbered traditional rights and liberties.[25] Citizens' allegiance to the protector-state became an important marker of membership within the new security regime. Tolerance for suspensions of such rights as habeas corpus became a criterion of belonging for those classified as deserving of protection. Those who openly criticized policy changes or challenged the national security state risked reclassification as enemies of the state. State manipulation of fear through the exaggeration of threats motivated "legitimate" residents to accept encroachments on their rights as a necessary condition for increased security. When doubts arose about the seriousness of impending threats in particular circumstances, legitimate residents were encouraged to accept the "new normalcy" of a perpetual war against terrorism.[26]

Just as the new security state approximated the draconian powers associated with *Leviathan,* so too did it occupy the seemingly benevolent position of masculine protector described by Stiehm, Peterson, and Young. Yet in what appears to be contradictory if not diametrically opposed logics, the benevolent protector also deployed dynamics of suspicion and demonization associated with an overtly oppressive state. Within the new security regime, the benign protector that positioned legitimate subjects as subordinate, feminized dependents in *need* of masculine protectors was not content to demonize external enemies. In an era when terrorists are mobile, deftly crossing national borders to inflict harm, the protectionist state emphasized that it must examine all who crossed its borders. Immigrants become a ready target for interrogation, and certain categories of immigrants surfaced quickly as "suspicious." Nonwhite immigrants were deemed to be particularly threatening, and good citizens were commanded to report "suspicious" activity. Deploying a form of racialization that blurs ethnic and national differences, "Middle Eastern," "Arab," "Pakistani," and Latina/o immigrants were increasingly constituted as "dangerous and threatening," and aggressive state actions were taken to restrict and control their every activity. Mobilizing fear of those suspicious "foreigners and aliens," the state placed them outside the scope of civic life, positioning them as enemies intent on disrupting social order. Once popular xenophobic fears had been set in motion, the state justified systematic abridgements of rights as necessary to safeguard public order. Suspension of habeas corpus, long-term detention without access to legal counsel, and rendition to external interrogation sites without due process of law were some of the state actions devised to treat those who "threatened" the dominant order. National security alerts also served as a powerful deterrent to protest from those citizens benefitting from state protection, who were expected to take comfort in the state's activity to eradicate threats.

Within its borders, the national security state selectively positioned citizens as feminine subjects in need of protection. Beyond its borders, the national security state emphasized that Afghani women were in need of rescue from a situation so dire that it legitimated a violation of international law concerning the nonintervention in the internal affairs of another nation. The justifications advanced by the State Department and the George W. Bush administration for engaging in war in Afghanistan and subsequently in Iraq described Afghani women as brutally oppressed by the Taliban, by Al Qaeda, by Muslim fundamentalists, and by Islamic governments. As the presidential radio address delivered by Laura Bush demonstrates, manly intervention by the United States was essential to end "the Taliban's war against women." Moreover, her positioning as the voice of the executive branch was coordinated with the release of the State Department's report entitled "The Taliban's War against Women," condemning the conditions of women and children under the Taliban and Al Qaeda.[27] In this report, the State Department reaffirmed this gendered logic for war by proclaiming:

> The United States Government, which has been the largest individual national donor to Afghan humanitarian assistance efforts, believes the Taliban's oppression of women must come to an end. The U.S. Government supports a broad-based government representative of all the Afghan people and which includes women in post-Taliban Afghanistan. Only Afghans can determine the future government of their country. And Afghan women should have the opportunity to play a role in that future.[28]

When President Bush signed the Afghan Relief Act, he too insisted, "The women and children of Afghanistan have suffered enough. . . . [T]his great nation will work hard to bring them hope and help."[29] Similarly, in his 2002 State of the Union address, the president declared, "The mothers and daughters of Afghanistan were captives in their own homes, forbidden from working or going to school. Today women are free."[30] Using the oppressive experiences of women living under the Taliban (conditions that were well documented as early as 1996 but prompted no U.S. response until after 9/11) as the justification for its invasion, the Bush administration embodied the benevolent patriarch intent on saving women and children. This gendered trope was offered as a condition of war as well as a measure of democracy in the United States, as a means to distinguish *us* from *them*. The freedoms of American women were contrasted with the oppression of Afghani women as an index of the inherent superiority of the American system. Within this framing, U.S. democracy and American civilization were constituted via gendered logic that imagined the United States as the benevolent masculine protector.

Within the United States, the benevolence of U.S. military intervention in Afghanistan and Iraq was coupled with recurrent refrains that military maneuvers abroad were also essential to "protect us from further terrorist attacks" and to "protect our way of life." This discourse not only gendered the state as the chivalrous and generous masculine protector abroad but equally constituted the subjects of protection as feminized subordinates in need of intervention. Despite explicit contrasts between free American citizens and oppressed Afghanis, the logic of protection subtly positioned U.S. citizens as defenseless subjects whose vulnerability to terrorists was comparable to the vulnerability of Afghani women under the Taliban. In this way, Americans at home (regardless of their actual sex) were constructed as feminized dependents in their relationship to the state in much the same way that women and children in Afghanistan were depicted as defenseless subjects in need of U.S. intervention. And just as particular immigrants were racialized and constructed as threats to domestic order, so too were Taliban and Al Qaeda operatives depicted as barbarians who posed an intolerable threat to the global order.

The outcome of such relationships severely encumbered immigrants but equally challenged the legal, political, and cultural foundations of modern citizenship. Docile citizens were expected to willingly trade their constitutional rights and civil liberties in return for protection. They were not expected to object to the 2001 passage of the USA PATRIOT Act, which gave law-enforcement officials broader authority to conduct electronic surveillance and wiretaps, to investigate and detain anyone associated with "domestic terrorism," and to confiscate the property of persons believed to be engaging in terrorism.[31] Passed by Congress within six weeks of 9/11 and in the wake of anthrax attacks that exiled several legislators from their offices, the act was passed with virtually no public hearing or debate and without conference or committee reports. This absence of proper investigation and deliberation indicates a willingness on the part of Congress to abdicate its decision-making authority to the executive office and the DOJ. Congress too assumed a feminized role, manifesting its willingness to enable the masculine protector state in the name of national security.

The state's assertion of masculinity in this post-9/11 atmosphere went further than protection, however, assuming an abusive character in relationship to its feminized dependents. In particular, new security measures were introduced and executed upon the bodies of gendered dependents at such places as airports, federal buildings, and other secured facilities. Implementing the state's logic of suspicion without qualification, "protected," "deserving," and "legitimate" citizens were subjected to increasingly invasive searches—literally being "roughed up" for their own protection.[32]

This manipulation of protected subjects for the sake of security was particularly evident in the sweeping changes made possible through the Transportation Security Administration (TSA), the federal branch of the DHS that had jurisdiction over the country's airports and major transportation facilities. Created in response to 9/11 and as part of the 2001 Aviation and Transportation Security Act, the TSA assumed responsibilities for passenger screening from private contractors who had previously operated under the supervision of the Federal Aviation Administration (FAA). By November 2002, the TSA had deployed more than 44,000 federal screeners and 158 federal security directors at 429 U.S. airports. In March 2003, the agency was subsumed under the DHS. The TSA, and by extension the DHS, assumed responsibility for the Computer-Assisted Passenger Prescreening System (CAPPS), which used a computerized database to review the names and itineraries of passengers and compare them to a government-provided "no-fly list" as well as a list of known or suspected terrorists. The computer-generated comparisons produced two categories of travelers—those who required additional security, or "selectees," and those who did not. Passengers designated as "selectees" were subject to additional screening, including more careful review of their travel history along with inspection of their bodies, which typically entailed at least partial disrobing, pat downs, electronic wand waves, and, in more extreme cases, body-cavity searches and x-rays. A proposal for even greater scrutiny (known as CAPPS II) was introduced by the TSA/DHS in 2003, only to be abandoned in 2004 after privacy concerns could not be successfully resolved.[33]

By 2010, the TSA not only was using physically invasive practices as part of its secondary screening but also had incorporated technology that produced virtual strip searches into its primary screening. In particular, the TSA adopted "whole body imagers" that scan travelers' bodies while they pass through a machine, producing images for TSA agents that reveal fully exposed bodies. Moreover, while TSA agents voyeuristically review these scans, travelers are asked to pose with their arms in the air, mimicking a mugging and completing the metaphoric protection racket described by Peterson.[34]

The new security strategies increasingly authorized the state to inspect, scrutinize, strip, scan, manipulate, harass, and, in the worst instances, penetrate the bodies of even its most protected (and gendered) subjects. In this capacity, the TSA and the DHS enacted a brutish mode of "masculine protection," deploying a rhetoric of benevolent protection for "American travelers" while violating the same passengers' bodies and privacy.

Demonizing and De-Americanizing Racial Minorities through Immigration Law and Policy

Even as it relegated the citizenry to feminized dependency, the security state employed a racialized logic that constituted Arab Americans, Muslims, and other nonwhite populations as foreign and threatening.[35] While race and ethnicity have long served as significant structuring divides within the scope of immigration law and policy, they became particularly salient to the processes of scrutiny, detention, and exclusion in the aftermath of 9/11.

In particular, racializing discourses embedded in immigration and naturalization policies established the legal boundaries of "American" identity while repeatedly defining nonwhites as marginal, subordinate, or excluded from full membership in the national community.[36] Even as the boundaries of whiteness shifted in legislation and in the infamous racial prerequisite cases, race remained a crucial axis upon which legal, political, and cultural membership turned.[37]

For Latinas/os—and Mexicans in particular—this process of exclusion manifested strongly in the legal and political discourse surrounding "illegal aliens," with repeated efforts to identify, target, and exclude "illegals" betraying a desire to purify the nation of brown bodies. As the North American Free Trade Agreement (NAFTA) inaugurated new opportunities for U.S. businesses south of the border and as U.S. agribusiness displaced increasing numbers of Mexican farmers, who migrated north in search of work, the political border between the United States and Mexico became a site of intensive policing. With growing attention given to undocumented workers in the national media, Mexican Americans as well as Mexicans were marked as perpetually foreign.[38] Redistributive policies in general and immigration-oriented policies in particular constituted Mexican immigrants as both "alien" and "undeserving."[39]

Bill Ong Hing argues that at certain critical junctures in American history, the racial subjectification of immigrants, nurtured by persistent demonization, has resulted in a process of "de-Americanization":

> De-Americanization is a process that involves racism, but unlike the racism directed at African Americans, with its foundations in the historically held beliefs of inferiority, de-Americanizers base their assault on loyalty and foreignness. The victims are immigrants or foreigners even though they may in fact be citizens by birth or through naturalization. Irrespective of the victim community's possible long-standing status in the country, its members are regarded as perpetual foreigners.[40]

Japanese immigrants and Japanese Americans were subject to racialized demonization and de-Americanization during World War II with the internment of more than 110,000 Japanese Americans.[41] During periods of economic depression in the Southwest, both Mexican immigrants and Mexican American citizens were de-Americanized through such programs as

"Operation Wetback" that resulted in their repatriation, regardless of their immigration status.[42] As noted in the opening to this chapter, in the months after 9/11, Muslims, Middle Eastern, and South Asian immigrants experienced demonization and de-Americanization, as they were constructed as potential "terrorists" and subjected to arrest, interrogation, and detention without cause.

Interrogation was only the beginning of a lengthy process of demonization for those who appeared to be Middle Eastern, or more specifically Arab and Muslim. In January 2002, the DOJ introduced the "Absconders and Apprehension Initiative," which deployed special teams of federal agents, members of the Immigration and Naturalization Service (INS), and local law-enforcement officers across the country to target six thousand "absconders" from "Al Qaeda" countries.[43] These immigrants were labeled "absconders" because they appeared in the National Crime Information Center (NCIC) database as having violated some aspect of immigration and/or criminal law. They were subsequently ordered deported but were never actually removed from the country. In December 2001, the INS announced that the names of 314,000 individuals with deportation orders would be entered into the NCIC database, which was accessible to more than eighty thousand federal, state, and local law-enforcement agencies across the country. According to a review conducted by the *Los Angeles Times,* approximately half of the 314,000 individuals were originally from Mexico. Most had incurred deportation orders for violating civil immigration laws and not criminal statutes.[44] Moreover, while the 1974 Privacy Act required the Federal Bureau of Investigation (FBI) to make reasonable efforts to ensure the accuracy, timeliness, and completeness of the NCIC database, the DOJ relieved the FBI of its duty to comply with this statute in 2002, virtually ensuring that incorrect information would leave immigrants vulnerable to false arrest, detention, and deportations.[45] This enhanced and unchecked NCIC database was used as the basis for the "Absconders and Apprehension Initiative."

Reports from immigration attorneys suggest that the same database was subsequently used by local law enforcement to pursue Mexican immigrants who had evaded deportation. The database has also served programs that have expanded the capacity of local law enforcement to act as immigration agents, such as the "287(g) agreements" facilitated through federal legislation passed by Congress in 1996. As the lines between local, state, and federal jurisdictions blurred, the NCIC was even used to conduct background checks on individuals during routine traffic stops. This database, which was intended to root out criminal offenders, instead increased the scrutiny of all immigrants, even in instances when their behavior did not constitute a criminal threat or a national security concern.[46]

In September 2002, the INS introduced a new "special registration" system that required foreign nationals from virtually all Arab and Muslim countries to submit to fingerprinting and photographing at yearly intervals. Those arriving in the United States for the first time would have to submit to such a registration at entry, thirty days after entry, and then again every year thereafter—despite the absence of any evidence that they had violated their immigration status or committed a crime. Following their registration, the activities of these immigrants were carefully scrutinized, ensuring that even a minor infraction of their immigration status would lead to detention and possible deportation. By May 2003, more than 2,700 Arab men had been detained in conjunction with the special registration, without any evidence of terrorist activity or any charges of terrorism being levied against them.[47] The DOJ's own inspector general condemned the abuses of more than 762 of these immigrants in detention facilities in New Jersey and New York and warned of potential constitutional violations that were occurring in their apprehension.[48] This litany of abuses signaled the beginning of a lengthy process of scrutinizing, detaining, and targeting immigrants. Subsequent chapters examine more closely the ways in which that process subsumed Latina/o immigrants and how it undermined due process protections for national-born citizens.

This process of racialized demonization is evident in the passage of various immigration policies during the twentieth century (the subject of Chapter 3) and in the terrorizing of Muslim, Middle Eastern, and South Asian immigrants, as described above. Race alone does not account for the myriad ways that subjects have been manipulated, abused, and encumbered by the national security regime. Feminization in the form of masculine protectionism and racialization in the form of demonization and de-Americanization are intertwined in the workings of the national security state and more explicitly within contemporary immigration politics. As a heightened state of fear becomes routine and the scrutiny of immigrants becomes commonplace, these processes become naturalized, falling below the threshold of visibility. By examining racialization and gendering processes, the following chapters seek to denaturalize everyday practices and formal state policies, demonstrating how racialized and gendered subjects are constructed by the national security state.

In distinguishing internal enemies from dependents worthy of protection, the state engaged in a process of ethnic and racial profiling, utilizing racial, ethnic, and religious markers to profile and exclude immigrants. Central to this distinction between protected subjects and threatening outsiders is the cultivation of fear aimed at Arab Americans, Muslims (particularly Arab and Muslim immigrants), and other immigrant populations, including Latinas/os. By promulgating images of detained suspects and unsubstantiated claims of potential terrorist attacks averted by their apprehension, the state legitimated its detention practices while cultivating fear of these "internal enemies." In the name of protecting legitimate citizens, the state subjected those designated as internal enemies to scrutiny, harassment, and, in the worst instances, abuse. As dependent subjects of the state were feminized in accordance with the logic of masculine protectionism (regardless of their actual sex), Arabs, Muslims, and increasingly Latinas/os were racialized as foreigners, regardless of their actual immigration status.

Conclusion

Race and gender figured centrally in the rise of the national security state in multiple ways. Appealing to a protectionist logic to justify aggressive actions at home and abroad in the war against terrorism, the state simultaneously cast itself as the chivalrous masculine defender of democracy while feminizing citizens as docile, obedient subjects. Justifying the need for aggressive (and often preemptive) defense, the security state constructed racialized demons, casting Arab, Muslim, South Asian, and Latina/o immigrants as potential terrorists and enemies of democracy. In this process, immigrants were terrorized and citizenship was redefined as civil liberties that provided legal protections and the foundations of political expression were eroded or suspended. Through simultaneous processes of racialization and feminization, the national security state altered the rights of immigrants and citizens alike.

The formation of the contemporary security state represents a moment of "constitutional" character and change.[49] Paralleling the narratives of "(re)founding" that have recurred throughout U.S. history, immigrants have once again been central to this rearticulation of national belonging. Marking the limits of democracy, constitutionality, and membership, immigrants and citizens targeted as "foreign" and "threatening" define the constitutive outside of American identity, serving as a potent disciplining mechanism for those who might consider opposing the national security state.[50] As Bonnie Honig has noted, those who are constituted as foreign—legally, politically, racially—are simultaneously persecuted for their foreignness.[51] They are positioned as terrorists at the moment that they are subjected to terrorizing practices by the state.

The contemporary security state is neither an anomaly nor a natural state of affairs. It arose from a particular confluence of forces built upon a longer history of immigration, naturalization, and citizenship in the United States. The next chapter situates the current state of immigration politics within this larger context, focusing on the changing status of Latina/o immigrants in relationship to the state.

3

Racialization of Latinas/os within American Immigration Law and Policy

> *Immigration policies are not simply reflections of whom we regard as potential Americans; they are vehicles for keeping out those who do not fit the image and welcoming those who do.*
>
> —BILL ONG HING, *Defining America through Immigration Policy*

In the late 1890s, almost fifty years after the signing of the Treaty of Guadalupe Hidalgo that ended the Mexican-American war and annexed half of Mexico to the United States, Mexican national Ricardo Rodriguez filed an application in a Texas court to become a U.S. citizen. His application was denied. Rodriguez filed the application believing that the ongoing interchange of people in this region, along with the established history of conferring U.S. citizenship on Mexicans under the Republic of Texas and subsequent U.S. law, would facilitate his naturalization.[1] Rodriguez is described in court documents as "a good man, of sound moral character, a hard worker, a peaceful law abiding citizen," who lived much of his adult life in San Antonio, Texas, and sought naturalization to vote and participate in the civic life of the country. In short, Rodriguez was a model applicant, possessing all the qualities of citizenship at the time, with one exception—he wasn't clearly "white."[2]

Working against Rodriguez's application was the 1790 Naturalization Act, which stipulated that naturalization, as distinct from immigration to the United States, was reserved for "free white persons."[3] In other words, under the terms of this law, only whites were permitted to become naturalized citizens. This restriction meant that Mexicans could migrate to the country, contribute labor and money to the economy, and even pay taxes, but they were prohibited from becoming citizens with the benefits and protections that designation entailed. In 1868, this law was amended with the ratification of the Fourteenth Amendment, which extended citizenship to all persons born in the United States. This amendment and subsequent federal legislation in 1879 extended citizenship to the millions of residents of African ancestry born in the United States under slavery or following its abolition, but deliberately excluded Asian immigrants. As the history of "racial-prerequisite cases" indicates, the terrain of "whiteness" shifted over time, but who was categorized as white was left largely to the discretion of the courts.[4] As a consequence, citizenship was conferred automatically on any person born in the United States, but only whites were permitted to acquire citizenship through naturalization. Rodriguez was born in Mexico. According to the state of Texas, he was "nonwhite," and as such, he was denied citizenship.[5]

Rodriguez appealed the decision to the federal district court, where again the terms of debate focused on the racialized nature of the law situating whites and persons of African descent as properly belonging to the nation, but excluding all others. T. J. McMinn and Jack Evans, San Antonio politicians, argued against Rodriguez's petition for naturalization, claiming that he did not qualify for citizenship because "he was not a white person, nor an African, nor of African descent, and is therefore not capable of becoming an American citizen."[6] Rodriguez argued that he was "pure-blooded Mexican" but neither a descendant of the indigenous people of Mexico nor of Spain or Africa, leaving open his racial identity. Rodriguez won his appeal in 1897 when Judge Thomas Maxey shifted Rodriguez's racial designation, maintaining that he and other Mexican Americans were, for the purposes of the law, racially white and as such fell within the boundaries stipulated in federal law for naturalization. Although Maxey's decision ceded Rodriguez's claim to citizenship, the case did not resolve enduring questions of immigration, naturalization, and citizenship for Latinas/os, nor did it contain the politics of racialization.

Rodriguez's case highlights several important elements of U.S. immigration politics in relation to Latinas/os. First, the case clarifies basic components of immigration politics, distinguishing between admissions policy, naturalization laws, and citizenship requirements. It also illuminates the various levels of governmental actors involved, including Congress, the courts, and local jurisdictions. Second, the case highlights the racialization of U.S. immigration policy. Although immigration policy has moved through several phases, it repeatedly privileges particular racial and ethnic groups who approximate a standard of "whiteness," while imposing restrictions on "nonwhites." Admissions policies, naturalization restrictions, and citizenship laws have not only discriminated against nonwhites; they have actively constructed "whiteness," defining American citizenship in relation to the property of whiteness. Periods of economic growth as well as economic crises have exacerbated this racialization process, alternatively drawing or deterring migration with shifting racial discourses about immigrants' places in American life. In the nineteenth and twentieth centuries, U.S. immigration policy privileged "whiteness" in ways that precluded Latinas/os and other nonwhites from full membership, even as the constructed meaning of whiteness changed over time.

Third, the execution of immigration policy plays a key role in the racialization of Latinas/os. The history of immigration politics is rife with contradictions, as Mexican laborers are drawn to the United States by direct appeals from farmers, growers, states, and even the federal government, only to be confronted by popular racism that restricts their rights once they arrive. Indeed, immigration policy has often created classes of Latina/o immigrants—organizing opportunities for specific national groups or economic elites while simultaneously encumbering others. The result is a complicated and often contradictory set of policies reflecting myriad clashing actors at work. The Rodriguez case also highlights tensions between policies that draw clear lines of demarcation between populations and geography dividing the United States from Mexico (and the rest of Latin America) and the history of the Southwest, where transnational flows of people, products, and cultures belie such simple divisions.

This chapter examines the relationship between U.S. immigration policy and Latinas/os in the United States, focusing particular attention on the experiences of Mexican immigrants and the U.S.-Mexico border in the twentieth century.[7] The examination highlights significant congressional acts, constitutional provisions, and federal and state execution of these laws that helped construct Latinas/os as racial outsiders and foreigners, laying the groundwork for shifts in immigration politics occurring in the contemporary state. Social scientists have a long history of examining patterns of immigration from Latin America, including the push-and-pull factors that help explain the flows of people across borders.[8] A similarly rich history documents European immigration patterns and experiences.[9] This chapter builds upon and deviates from these works by focusing on the constitutive *relationship* between the population of Latinas/os and immigration policy, tracing how processes of racialization, informed by shifting political and economic terrains, altered the political standing of Latinas/os in the United States.

Following the maxim that the past is prologue, this chapter identifies the foundation for the war on terror in the racialized demonization of Latina/o immigrants tied to a complicated history of exclusions established by U.S. immigration policy. The terrorization of immigrants by the contemporary security regime is grounded in shifting immigration policies, practices, and discourses that surfaced in the 1990s, but whose roots stretch back much further. The events surrounding 9/11 served as a common focal point for the war on terror and the surge of national security in the United States, but they were not the origin of these practices. The escalation of border enforcement, the passage of federal legislation aimed at restricting immigrant rights and services, and the extension of immigration enforcement to local law-enforcement officers emerged in the last decade of the twentieth century, establishing precedents for the war on terror. Yet the systematic demonization and the imposition of restrictions on Latina/o immigrants have much longer histories. Calling attention to similarities and differences, the chapter assesses what is new in recent immigration policies and what is tied to a much longer tradition of racialization in the construction of citizenship and national identity.

The formation of immigration policy is unique in that the power to enact immigration law rests exclusively with Congress, as mandated by the U.S. Constitution. Despite Congress's sole responsibility to legislate terms of citizenship, execution of these laws, implementation of policy, and adjudication rest with myriad federal agencies, immigration courts, and local jurisdictions. Immigration law and policy involve interlocking questions about membership, belonging, status, restriction, and removal. The following analysis focuses on shifts in admission and naturalization policies corresponding to U.S. territorial expansions between the last half of the nineteenth century and 2001, tracing how changes in law and policy altered the racialization and the status of Latina/o immigrants in the country.

U.S. Territorial Expansion into Latin America and the Formation of U.S. Latina/o Communities

Wars between the United States and Mexico (1846–1848) and the United States and Spain (1896–1898), and the resolution of those wars through treaty agreements, dramatically reconfigured the relationships of Latinas/os, particularly Mexicans, Puerto Ricans, and Cubans, with the United States. During the same period, the growth of mining, agriculture, and transportation industries in the Southwest prompted calls for labor, which actively recruited immigrants from Latin America and Asia. These colonial enterprises resulted in the first wave of Latina/o immigrants to the United States, the formation of the first Latina/o communities in the United States, and a renewed debate about the proper levels of naturalization for Latinas/os and other nonwhite populations.

The first wave of Mexicans in the United States did not consist of a migratory passage or any movement of Mexican nationals across an international border. In a common mantra from the Chicano movement, "We [Mexican Americans] didn't cross the border; the border crossed us!" Several generations of Mexicans lived in the Southwest before 1848, but these residents became U.S. communities only at the end of the Mexican-American War with the signing of the 1848 Treaty of Guadalupe Hidalgo. Under the terms of this treaty, more than half of the territory belonging to Mexico was ceded to the United States, including much of the current Southwest. The estimated one hundred thousand Mexicans living in the territory were given a choice: return to the newly configured territory of Mexico or stay in the United States and receive the protection of U.S. citizenship, including property and grazing rights.[10] Thus, the first Mexicans to become U.S. citizens were not immigrants but long-term settlers already in the territory as a consequence of Spanish colonization who were granted citizenship as a result of war with the United States. This colonial relationship afforded Mexicans compromised inclusion with profound consequences for subsequent relations between the United States and Mexican immigrants throughout the twentieth century, a relationship that Raymond Rocco has dubbed "inclusionary exclusion."[11] The establishment of the border between Mexico and the United States separated the population living in the region from their national origins, cemented the U.S. position as regionally dominant, and constructed a Mexican American minority population.

While the signing of the Treaty of Guadalupe Hidalgo established a political border, marking the formation of the first Mexican American communities in the United States, the border as we know it today did not emerge until the twentieth century with the advent of the Border Patrol and the restriction of Mexicans entering the United States. Between 1848 and 1880, life along the border was characterized by shared economic and cultural ties and the daily flow of goods and people with little to no impediment. An increase in the population of Mexican immigrants entering and settling in the United States occurred around 1849 with the discovery of gold in California and the expansion of agriculture and transportation industries in the West. Young men arrived from Mexico, Chile, and Peru—locations where long-term mining generated skilled workers necessary to fulfill the labor demands prompted by the gold rush.[12] The expansion of mining and agricultural opportunities, along with the need for improved transportation, fueled demand for greater numbers of cheap laborers in Hawaii, California, and the Pacific Coast. Along with the growing population of Mexicans, Chinese, Japanese, and subsequently Filipino, Korean, and Indian male laborers emigrated to the United States.[13]

As the geographic origin of immigrants shifted away from Britain, Germany, and the Nordic states, racialized fears multiplied, generating calls for restrictions on admission and naturalization. Although the 1790 Naturalization Act barred Asian entrants from naturalization, additional restrictions pertaining to work and property ownership were created by local ordinances, state laws, and federal legislation.[14] As nativist sentiment expanded, so too did efforts to regulate and restrict the entrance of nonwhite immigrants, shoring up cultural and political preferences for "white" immigrants. In particular, the focus on centralizing admissions policy brought with it a preference for admitting those who were healthy, employable, unlikely to become public charges, and most easily "assimilable," possessing cultural, religious, and racial qualities approximating the politically dominant Anglo-Saxon population.

These racialized sentiments resulted in passage of the first general immigration act in 1870 as well as a series of immigration laws restricting Asian immigrants, laws that were not fully removed until 1965. Most notable among these was the 1882 Chinese Exclusion Act, which prohibited for ten years the entry of Chinese laborers who had not previously been in the United States (with the exception of businessmen and their families) and reiterated the ban on foreign-born Chinese acquiring U.S. citizenship. Although the Chinese Exclusion Act was not the first attempt to restrict admissions of Chinese immigrants, it proved to be one of the most widespread and successful. Along with the Immigration Act of 1870, it represented the first federal attempt to exclude immigrants predicated on national origin. Passage of the Chinese Exclusion Act resulted in a significant loss of labor in the agricultural, mining, and transportation industries of the Pacific West, prompting a series of racially targeted exclusions, such as the 1907–1908 "Gentleman's Agreements" designed to halt Japanese immigration to the United States.[15] The practice of explicitly and deliberately excluding Chinese immigrants from entering U.S. territory expanded the history of racialized exclusion in naturalization policy enacted in the 1790 Naturalization Act. Those who had once been denied access to citizenship were now denied access to entry, as white privilege justified exclusions predicated on race, ethnicity, and national origin.

The colonial relationship between the United States and Latin America and the subordinated political status of Mexican immigrants was extended to Puerto Ricans and Cubans with the eruption of the Spanish American war. In 1896, incited by the desire to expand its growing economy to the Caribbean islands, the United States entered into a two-year war with Spain, which ended with the signing of the Treaty of Paris in 1898. As a condition of the treaty, Spain ceded control over Puerto Rico, Cuba, and the Philippines to the United States. Consolidating U.S. colonial rule over the islands of Cuba and Puerto Rico required transforming their political systems, legal codes, and economies and establishing an Americanization campaign marked by universal education in English.[16] Colonial control over Puerto

Rico prompted a small population of industrial and agricultural contract laborers (along with an even smaller group of merchants, skilled workers, and political activists) to leave the island. The largest bulk of these migrants settled in New York and other metropolitan centers along the East Coast. Their migration and subsequent trips back to the island established a social network that facilitated future Puerto Rican settlement on the mainland, building a transnational cyclical economy.

By the end of the nineteenth century, immigration policy—both the establishment and supervision of admission and naturalization laws—were fully consolidated under federal control. With passage of the 1891 Immigration Act, Congress established the first permanent administration for the national control of immigration in the form of a superintendent of immigration in the Treasury Department and the Office of Immigration. The marginalized status of Latina/o immigrants as racialized outsiders was institutionalized through colonial expansion and subsequent treaty agreements, which lessened their purchase on citizenship, property, and belonging.

Citizenship as the result of colonial conquest and U.S. imperialism racialized Latinas/os, but this form of racialization paled in comparison to the restrictions imposed by Congress in subsequent eras. Although intended to purify the racial composition of incoming immigrants, contradictory provisions in these laws had the effect of expanding economic opportunities for Mexican Americans and Puerto Ricans and increasing the population of Latinas/os in the United States.

Expanding Racial Restrictions on Nonwhite Immigrants and Opportunities for Latinas/os

Between 1900 and 1910, immigrants constituted a larger percentage of the U.S. population than at any other point in U.S. history, with Southern and Eastern Europeans constituting the majority of newcomers. The rapid increase in immigrants, most of whom were legally defined as nonwhite, alarmed nativists and eugenics advocates already concerned with the growing number of Asian laborers. As a consequence, three separate federal laws were enacted by Congress—the 1917 Immigration Act, the 1921 Quota Act, and the 1924 National Origins Act—setting the standard for immigration restriction for the first half of the twentieth century. These laws consolidated the pattern of racial privilege accorded to Anglo-Saxons, further defining the boundaries of American national identity for decades to come. By 1924, immigration and naturalization laws constricted the opportunity for becoming a "real American" by constructing a new definition of whiteness.

The creation and passage of these key pieces of racially and ethnically restrictive federal legislation were supported by findings from the first large-scale government investigation of immigration conducted under the U.S. Immigration Commission, chaired by John Dillingham. The commission determined that too many immigrants to the United States were coming from the "wrong places" and endorsed the use of literacy tests to cull admission. The commission also recommended that numerical limits be placed on previously unrestricted immigrants from Southern and Eastern Europe, but it encouraged immigration from Northwestern Europe—most notably the British Isles, Germany, and Scandinavia.[17]

Efforts to restrict the population of unskilled and nonwhite immigrants and to cull the "divided loyalties of hyphenated-Americans" led to passage of the Immigration Act of 1917, which required all new arrivals to the United States older than sixteen to demonstrate an ability to read or be turned away. The law broadened the geographic area from which Asian immigrants could be excluded, denied admission to persons advocating sabotage or belonging to revolutionary organizations, and mandated deportation of any immigrant in the United States found preaching or supporting such doctrines.[18] Much like the provisions for detention and exclusion targeted at immigrants in the 1798 Alien and Sedition Acts, and the restrictions against anarchists and other revolutionaries spelled out in 1903 Immigration Act, the newest provisions established a basis for politically motivated targeting of immigrants in the name of national security—provisions that would be radically expanded by the end of the twentieth century and even more so during the war on terror.

Although the 1917 Immigration Act went further than any previous federal policy in its attempt to restrict immigration, for nativists and restrictionists it failed to sufficiently limit the number of "unassimilables"—notably, immigrants from Southern and Eastern Europe. Calls for racialized restrictions mounted, and in the process the construction of the ideal immigrant (and, by extension, the real American) became more closely linked to biologically determinist constructions of race, which limited to an even greater extent who could qualify as white and claim membership in the national community. Congress passed two acts restricting immigration by national origin that encompassed the restrictions called for by nativists. The 1921 Quota Law limited the annual number of entrants of each admissible nationality to 3 percent of the foreign-born of that nationality as recorded in the U.S. census of 1910, limiting the total number of visas issued to approximately 350,000.

Due to pressure from agricultural and manufacturing industries, Latinas/os—specifically, Mexican Americans and Puerto Ricans—were exempt from the restrictions on admission and naturalization emanating from these new federal laws. Nonetheless, they still felt the impact of the racialization of immigration. Desire for their labor in the form of military service and fieldwork prompted exemptions in the federal law and extensions of citizenship. Yet these provisions came with a price, relegating the population to second-class standing legally and politically.

For Puerto Ricans, the military buildup and security concerns surrounding World War I translated into passage of the 1917 Jones-Shafroth Act, which conferred U.S. citizenship on the people of Puerto Rico. Passage of the act facilitated conscription on the island, and more than twenty thousand Puerto Ricans were enlisted in the U.S. Army during World War I. Although the Jones Act permitted ease of travel between the island and the mainland, thereby expanding the population of Puerto Ricans living in the East Coast, it failed to extend to Puerto Ricans all rights of native or naturalized citizenship. For example, Puerto Ricans were empowered to elect a resident commissioner to the United States to represent the island in the U.S. House of Representatives with a voice but not a vote. Citizenship was conferred by statute rather than constitutional mandate, making claims of belonging and purchase on rights far more vulnerable and subject to congressional action.[19]

For Mexican Americans, the 1921 Quota Law expanded opportunities for legal admission, as key provisions in the law exempted immigrants from countries in the Western Hemisphere from exclusion. Responding to pressure from Southwest growers, railroads, and mining interests that depended on unskilled seasonal laborers from Mexico, including the Raisin Growers Association and the American Farm Bureau Federation, Congress created a loophole allowing for legal immigration from countries in the Western Hemisphere, such as Mexico and Canada.[20] This exemption for Western Hemisphere immigrants generated aggressive outreach to Mexican laborers, particularly within agricultural sectors. But the nativist sentiment that generated the restrictions was still present once the immigrants arrived in the United States. Biological determinists proclaimed Mexicans to be docile, indolent, "obedient[,] and cheap." Restrictionists claimed that Mexicans possessed a "birthright of laziness" and "indefinite powers of multiplication" that threatened the country.[21] Mexican immigrants were not denied admission to the United States in the same manner as other immigrants, but they faced social, cultural, and political marginalization in the country.

In the worst instances of racialized targeting, Mexicans and Mexican Americans were rounded up en masse and deported without hearings or administrative reviews. Such incidents occurred in 1913 and 1921 as well as during the Depression era and in the 1950s. The most virulent cases of mass deportation occurred during the Great Depression in 1931 and under the auspice of "Operation Wetback" in 1954—both of which took place in accordance with policy developments discussed in detail in Chapter 5.[22]

The 1921 Quota Law was initially set to expire in 1922 but was extended by Congress to 1924.[23] Despite its extension, the 1921 Quota Law was insufficient to assuage the fears of nativists. In 1924, it was replaced by a new racial formula for determining admission in the form of the National Origins Act. The National Origins Act further restricted immigration by setting admissions quotas at 2 percent of the foreign-born of any nationality as recorded in the 1890 census. The act also barred from entrance all immigrants "ineligible for citizenship," reinforcing the exclusion of Chinese immigrants as well as other Asians declared racially ineligible for naturalization. Under the National Origins Act, the ethnic and racial composition of new immigrants was further constrained. Of the 150,000 visas for entrance issued each year, 82 percent went to immigrants from Northern and Western Europe, 16 percent from Southern and Eastern Europe, and 2 percent from all remaining quota-receiving nations.[24] The total number of immigrants entering the United States—those entering under the quotas and exempted "nonquota" immigrants—fell from 805,000 in 1921 (prior to the quota restrictions), to an average of 513,000 between 1921 and 1924, to an average of 294,000 in the first six years after passage of the National Origins Act.[25]

As with the 1921 Quota Law, the National Origins Act was designed to engineer a strict code of racial hegemony that privileged whiteness. The provisions of the 1924 act barred broad sectors of the global population from entrance to the country. As Roger Daniels and Otis Graham note, "If anyone requires evidence that Congress regarded the US as a 'white man's country' . . . subdivision 'd' of Section 11 of the Immigration Act of 1924—provides it. Persons descended from Africans, Native Americans, and Asians were simply defined as not members of the American Nation."[26]

Despite its clear exclusionary intent, the National Origins Act continued the exemption for Western Hemisphere immigrants, thereby facilitating the entrance of a growing number of Mexican Americans into the United States. In fact, the largest increases in immigration in this period occurred among Mexicans, whose population rose from 0.6 percent of all legal admissions to the United States between 1900 and 1910, to 3.8 percent between 1911 and 1920, to 12.4 percent by 1924. The year that the National Origins Act was passed, Mexican immigrants constituted approximately 45 percent of all legal admissions.[27] The increase of Mexican immigrants represented more than a demographic shift in the Southwest; it signaled the centrality of Mexican labor, particularly within the growing agricultural, manufacturing, and transportation industries—a relationship that would eventually be formalized in a long-standing guest-worker program between the United States and Mexico.

Growing Latina/o Labor, Expanding Large-Scale Raids, and Framing Immigrants as Political Threats

By 1924, the restriction of Asian, Eastern and Southern European, and African immigrants coupled with the exemptions for Western Hemisphere immigrants led to the development of an unofficial labor-importation program that increased rapidly as agribusiness, manufacturing, and transportation industries became more dependent on unskilled Mexican labor. While this relationship between business and Mexican laborers existed informally from 1924 to 1942, it was formalized with the creation of the Bracero Program in 1942.

The Bracero Program was the largest guest-worker program in U.S. history and led to the importation of approximately 4.6 million Mexican workers between 1942 and 1964.[28] The program was formalized through a series of bilateral agreements between the United States and Mexico; state-level statutes and contracts with individual employers governed day-to-day operations and working conditions. The majority of braceros labored on farms in five states—Arizona, California, Nevada, Utah, and Texas. While the workers were supposed to fill a temporary shortage of laborers, as many as one-third remained in the United States on a permanent basis.[29]

The initial rights and working conditions of Mexican braceros were outlined in the international executive agreement signed between the United States and Mexico in August 1942. This agreement was implemented and regulated by the Bureau of Migratory Labor Affairs in Mexico and the U.S. Department of Labor. Over time, the terms of the Bracero Program changed, particularly with subsequent legislation intended to fine-tune the implementation and give greater leverage to U.S. interests in such areas as recruitment and regulation.[30] Standard rights afforded to braceros through the program included "the right of the worker to choose the type of farm work he desires," "guaranteed wages at the prevailing rate paid domestic workers for similar work," the right to make a sufficient "living wage," and "the right to elect their own representatives who shall be recognized by the employer 'as spokesmen' . . . for the purpose of 'maintaining the work contract.'"[31] As noted political historian Ernesto Galarza documents in a series of investigations into the lives of farmworkers, however, most of these commitments were violated or sporadically implemented during the tenure of the Bracero Program. Workers regularly experienced substandard working conditions, persistent discrimination, and life-threatening hazards.[32]

While the preponderance of Mexican laborers who entered the country in this era were legally authorized through the Bracero Program, agricultural and manufacturing industries simultaneously facilitated a black market for undocumented labor. By using unauthorized laborers, employers could avoid transportation or subsistence costs, pay lower wages, extend working hours, evade or weaken rules on working conditions, and keep braceros in the United States beyond the terms of their contracts. Unauthorized workers lived under the constant threat of exposure and thus had even less leverage to press for decent working conditions, wages, and basic services. Unauthorized workers provided an ample supply of underpaid labor that could be easily manipulated to meet the interests of employers.

Evidence of unauthorized workers entering the country throughout the program exists; however, their numbers increased substantially during lapses in the authorizing legislation. Thus, while the Bracero Program was initiated via bilateral agreements and congressional legislation between 1942 and 1946, this initial agreement lapsed in 1946, with no new legislation until 1947. During this lapse, demand from the agricultural and manufacturing sectors and social networks of Mexican communities in the United States supported continued migration from Mexico, albeit without legal authorization. Statistical data from the Immigration and Naturalization Service (INS) indicate a 50 percent increase between 1946 and 1947 of the numbers of deportable Mexican immigrants apprehended.[33] During subsequent lapses in the program, agricultural and manufacturing sector lobbyists pressured INS to open the border or to do away with head tax and other immigration restrictions to facilitate the continued flow of Mexican laborers, and the U.S. government complied.[34] In fact, during the 1946–1947 lapse, the federal government enabled this flow of unauthorized workers by ordering INS to deliberately cut back on the number of border-enforcement agents, thereby leaving the border porous and easier to cross. Lapses in authorizing legislation became more frequent, with additional gaps occurring between 1951 and 1953 and between 1954 and 1959. These lapses were prompted in part by fears of growing Mexican communities, coupled with periods of economic slowdown, that resulted in racial scapegoating on a scale comparable to that targeting Asians and Southern European laborers in previous years.

The continued entrance of Mexican laborers during these lapses intensified existing racialized fears and prompted large-scale immigration sweeps and military-style roundups within Mexican communities. One of the largest sweeps occurred prior to the formalization of the Bracero Program in 1931, when more than five hundred thousand Mexicans (immigrants and American citizens) were rounded up and summarily deported. Much like the previous targeting of Asian laborers, the restrictions aimed at Mexican immigrants were rooted in public fears, supported by pseudoscientific studies, and institutionalized via public law and policy.[35]

This racialization of immigration policy was once again apparent in "Operation Wetback," the largest roundup of Mexicans in U.S. history, authorized by President Dwight Eisenhower in 1954. Led by retired U.S. Army General Joseph Swing, this initiative deployed eight hundred border-enforcement officials, working with local police, press, and farmers, into Mexican communities and ranches throughout the Southwest. Border-enforcement agents swept through market places and homes, often rounding up anyone who merely looked Mexican (regardless of individuals' actual statuses or ethnic backgrounds), transferring them to a processing center, and deporting them to Mexico.

In conjunction with Operation Wetback, INS experimented with a new deportation practice that would export deportees deep into the interior of Mexico in the hopes that such distance from the U.S.-Mexico border would discourage return migration. The result was a generalized terror among Mexican communities, as families were separated, individuals disappeared, and hundreds of Latinas/os were deported without even an administrative hearing to determine whether they were in the country legally. The practice of unleashing federal agents in Mexican communities became a hallmark of immigration-policy enforcement throughout the remainder of the twentieth century. This practice effectively "de-Americanized" Mexican Americans, designating them as potential "aliens" who could be deported at will and setting a pattern replicated forcefully in the post-9/11 era. Ultimately General Swing's efforts were deemed so successful that Congress rewarded INS with a supplemental appropriation of $3 million and extended the program until 1959.[36]

The Bracero Program was renewed in 1959 but came to a formal end in 1964, despite efforts for more than a decade to revive the guest-worker program. By the time of its demise, the Bracero Program had established a significant political change in admission policy for Mexican workers. The largest guest-worker program in U.S. history consolidated the status of Mexicans as "temporary" workers while altering the composition of Latina/o communities in the United States. The rapid increase and growing dependence of U.S. industry on Mexican labor reignited racialized fears, prompting a series of large-scale raids and roundups intended to intimidate, cower, and systematically remove Mexican immigrants from the United States. The demand for migrant labor coupled with racialized demonization, alienation, and threat of removal set a precedent for immigration enforcement in the late twentieth century and during the war on terror.

This period of immigration politics was also marked by a shift in immigration legislation away from a unified focus on restricting nonwhites toward restricting potential political subversives who threatened national security. Beginning in 1940, Congress modified immigration policy to meet what it defined as the security needs of the country, specifically addressing the perceived threat of foreign subversives. Congress passed the Alien Registration Act in 1940 requiring that all immigrants register, be fingerprinted, keep the government informed of their addresses, and possess internal passports. The act also stipulated provisions for a peacetime sedition act, also known as the Smith Act, which made it a crime to "knowingly or willfully advocate, abet, advise, or teach the duty, necessity, desirability, or propriety of overthrowing or destroying any government in the United States by force or violence" or "to organize . . . any . . . assembly of persons who teach, advocate, or encourage the overthrow or destruction of any government in the United States by force or violence."[37] The act authorized American consuls to refuse visas to applicants who might endanger "the public safety" and empowered the president to deport any immigrant whose departure was "in the interest of the US." Collectively, these changes sanctioned fear of immigrants as threatening subversives and traded upon this fear to legally encumber immigrants' rights in the name of national security.[38]

The growing fear of political subversives intersected with the fear of non-white foreigners during World War II, culminating in the internment of persons of Japanese origin living in the United States. Through the administration of executive order 9066, 110,000 persons of Japanese ancestry were incarcerated on the threat that they constituted a "fifth column." More than 70,000 of those interned were U.S. citizens; the remaining persons were foreign-born residents, none of whom demonstrated any actual threat to national security. As Natsu Saito notes, in the process of internment, individuals of Japanese descent in the United States became racialized as foreign and threatening, regardless of their actual immigration status.[39] This intersection of racialized fears and political targeting of potential subversives would emerge again powerfully in the period after 9/11; however, the weight of that intersection would be felt most prominently by persons of Arab descent, regardless of their immigration statuses or actual affiliations with foreign entities. However, the equation of immigration and immigrants with threats to the country and the escalation of security discourse that enabled the racialized demonization of nonwhites would be replicated broadly in the twenty-first century. Much like the summary roundups and deportations of Mexican Americans, this racialization of Japanese persons was deeply embedded in public sentiment, supported in formal academic discourse, institutionalized in law, and upheld by the courts.[40]

With the advent of the Cold War, Congress began repealing open restrictions on admission, birthright citizenship, and naturalization based on race in exchange for more subtle forms of racialization predicated on national security. In 1952, Congress passed the McCarren-Walter Act, which stated that "the right of a person to become a naturalized citizen of the US shall not be denied or abridged because of race or sex or because such a person is married."[41] This legislation ended the total exclusion of Asian immigration and in theory made all races eligible for naturalization.

Yet in moving away from race-based restrictions, the 1952 McCarren-Walter Act introduced belief-based exclusions, restricting immigrants who were potential political subversives. Building upon the Alien Registration Act and the Smith Act, the 1952 legislation provided for the exclusion of foreign-born persons who were anarchists, Communists, and/or advocated or taught opposition to organized government. The McCarren-Walter Act also barred from entry "aliens who write or publish, or cause to be written or published, or who knowingly circulate, distribute, print, or display . . . any written or printed matter, advocating or teaching opposition to all organized government, or advocating or teaching . . . the overthrow by force, violence, or other unconstitutional means of the Government of the United States or all forms of law."[42] The act gave broad latitude to the Department of Justice (DOJ) and INS to restrict and encumber foreign-born students, intellectuals, and lay persons who studied, taught, or promoted ideas politically unfavorable to the United States. It extended and seriously fortified provisions for excluding immigrants during periods of national security concern, particularly those whose political views were perceived as challenging, threatening, critical, or in any way oppositional to the country. In so doing, the McCarren-Walter Act further entangled matters of immigration with security and defense concerns.

Reforming Immigration Policy, Expanding Globalization, and Militarizing the U.S.-Mexico Border

Between 1965 and 1995, immigration politics was dominated by three significant developments: (1) broad-scale reforms in immigration legislation ending the openly racist practices of the National Origins Act, (2) expanding globalization in the Western Hemisphere facilitated by government programs and trade agreements, and (3) increased attention to border security, including a large-scale infusion of resources to fortify the U.S.-Mexico border. For Mexican immigrants specifically and Latinas/os generally, these shifts had the effect of placing administrative barriers on admission while steadily increasing the flow of new immigrants due to economic displacement and extensions of transnational social networks through globalization. Increased border security coupled with the militarization of immigration enforcement also situated these immigrants as aliens who posed cultural and economic threats to the country. The confluence of economic displacement in migrants' home countries and restrictive immigration enforcement in the United States further marginalized the population.

Among broad reforms in immigration legislation, the 1965 Hart-Cellar Act and the 1986 Immigration Reform Act stand out for their lasting impact, particularly on Latina/o immigrants in the United States. Passed in the aftermath of increases in both legal and unauthorized Mexican immigration associated with the Bracero Program, the Hart-Cellar Act of 1965 was a response to efforts to end de jure racial discrimination at the heart of the civil rights and Chicana/o movements. Under the terms of this legislation, the national-origins quota system for individual nations was abolished, and admissions standards were shifted to favor family reunification. The new immigration act provided for the admission of certain close relatives of American citizens and legal permanent residents without numerical limitations.[43]

Yet the act also imposed limits on immigration from Western Hemisphere countries, the first of its kind in federal immigration legislation. The 1965 law set an initial quota of 120,000 visas per year for the entire Western Hemisphere. This numerical restriction coupled with the more than forty years of intensive labor recruitment and expanding social networks between U.S. and Mexican communities guaranteed that the number of requests from the region far exceeded the number of available visas. By 1976, a severe backlog in visa applications yielded a waiting list of approximately three hundred thousand names and an average waiting period of approximately three years.[44] For Mexican immigrants, the impact was experienced in terms of not only the limit on visas and the increasing application backlog but also the shift in political relationships: They were no longer a favored immigrant group exempted from quota restrictions.

Visas were allocated on a first-come, first-served basis, and applicants still had to meet strict labor-certification requirements and demonstrate that they would not be displacing U.S. workers. As the numbers of Mexican immigrants who were denied visas increased, and the waiting lists expanded, an increasing number of immigrants entered the United States without proper authorization. The 1965 law changed the face of immigration to the United States. Prior to the law, more than 60 percent of immigrants to the United States came from Europe, with approximately 35 percent arriving from South and Central America and 3 percent from Asia. After 1965, European immigrants accounted for approximately 19 percent of the immigrant population, South and Central Americans represented 43 percent, and Asian immigrants were 34 percent of the immigrant population.[45]

The end of the Bracero Program raised new questions about how to handle the increasing numbers of unemployed Mexican laborers descending on border towns, such as Matamoros and Ciudad Juarez in Mexico, and the increased flow of unauthorized laborers into the United States. The termination of the Bracero Program did nothing to stop the need for low-income, manual labor, particularly in the burgeoning agricultural and manufacturing sectors of the United States, nor did it disrupt the social networks and patterns of flow long established after more than four decades of migrant traffic.

In 1965, with the support of international lending institutions, the Mexican government initiated the border industrialization program (BIP), creating a series of trade zones along the U.S.-Mexico border to encourage the establishment of large-scale manufacturing plants by offering lucrative tax breaks to foreign-owned companies. Modeled after export-processing zones, the program created employment for thousands of out-of-work laborers in northern cities by allowing wholly owned foreign subsidiaries to enter Mexico and set up processing plants in industrial parks along the border. These plants, or *maquilas,* were dedicated to manufacturing and assembly production, employing workers at wages significantly below those earned by their American counterparts.

Although the BIP was intended to alleviate the economic pressure of thousands of unemployed men returning from the Bracero Program, it did nothing to lower the rates of male unemployment, because plant owners almost exclusively employed young women. Owners suggested that women were better workers, who tended to have more formal education. Activists and advocates for the women workers argued that they were more vulnerable and pliable as workers and subject to greater levels of mistreatment.[46]

Largely due to tax abatements afforded to companies participating in the program, the BIP did not contribute to economic development of the region as planners had hoped. Overall, 80 percent of the plants were owned by U.S. companies making products purchased primarily by Americans. The wages paid to employees through the BIP did not prompt the anticipated growth, because wage levels were so low that many of the laborers could not afford to buy the products they were making. Border cities became tethered to these *maquilas* with little diversification. When plants shut down or fired workers, the towns were left to absorb the consequences with few sources of alternative employment.

The *maquiladora* industry was part of a larger push toward globalization in the region. Marked by an increase in export-oriented production, the growth of transnational industry, and a weakening of the state and expanded privatization, the BIP represented an intensification of neoliberal economic reforms in Mexico and Latin America. These reforms were prominent in the 1994 North American Free Trade Agreement (NAFTA) as well as the proliferation of regional trade agreements, such as CARICOM, the Caribbean Basin Initiative, and MERCOSUR. These reforms had serious economic and political consequences for the region, not the least of which was the increased displacement of poor, rural, working-class farmers and indigenous populations and a subsequent increase in the numbers of Latin American migrants entering the United States.[47]

The steady increase of unauthorized migrants, coupled with increasing numbers of immigrants fleeing civil unrest in Central America (particularly El Salvador, Guatemala, and Nicaragua), prompted a renewed call for Congress to tackle immigration reform. The Immigration Reform and Control Act (IRCA) of 1986 represented a compromise between enforcement advocates who wanted stronger controls placed on employers they believed were responsible for the expanding immigrant communities and immigrant advocates who sought legalization for the millions of unauthorized immigrants and their families already in the United States.

IRCA created a dual amnesty program as well as a diversity program benefiting millions of immigrants and added new restrictions and penalties for employers who hired unauthorized laborers. The larger of the amnesty measures provided permanent residency to persons who could demonstrate they had continuously lived in the country since December 31, 1981. The second measure, also known as the Special Agricultural Worker (SAW) program, enabled undocumented immigrants who had worked in agriculture for at least ninety days between May 1985 and May 1986 to legalize their status and become permanent residents.[48]

The legalization provisions in the act were paired with restrictions on employers. IRCA created sanctions prohibiting employers from "knowingly hiring, recruiting or referring for a fee aliens not authorized to work in the U.S." In particular, employers were required by the law to verify that a new employee was eligible to work by completing an I-9 form. Moreover, employers who violated these provisions were penalized with fines ranging from $250 to $10,000 per unauthorized worker, and employers who habitually violated the act faced criminal penalties.[49] Subsequent legislation in 1990 refined aspects of these employer sanctions while strengthening protections against discrimination for workers.[50]

Almost three million immigrants applied for legalization through the pre-1982 amnesty provisions as well as the SAW program (1.7 million under the pre-1982 provisions and 1.2 million SAW applicants). In addition to completing a lengthy application and providing supporting documentation, each applicant had to pay a significant filing fee, receive a medical examination, get fingerprinted and photographed, and pass an interview. Persons submitting applications through the pre-1982 process were also required to demonstrate English-language proficiency and knowledge of U.S. history and government. Those who filed their applications were typically given temporary employment authorization for approximately six months, followed by permanent residency cards if their applications were successful. Beneficiaries of the act were disproportionately Latina/o, as more than 72 percent of the applicants were Mexican, followed by Central Americans (Salvadorans and Guatemalans), Haitians, and Asian Indians.[51]

By the early 1990s, the failure of previous immigration policies to control the flow of undocumented immigrants, coupled with demands to regulate the increased traffic of goods, services, and people associated with global-ization, prompted a new national border-patrol strategy. Beginning in 1994, the INS announced a shift away from its previous focus on apprehension to a strategy focused on control and prevention through deterrence. The policy was executed primarily through the use of "concentrated enforcement" in the most visible and highly trafficked routes for undocumented immigrants and smugglers. Concentrated enforcement took the form of large-scale increases in the number of Border Patrol agents and increased time spent on border-control activities, installation of fencing and physical barriers, and use of advanced electronic surveillance equipment (e.g., state-of-the-art sen-sors and video equipment, infrared night-vision devices, forward-looking infrared systems, and unmanned aerial vehicles).[52] The strategy was meant to deter the traffic of undocumented immigrants by making passage in the usual corridors so difficult and channeling them into territory so challeng-ing to navigate that it would make apprehension easier. Animated by the anti-immigrant fervor set off in California in response to the slowdown in the state's economy and the scapegoating of immigrant workers prominent in the California governor's race, these policy changes were also linked to efforts by Democratic politicians eager to hold onto gains made in the 1996 midterm elections.

In conjunction with the shift to concentrated enforcement, regional Border Patrol supervisor Silvestre Reyes initiated Operation Blockade (later known as Operation Hold the Line) in the El Paso, Texas, area. As part of the operation, Border Patrol agents were stationed along the Rio Grande in a concentrated lineup with closely spaced vehicles to intimidate entrants. The blockade served as a model to the INS as it sought to implement the new national policy. Operation Blockade was quickly followed by several other operations intended to create similar deterrents in high-traffic corridors, including Operation Gatekeeper, initiated in October 1994 in San Diego, California; Operation Safeguard, initiated in October 1994 in Tucson and Nogales, Arizona; and Operation Rio Grande, initiated in August 1997 in Brownsville, Texas.[53]

These operations were intended to deter undocumented immigrants, thereby reducing the number of apprehensions by Border Patrol, but the results were inconsistent. In the California region covered by Operation Gate-keeper, apprehensions fell in San Diego but increased in the nearby eastern area of El Centro. In Arizona and Texas, apprehensions increased significant-ly over the five years following the operation's launch, but the program also pushed undocumented immigrants into more challenging terrain, increasing the number of deaths from exhaustion, exposure, and dehydration.[54]

In the six years after the implementation of Operations Blockade, Gatekeeper, and Safeguard, the number of migrant deaths documented along the border due to hypothermia, heat stroke, drowning, accident, or homicide increased from 27 in 1994 to 140 in 2000.[55] Border Patrol agents acknowledged that the number of recorded deaths was conservative and underestimated much larger numbers of bodies that were never discovered in the rough terrain.

Expanding the National Security Regime, Framing Immigrants as Terrorists, and Extending Enforcement to Local Officers

Although changes in immigration policies after 9/11 reflected longer trajectories of racialization, they grew most directly from legislative and policy changes enacted in the 1990s. By 1996, efforts to deter undocumented immigrants through Operation Gatekeeper and similar programs had effectively militarized the border. Employer sanctions and worksite raids resurfaced as a favored strategy for immigration enforcement. Then, in 1996, Congress passed three pieces of legislation that dramatically intensified restrictions on immigrants: the Anti-Terrorism and Effective Death Penalty Act (AEDPA), the Personal Responsibility and Work Opportunity Reconciliation Act (PRWORA), and the Illegal Immigration Reform and Immigrant Responsibility Act (IIRIRA). Together, these laws increased scrutiny of immigrants, raised penalties for unlawful presence, severely restrained judicial review and due process, facilitated higher numbers of detentions and deportations, and created a system to expand immigration enforcement by deputizing local law enforcement as immigration agents. The new legislation also capitalized on the still-pervasive framing of immigrants as economic burdens, denying a host of federal benefits to immigrants as part of welfare reform. But, most significantly, these bills portrayed immigrants as terrorist threats. Following the lead of the federal government, states across the Southwest also became increasingly aggressive in establishing and enforcing new statutes that denied public services to immigrants. In other words, the punitive policies that terrorized immigrants after 9/11 were rooted in racially restrictive legislation prevalent throughout the twentieth century, especially those laws enacted in the late 1990s.

Capitalizing on the fear of terrorism reignited in the wake of the 1995 Oklahoma City bombing, the AEDPA targeted immigrants suspected of terrorism by establishing a new court to process the removal of immigrants certified by the attorney general as posing a threat to national security and giving broad latitude for the detention and imprisonment of such immigrants. With nothing more than the attorney general's certification that an immigrant posed a threat, the law denied other forms of relief, including asylum, voluntary departure, and habeas corpus.[56]

In addition to creating new forms of scrutiny, the changes initiated in 1996 denied services to immigrants (both documented and undocumented), particularly through the PRWORA, popularly known as welfare reform. This new legislation reconfigured government assistance for low-income families by eliminating the long-standing Aid to Families with Dependent Children (AFDC) and replacing it with a decentralized program called Temporary Aid to Needy Families (TANF). Signed into law by President Bill Clinton, the law sought to reduce the number of persons on welfare by placing time limits on the amount of aid received, strengthening work requirements, shifting the funding from an open-ended federal entitlement program to a series of capped state block grants, and providing performance bonuses to states that successfully moved recipients into jobs.

Title IV of the legislation outlined eligibility requirements, underscoring the continual perception of immigrants as burdens to the state and emphasizing the language of "self-sufficiency," stating:

> Self-sufficiency has been a basic principle of United States immigration law since this country's earliest immigration statutes. It continues to be the immigration policy of the United States that aliens within the Nation's borders not depend on public resources to meet their needs, but rather rely on their own capabilities and the resources of their families, their sponsors, and private organizations, and the availability of public benefits not constitute an incentive for immigration to the United States.[57]

Following this logic, noncitizens were denied access to most federal public benefits, including "grant, contract, loan, professional or commercial licenses" as well as "retirement, welfare, health, disability, public or assisted housing, postsecondary education, food assistance, unemployment benefit, or any other similar benefit."[58] As a condition of these tightened eligibility requirements, noncitizens were denied access to food stamps as well as supplemental social security income.[59] Passage of PRWORA opened avenues for states to extend these restrictions by barring undocumented students from receiving in-state tuition rates and restricting Medicaid to legal immigrants. The legislation legitimized the presumption that immigrants were an economic burden rather than an asset or a stimulus, a theme taken up by states as they rapidly expanded legislation and initiatives to deny access to virtually every public service.

Of the three statutes passed, the IIRIRA had the most significant impact on immigration politics by increasing the militarization of the border, detentions, deportations, and joint operations between local law enforcement and the federal government. The act extended the project of concentrated border enforcement initiated with Operation Blockade by dramatically increasing Border Patrol personnel (adding five thousand new officers) and providing $12 million for additional fencing (extending Operation Gatekeeper). The act also provided state-of-the-art technology, including aircraft, helicopters, night-vision goggles, and four-wheel-drive vehicles. It enacted new penalties for entering the country without inspection, including a $250 fine, and a five-year prison sentence (and deportation) for persons attempting to evade capture through high-speed chase. The act significantly increased the high-tech scrutiny of immigrants, with the issuance of new border-crossing identification cards complete with biometric identifiers; the creation of a new automated entry/exit control system that recorded the entrance and departure of all immigrants, facilitating the apprehension of people overstaying their visas; and the addition of "pre-inspection stations" in five foreign airports responsible for sending the largest number of inadmissible immigrants. New databases scrutinizing employment eligibility were also authorized through the law, as was the collection and scrutiny of the records of student visa holders. Adding to this new level of scrutiny, the act authorized the hiring of three hundred INS employees to target immigrants who had overstayed their visas.[60]

The act created a new category of "unlawfully present" persons and levied increased penalties for migrants who entered and stayed in the country without proper documentation. These sections of the law dealt with immigrants who had entered the country legally but whose status had changed (e.g., due to an expired visa), rendering them no longer lawfully present. As a condition of the act, immigrants caught without proper documentation for more than 180 days but less than a year would be deported and barred from returning for a minimum of three years. Those who had been in the country without proper documentation for more than a year would be deported and required to remain outside the United States for a minimum of ten years. Failure to abide by these terms precluded the individual from applying for a waiver for a minimum of ten years. There were no possibilities for appealing an INS decision on bans on readmission. With respect to removals, the law broadened INS discretion beyond the initial screening phase to permit expedited removal, which allowed an individual INS officer to unilaterally rule that an immigrant was inadmissible and to remove him or her without a hearing.[61]

The statute broadened the definition of an aggravated felony and stipulated that conviction of this crime warranted automatic deportation—and applied these broadened definitions retroactively.[62] Under the terms of this act, a relatively minor offense, such as shoplifting, which had previously been grounds for possible fines and imprisonment, could result in immediate deportation. The IIRIRA also constructed several new grounds for exclusion of immigrants, such as failing to have vaccinations for such diseases as measles, polio, and hepatitis B. It denied entrance altogether to those suspected of inciting terrorism, falsely claiming U.S. citizenship, unlawfully voting in the United States, or being convicted of domestic violence or stalking.

One of the most contentious elements of the bill was section 287(g), regarding the performance of immigration-officer functions by state officers and employees. Specifically, the law authorized the secretary of the U.S. Department of Homeland Security (DHS) to enter into agreements with state and local law-enforcement agencies, "permitting designated officers to perform immigration law enforcement functions, pursuant to a Memorandum of Understanding (MOU), provided that the local law enforcement officers receive appropriate training and function under the supervision of sworn U.S. Immigration and Customs Enforcement (ICE) officers."[63] Originating in the 1996 legislation, this program was fully realized only in 2002, when Florida became the first state to enter into a 287(g) agreement with the federal government. Since that time, more than sixty-six such agreements have been signed in twenty states, producing more than one thousand local officers trained to serve as immigration agents in their localities.

These 287(g) programs have come under intense scrutiny in recent years. Reports from the DHS inspector general, the General Accounting Office, and independent agencies allege widespread racial profiling, insufficient oversight from the federal government, inadequate training, and incidents of abuse. One independent report issued by the University of North Carolina School of Law found that the programs were being used to "purge towns and cities of 'unwelcome' immigrants . . . resulting in the harassment of citizens and isolation of the Hispanic community."[64]

These joint operating agreements instantiate the central dynamic of racialized demonization of immigrants, which has become a cornerstone of the war on terror and the national security regime. Predating the events of 9/11, these programs were intensified and escalated thereafter. The following two chapters demonstrate how framing immigrants as threats to the country was expanded through new legislation as well as implementation of 287(g) agreements through large-scale raids and roundups.

Conclusion

The reforms initiated in 1996 continued practices of racialization central to U.S. immigration policy since its inception. They continued the long-standing discursive construction of Latina/o immigrants as threats, not only framing Latina/o immigrants as cultural, social, and economic burdens but also introducing language constructing them as threats to the nation—as potential terrorists. In keeping with unrelentingly negative framing, this legislation set new boundaries on eligibility for government services, denying both documented and undocumented immigrants access to aid. These tendencies, constituting immigrants as terrorist threats, subjecting them to heightened scrutiny, and restricting their access to government services, would become a hallmark of legislation, policy directives, and ICE operations after 9/11. Endorsed by the federal government, these policies gave license to states, localities, and private political actors to impose restrictions on documented and undocumented immigrants, excluding them from national belonging as inherently suspicious.

In the next chapter, I examine how these changes were intensified in legislation passed by Congress in the 107th to 110th legislative sessions and how they were punitively executed in a range of operations on the ground, which resulted in thousands of Latina/o immigrants being rounded up, detained, interrogated, arrested, and frequently deported.

4

Securitizing Immigration Legislation

For years, Tom Tancredo has been a vocal advocate for stricter immigration enforcement in the country. As a House representative from Colorado, Tancredo made illegal immigration—and, more specifically, efforts to restrict Latina/o immigrants—a centerpiece of his congressional activity. Even before 9/11, Tancredo sponsored several pieces of legislation aimed at enhancing border security, promoting English-only education, and limiting access to government services for all immigrants in the United States. He was an ardent supporter of state initiatives and legislation targeting Latina/o immigrants, such as proposals to limit bilingual education and to deny driver's licenses to unauthorized immigrants. Tancredo was not shy in expressing his views and was notorious for headline-grabbing hyperbole.

Given his single-minded attention to immigration, it was of little surprise when Representative Tancredo announced his plans to host a 2002 community vigil commemorating the 9/11 terrorist attacks, opposing the increase of unauthorized immigrants in the country, and supporting individuals who were "victims of illegal immigration and open borders." His guest list included "relatives of 9/11 terrorist attacks, people who lost their jobs to undocumented immigrants, and people injured by undocumented immigrant drunk drivers and criminals." Although the event failed to materialize, Tancredo's discussions of his proposed vigil articulated beliefs circulating widely in Congress that conflated immigrants with terrorism and constructed unauthorized Latina/o immigrants as threats to the homeland. Tancredo's position at the forefront of anti-immigrant activity signaled that the long-standing racialization of Latina/o immigrants cultivated within immigration politics had been fully integrated into the expansion of the national security regime, prompting a restructuring of immigration politics and its administration as well as a host of new restrictions.

This chapter examines the rise of anti-immigrant legislation in Congress in the years after 9/11 and through the height of the war on terror. I am particularly concerned with the construction of Latina/o immigrants as threats to national security in legislation passed during the 107th to 110th legislative sessions from 2001 to 2008. Immigration legislation (as well as department directives, executive orders, and policy) racialized and demonized Latina/o immigrants and generated new levels of restriction. This chapter draws attention to the unique intersections of gendered rights and immigration restrictions within the securitization process, paying particular attention to the 2005 reauthorization of the Violence Against Women Act (VAWA) and the 2003 Trafficking Victims Protection Reauthorization Act (TVPRA).

Prominent national advocacy organizations noted mounting hostility toward immigrants in congressional legislation.[1] This chapter builds upon these insights to provide a comprehensive review of key legislative changes pertaining to immigration in the bills passed by Congress. Just as the commemoration planned by Representative Tancredo positioned Latinas/os as potent threats to the American public, congressional discourse constructed immigrants as terrorists and created new technologies to restrict and control those threats.

Congressional Legislation, 2001 to 2008

Between September 11, 2001, and the end of the George W. Bush administration in January 2009, more than 2,000 bills dealing with immigration were introduced in Congress. Of these, 144 were passed by both the House and Senate and signed into law.[2] Among those bills that made it out of Congress and to the president's desk, most included restrictive language, although the types of restrictions aimed at immigrants varied. These restrictions reflected a mix of priorities with regard to security but generally aimed at increasing the degree to which immigrants were monitored, detained, confined, and policed. The most common types of restrictions appeared in five areas:

1. Increased scrutiny of immigrants, including policing and scrutiny related to immigrants' work authorization; more federal agents (e.g., Border Patrol, fugitive operations teams); higher budgets and more resources (e.g., unmanned aerial vehicles); creation of special programs designed to cull additional identifying information on immigrants (e.g., TIPS, US-VISIT).

2. Increased possibilities for detention, arrest, and/or deportation (resulting in part from the increased scrutiny and capacity for monitoring immigrants), including increased arrests for violations that involved charges that would not have required detention prior to 9/11; use of operations intended to fight domestic or international terrorism to apprehend persons of unknown origin, fugitives, and gang members.

3. Increased militarization of the border region (including increased capacity at the border in the form of additional Border Patrol agents, personnel, and new technology and infrastructure); expansion of physical barriers along the U.S.-Mexico border.

4. Increased restrictions and/or constraints on federal services and benefits to immigrants. Congress enacted multiple bills preventing immigrants from receiving federally authorized and funded services, such as social security benefits, while also restricting employment opportunities for legal immigrants and barring them from accessing information about themselves stored in federal databases. Several bills increased the cost of services to immigrants (including fees for entry).

5. An expansion of immigration enforcement, specifically through the empowerment (or extension of capacity) of local- and state-level law enforcement to execute greater levels of investigation, review, apprehension, and/or cooperation with federal immigration authorities. This expansion included legislation authorizing or obligating immigration-enforcement duties (including reporting of apprehensions/detentions); language encouraging cooperation between local and federal law enforcement; increased training and/or resources for local law enforcement to act in immigration-related matters not previously executed; and the creation of and/or participation in joint task forces between local and federal agents.

Each of these kinds of restriction substantively altered the landscape of immigration politics. Although some of the legislative language appeared facially neutral and politically innocuous, the creation of new modes of restriction contributed to the racialization of Latinas/os as threats and terrorists, justifying expansion of the security regime.[3]

Increased Scrutiny and Review of Immigrants

The expansion of state authority as part of the war on terror facilitated increased scrutiny of multiple subjects, most notably immigrants in the

United States. Careful monitoring of virtually all aspects of immigrant life was made possible through an expansion of funds, information, personnel, technologies, and sharing of these resources across departments, agencies, and law-enforcement jurisdictions.

Particular attention was paid to reviewing and recording the daily activities of immigrants, as all travel and entry documents, including visas, issued by the United States and all work-authorization permits for refugees and asylees were required to be machine-readable and tamper-resistant and to include a standard biometric identifier.[4] Although immigrants admitted to the country have often been subject to invasive state inspections, particularly nonwhite and poor immigrants defined as politically or medically threatening, this new legislation expanded the scrutiny of immigrant bodies with more invasive technology and preserved personal data for myriad practices from admission to deportation.

At the same time that immigrant bodies were being monitored, culled, and made subject to new classifications, the number of immigration agents, investigators, inspectors, affiliates, and associated personnel was repeatedly expanded through new legislation. The Enhanced Border Security and Visa Entry Reform Act of 2002 substantially increased the number of immigration investigators and inspectors. Additional supplements were mandated by the act through 2006.[5] This legislation also provided for more training, facilities, and "security-related technology" for such personnel.[6] Similarly, legislation passed in 2005 increased the number of diplomatic security personnel assigned exclusively to the function of preventing and detecting fraud by applicants for visas.[7]

In immigration-reform legislation passed between 2001 and 2008, Congress authorized the creation of new structures dedicated to the review and monitoring of immigrants, such as the Terrorist Lookout Committees established at each U.S. mission. These committees provided training for consular staff in immigration-enforcement matters while also sharing terrorist-related intelligence to assist in the performance of such work.[8] The Enhanced Border Security and Visa Entry Reform Act of 2002 created plans for a "North American National Security Program," linking the United States, Mexico, and Canada and creating additional preclearance and pre-inspection reviews for immigrants seeking admission.[9] The Intelligence Authorization Act for Fiscal Year 2003 created new federal agencies, centers, and databases to monitor the activities, financial capabilities, and practices of foreign individuals and groups believed to be associated with terrorism.[10] Congress also authorized expanded review of immigrants in custody through the creation of the Office of the Federal Detention Trustee in 2004. The trustee works with officials in the Bureau of Prisons to oversee the detention of immigrants and collect information related to federal prisoners in nonfederal institutions.[11] Although each of these various agencies and programs performed a variety of functions, individually and collectively, they added new layers to the pervasive system of surveillance designed to maintain a firm grasp on immigrant activity.

Additional scrutiny of immigrant bodies was advanced through stricter reporting and registration requirements for foreign students and for passengers and occupants of commercial aircraft and vessels (including trains and buses) traveling by land, air, or water.[12] These practices included expanded monitoring of foreign students' registrations, courses, and participation in college and university activities as well as additional review of institutions approved to accept foreign students and/or exchange visitors.

Monitoring of immigrant labor was expanded through extensions of the "Basic" employment-verification system that performs electronic checks of Social Security Administration and Immigration and Naturalization Service (INS) databases to verify the eligibility of new employees. The program, which was extended to all fifty states in 2004, created additional review of immigrants' documents, work histories, and employment relationships with the aim of preventing unauthorized immigrants from working in the United States. In addition, the expansion act passed by Congress in 2003 heightened scrutiny of the immigration investor program authorized under the Basic Pilot Program, which required "information on the number of such immigrants, and their country of origin, settlement locality, and employment created by them."[13]

This expanded scrutiny and documentation of immigrant activity produced a need for new mechanisms to store and share information. Several acts passed by Congress between 2001 and 2008 enabled the construction of new databases of information pertaining to visas, admissibility of immigrants seeking entrance, and deportation. Legislation created provisions for sharing (and making interoperable) these databases across federal departments, agencies, and U.S. law-enforcement jurisdictions. The Chimera system, one of the most famous new databases, included provisions for name matching in at least four different languages, which was deemed a priority for immigration management. By integrating information across existing sources and adding new details obtained from heightened scrutiny and review of immigrants in the United States, new modes of information management promised to produce smarter and more efficient systems of immigrant tracking and control.[14]

Another controversial database, initiated by the Department of Homeland Security Appropriations Act of 2004, extended the screening of airline passengers to delay or prohibit those who posed a threat from boarding a flight. The Computer-Assisted Passenger Prescreening System (CAPPS II) allowed the Transportation Security Administration (TSA) to mine government and commercial databases and flag passengers according to their presumed threat levels, thereby preventing them from boarding an airplane. Concerns over privacy and curtailing of personal liberties as well as the high number of false threats generated by CAPPS II led to its termination in 2005. It was replaced by an upgraded prescreening system called Secure Flight.[15]

Sharing information across jurisdictions was facilitated through such initiatives as the Homeland Security Information Sharing Fellows Program, which made training with the Office of Intelligence and Analysis available to local, state, and tribal law-enforcement officials. The same legislation that created the Sharing Fellows Program established the State, Local and Regional Fusion Center Initiative along U.S. borders, which required the Department of Homeland Security (DHS) to assign officers and analysts from Customs and Border Protection (CBP), Immigration and Customs Enforcement (ICE), and the Coast Guard to such centers.[16]

Increased Detention, Incarceration, and Criminalization

Immigration legislation passed by Congress between 2001 and 2008 expanded the grounds on which immigrants could be rendered inadmissible to the United States, detained, or incarcerated. Congress also expanded the grounds on which naturalized citizens could have their citizenship revoked.

The Enhanced Border Security and Visa Entry Reform Act of 2002 created provisions rendering immigrants from countries designated as "state sponsor[s] of international terrorism" inadmissible to the United States.[17] According to the legislation, it was the prerogative of the United States to define terrorism and to determine which states sponsored international terrorist activity. Legislation passed in 2005 excluded from admission to the U.S. immigrants determined by the DHS secretary to have provided any support to rebel forces in Colombia, including the Revolutionary Armed Forces of Colombia (FARC), the National Liberation Army (ELN), or the United Self-Defense Forces of Colombia (AUC). Support could include "taking actions or failing to take actions which allow, facilitate or otherwise foster the activities of such groups."[18] Ignoring the long history of political conflict in Colombia that had fueled low-intensity war for more than fifty years, Congress empowered the DHS to classify *any* type of support for a specified party to this war to serve as grounds for denial of visas, thereby denoting potential immigrants inadmissible to the United States. By specifying factions of the Colombian civil war, this act blurred the boundaries between the long-standing "war on drugs" and recently proclaimed "war on terror" to create another obstacle directed at Latina/o immigrants.

The Identity Theft Penalty Act of 2005 amended the federal criminal code to augment penalties associated with identity theft (including theft related to immigration offenses and false statements regarding social security and Medicare benefits). The law expanded the existing identity-theft definitions to include possession of another person's identification with intent to commit unlawful activity, linking identity theft to forms of domestic terrorism. This legislation increased the criminal penalties associated with document fraud, a frequent violation among unauthorized immigrants. Any undocumented immigrant who resorted to identity theft (or intended to do so) to gain employment or access to benefits, such as Medicare, would face additional penalties, including extended incarceration and deportation.[19]

Legislation passed in 2004 established grounds for revoking the citizenship of immigrants who became naturalized through military service: leaving the armed forces under any circumstance other than honorable conditions and serving fewer than five years honorably.[20]

Appealing to the need for tightened restrictions due to potential harm to national security, the new legislation placed immigrants at greater risk of detention, incarceration, and deportation. Yet this legislation also created a troubling double standard, allowing U.S. citizens to receive lesser penalties for the same actions. The Terrorist Bombings Convention Implementation Act of 2002, for example, altered the federal criminal code to prohibit the detonation of an explosive in a public space with the intent to cause bodily harm or destruction of property. Yet the law exempted "offenses committed by U.S. citizens within the United States, where the alleged offender and the victims are U.S. citizens and the alleged offender is found in the U.S.," despite a long history of domestic-terrorist episodes in which militant American citizens attacked government agents and institutions.[21] In addition to provisions that established harsher penalties for terrorist bombings committed by noncitizens, the law also created another form of inequality: Immigrants were denied access to information or resources that could protect them, particularly from unwarranted scrutiny that could lead to their detention.[22]

Increased Militarization of the Border

The restrictive legislation enacted between 2001 and 2008 contributed to heightened militarization of the U.S.-Mexico border. Securing the physical and symbolic borders of the homeland became a key feature of the securitization process, building upon a decade-long concentration on border-enforcement efforts. The two-thousand-mile U.S.-Mexico border was highlighted in several pieces of legislation, but the borders constituted in airports and other ports of entry also became sites of heightened security.

Militarization was most commonly achieved through expanded numbers of Border Patrol agents, immigration personnel, and staff at ports of entry and along the U.S.-Mexico border.[23] Legislation required new background checks (including a criminal-history check and review of law-enforcement databases) for any person who regularly had access to airports or secured areas around airports. These changes placed persons with jobs unrelated to transportation (particularly people in service professions) under intense scrutiny and review by federal authorities and heightened prospects of detention and removal if their documentation was determined invalid.[24] Unauthorized immigrants working in janitorial or service capacities in and around many of the country's airports after 9/11 were hit particularly hard by this legislation. Through a series of enforcement initiatives, discussed in subsequent chapters, immigrants who were found to be working with invalid documentation were apprehended, detained, fined, and frequently deported. The presence of persons without proper documentation was repeatedly described as a homeland-security risk—a threat from "persons of unknown origin"—and their apprehension was justified as a form of terrorist prevention, despite the absence of evidence linking any of those immigrants apprehended to actual terrorist activity.

Militarization was also facilitated through expanded training for Border Patrol, immigration, and customs enforcement agents and the expansion of security-related technology (including vehicles, aircrafts, and infrastructure) for Border Patrol detention and removals as well as for gathering intelligence via investigations and inspections.[25] The Secure Fence Act of 2006 directly and thoroughly militarized the border region, transforming unlawful immigrants crossing the border into terrorists and military threats. Under the terms of this act, the DHS secretary was directed to "take appropriate actions to achieve operational control over U.S. international land and maritime borders." Operational control was defined as "the prevention of all unlawful U.S. entries, including entries by terrorists, other unlawful aliens, instruments of terrorism, narcotics, and other contraband." Securing control was to take place via "systematic border surveillance," made possible with the use of additional personnel and technology (including unmanned aerial vehicles, sensors, satellites, radar, and cameras) and the fortification of fencing along the border to include a minimum of two layers. The legislation made clear that the suspected security threats were Mexican immigrants, as the additional fencing and physical barriers were exclusively designated for areas along the U.S.-Mexico border, particularly in California, Arizona, New Mexico, and Texas.[26]

Increased Restrictions on Federal Services and Benefits

Several states restricted immigrants' (particularly undocumented immigrants') access to state services beginning in the 1990s. Launched by citizen-sponsored initiatives, such as Proposition 187, which passed in California in 1994, these restrictions increased rapidly between 2002 and 2007. State legislatures considered thousands of bills proposing to restrict immigration and to bar immigrants from receiving any state-subsidized benefits.[27] Restricting immigrants from accessing services and benefits became a hallmark of state legislatures by 2008. Expanding on the restrictions on immigrant access to benefits created by "welfare reform" and "immigration reform" legislation in 1996, federal legislation also barred immigrants from accessing federally authorized grant programs for research, development, and research fellowships through the National Science Foundation (NSF) and the secretary of Commerce.[28] Additional legislation denied social security benefits to persons not authorized to work in the United States,[29] restricted employment as security screeners at airports and other federally security facilities to U.S. citizens, and required that companies providing security at airports and other sensitive locations be owned and controlled by U.S. citizens.[30] Other legislation prevented anyone other than U.S. citizens and permanent residents from requesting information about themselves from the operational files of the National Reconnaissance Office.[31] The Maritime Transportation Security Act of 2002 restricted access to security files from immigrants who "*may be* denied admission to the United States or removed from the United States under the Immigration and Nationality Act . . . or otherwise poses a terrorism security risk to the United States."[32]

Congress characterized this restriction as reasonable and necessary in the wake of terrorist attacks on the United States. The language of this provision was so broad, however, that it excluded persons who "may be denied entrance" and who posed a "risk" without clearly delineating the grounds for denying entry or the criteria for posing a risk. Under this provision, even the possibility of being denied admission (an increasingly probable occurrence for many Latina/o immigrants, given the additional levels of scrutiny and security) would prevent immigrants from accessing important information about themselves housed in federal databases. The vagueness of the language provided broad latitude for denying information that could be erroneous or exculpatory to individuals based largely on their immigrant status.

In addition to legislation that prevented or restricted access to government benefits and services, some legislation increased the "costs" of participation. Fees for services related to entry were increased (e.g., entry fees for persons arriving by airplane and on commercial vessels as well as increased land-border inspection fees).[33] Reflecting a different kind of "cost," legislation was passed that required immigrants who were trafficking victims to assist with federal, state, and/or local law-enforcement investigations to be eligible for victim benefits and services.[34] In the context of the criminal syndicates involved in trafficking, mandatory cooperation with U.S. law enforcement could put trafficking victims and their relatives in their countries of origin at grave physical risk.

Ironically, at the same time that immigrants were being barred from various services and opportunities, avenues for naturalization were expanded for military personnel. The Department of Defense Appropriations Act of 2004 reduced the period of required service for immigrants seeking naturalization through service in the armed forces from three years to one year; prohibited the imposition of fees on such persons seeking naturalization through military service; expanded the resources available for processing "applications, interviews, filings, oaths, ceremonies, or other proceedings" of immigrant service members in U.S. embassies, consulates, and military installations overseas; and extended posthumous benefits associated with citizenship to surviving spouses, children, and parents of the servicemen and servicewomen seeking naturalization.[35] Although most post-9/11 legislation positioned immigrants as threats, these provisions allowed immigrants to enroll in the U.S. military as a means to avoid suspicion. In 2007, legislation implementing recommendations from the 9/11 Commission authorized "visa-free travel privileges" to "nationals of foreign countries that are partners in the war on terrorism." Immigrants associated with countries serving the U.S. security state were afforded treatment in terms of access to and reception in the country that was far different from the treatment afforded to those whose racial, religious, or immigrant statuses targeted them as potential threats.[36]

Empowering Local Law Enforcement to Act as Immigration Agents

Despite the daunting effect of the changes in immigration politics outlined above, the most significant shift in post-9/11 legislation empowered local law enforcement to act as immigration agents. Although legislation enacted prior to 2001 initiated this shift, particularly anti-terrorist and immigration reform legislation passed by Congress in the mid-1990s, after 9/11 this process gained renewed attention and vigor as additional MOU were crafted between federal agencies and local law enforcement, and state and local personnel were granted security clearances required to access secured information in federal databases.[37] Once discouraged or barred from enforcing immigration guidelines, by 2008, state, local, and even tribal law-enforcement agents had become thoroughly intertwined with federal immigration enforcement. Constructed as threats to national security, immigrants were now exposed to arrest and detention for even minor infractions of local ordinances.

Empowering local law enforcement to act as immigration agents occurred through various processes, most notably the coordination of law-enforcement activities between federal, state, and local departments, agencies, and personnel, including collecting and sharing information, conducting surveillance related to immigrants (such as information on immigrant inadmissibility and deportation) and security threats, and producing and deploying the Chimera system, an integrated, interoperable computer system for the INS.[38] Other legislation created, facilitated, or extended joint law-enforcement task forces, teams, and committees to further share intelligence related to foreign persons and to identify and remove homeland-security and terrorist threats.[39] Some resources were shared through task forces and committees comprising enforcement agents from multiple jurisdictions; other resources, such as technology items and enforcement equipment, were transferred directly to state and local first responders in support of homeland security.[40]

One of the more common vehicles for transferring authority came through grant allocations to local law enforcement. Billions of dollars were spent to enhance communication and cooperation with federal law enforcement on terrorism and immigration-related matters[41] and to fund technology, intelligence, construction, and personnel designed to respond to terrorist threats, particularly along the Southwest border.[42] Federal funds were also allocated for highway patrol officers to conduct investigations related to immigration and terrorism, including "license fraud detection and prevention, northern border safety and security."[43]

The 2001 Aviation and Transportation Security Act required air carriers to conduct reviews of passengers who might be threats to national security and to take action if a person was identified, extending the review, scrutiny, and detention of potential threats to non-law-enforcement personnel.[44]

Configurations of Race and Gender within Immigration Legislation

Racialization and gendering intersected in the creation of new legislation that expanded gender-based rights, particularly protections, access, and opportunities for immigrant women and children, in the context of heightened scrutiny of immigrants. The Violence Against Women and Department of Justice Reauthorization Act of 2005 (VAWA) and the 2003 Trafficking Victims Protection Reauthorization Act (TVPRA) provide powerful examples of these intersecting dynamics.

The 2005 reauthorization of the VAWA extended protections, rights of admission, and legalization to immigrants who were victims of sexual assault or trafficking in the United States, a population constituted disproportionately by women and children. In reinstating the VAWA, originally passed in 1994, the 2005 bill provided $1.6 billion for the investigation and prosecution of violent crimes against women (including but not limited to domestic violence, dating violence, sexual assault, and stalking) and established the Office on Violence against Women within the Department of Justice (DOJ).[45]

The VAWA grew out of the mobilization of extensive grassroots efforts in the late 1980s and early 1990s, as advocates and professionals involved with the battered women's movement, sexual-assault prevention, victim services, law-enforcement agencies, prosecutors' offices, and the courts urged Congress to adopt legislation to address domestic and sexual violence. Women of color and immigrant women were well represented within the coalition advocating for the bill's passage and legislative enactment in 1994. Subsequent reauthorizations in 2000, 2005, 2012, and 2013 were celebrated as important victories for women's rights.

One of the act's greatest achievements was creating support networks and comprehensive community responses to the kinds of gendered violence covered by the legislation. As a function of the act, law-enforcement agents worked closely with courts, victim services, and community-based organizations to offer coordinated relief previously nonexistent on the state and local levels. Providing culturally and linguistically competent services, particularly to immigrant women and women of color, became an important feature of the VAWA's implementation. The VAWA "afforded benefits to abused foreign nationals and allowed them to self-petition for lawful permanent resident (LPR) status independently of the U.S. citizen or LPR relatives who originally sponsored them."[46] In the 2000 reauthorization of the VAWA, Congress created the U visa for immigrants who were victims of abuse and assisted law enforcement, making it easier for battered immigrant women to enter and remain in the United States.

The reauthorization of the VAWA was particularly important for the protection of abused immigrant women who entered the United States on spouse-dependent visas or who entered the country without proper documentation, rendering them largely ineligible for many existing legal protections. The intersecting burdens immigrant women experience due to lack of citizenship, economic insecurity, and racial marginalization heighten the difficulties in abusive relationships, influencing the victim's ability to leave a batterer. Without the opportunities and protections provided by the VAWA and its subsequent reauthorizations, many immigrant women became "bodies without rights."[47] The 2005 reauthorization of the VAWA provided significant relief to many of these women, granting access to work authorization visas "if they [could] demonstrate they ha[d] been subjected to battery or extreme cruelty by a foreign worker-spouse."[48]

Although the initial legislation and the 2005 reauthorization expanded the rights of women and children (and especially immigrant women and children), the 2005 legislation adopted additional provisions extending restrictions on immigrants, thus echoing other congressional legislation passed during the height of the war on terror. The 2005 reauthorization extended the practice of empowering local law-enforcement officials to act as immigration agents, a key feature of the surge in immigrant-related raids and roundups. Thus the coordinated response teams that were the hallmark of the VAWA's initial success became a vehicle to facilitate additional scrutiny, harassment, and apprehension of immigrants after the bill's reauthorization in 2005.

The 2005 reauthorization integrated local offices, officers, and resources with federal immigration agents by reauthorizing appropriations for the "state criminal alien assistance program," which allowed local agents to conduct raids in residential neighborhoods that targeted immigrants previously convicted on criminal charges. Although supporting raids aimed at "criminals" seemed reasonable when taken at face value, the boundaries and definitions of "criminality" were significantly expanded by this legislation, blurring the lines between persons who constituted a public threat and immigrants caught up in a state of hypersecuritization.[49]

The 2005 reauthorization of the VAWA also directed the DOJ to study and report on state and local assistance in "incarcerating undocumented criminal aliens." Designed to facilitate local officers' communication with federal agents to enable the transfer of immigrants from local jails to federal holding facilities, this provision was particularly important to the Secure Communities Program.[50] The legislation also provided funding to local law enforcement for new technology and training aimed at expanding antiterrorism efforts.[51]

Another example of gendered legislation that advanced immigrant racialization and restriction is the 2003 Trafficking Victims Protection Reauthorization Act (TVPRA). Modeled on VAWA, the initial Trafficking Victims Protection Act of 2000 emerged from a broad coalition of anti-trafficking advocates, service providers, and law-enforcement supporters who pressed Congress to create an expansive support network to identify and rescue trafficking victims (domestically and internationally) and to punish perpetrators. In addition to establishing the State Department Office to Monitor and Combat Trafficking in Persons, the TVPRA authorized the annual Trafficking in Persons report, which united federal, state, and local law-enforcement investigators and prosecutors in interagency task forces designed to comprehensively address the problem of human trafficking.

However, like the reauthorization of the VAWA, the 2005 TVPRA deployed security discourses characteristic of post-9/11 legislation. The

TVPRA expanded the reach of immigration enforcement by allowing foreign nongovernmental organizations (NGOs) to work with "border guards, officials, and other law enforcement" personnel to review and scrutinize immigrants crossing the border.[52] Moving well beyond providing such services as shelter and aid to victims of trafficking or creating prevention and education programs, the language of the 2003 reauthorization empowered NGOs to take on enforcement duties, literally serving as vehicles for "border interdiction."[53] Thus legislation explicitly designed to promote women's rights became a vehicle for securitization.

The reauthorizations of the VAWA and the TVPRA were celebrated as significant advancements of gendered legislation and women's rights. As Sharmila Lodhia notes, "This legislation was a significant victory of advocacy and highlights the importance of legal advocacy."[54] The problem with both acts, however, was that they blurred the boundaries between antiviolence/anti-trafficking legislation and securitization and anti-terrorism initiatives. Through the expansion of law-enforcement powers, women's rights legislation becomes a means of targeting immigrants, constructing them as potential threats to the homeland and creating new mechanisms for their control. Both the TVPRA and the VAWA contributed to the racialization of immigrants by expanding securitization practices aimed at restraining and restricting them.

Examining the racialized and gendered configurations of the legislation exposes these hidden burdens and disadvantages while also pointing to complex and contradictory ways that immigrants were constructed in post-9/11 legislation. Immigrant women and children were depicted as innocent victims worthy of state protection, including admission to the country and access to a range of social services. At the same time, the state traded on a benevolent gendered theme to construct other immigrants, regardless of their statuses, as violent, threatening, suspect, and potential terrorists. The veracity of gendered rights ensconced in the legislation is called into question, as these laws provided no protection for women and children who were caught up in the raids facilitated by these acts. As the raids and roundups increased after 2006, increasing numbers of women were apprehended, subjected to abuse in detention facilities, deported, or left as single parents, and growing numbers of immigrant and U.S.-born children were traumatized. Neither act provided recourse to the states' own terrorizing practices.

In addition to immigration legislation, several post-9/11 laws were so comprehensive that they deserve closer scrutiny. Three pieces of legislation in particular heightened multiple forms of restriction and intensified the language of racialized demonization, significantly recasting contemporary immigration in the context of the war on terror.

2001 USA PATRIOT Act

In the aftermath of 9/11, passage of the USA PATRIOT Act launched the domestic war on terrorism, altering the meaning and boundaries of U.S. citizenship and civil liberties while imposing new layers of restriction upon immigrants. Touted as one of the largest enhancements of law-enforcement capabilities ever enacted, the law granted new powers to federal and local authorities to fight "domestic and international" terrorism, including broader authority to conduct electronic surveillance and wiretaps; investigate and detain anyone associated with suspicious persons, groups, or activities; and confiscate the property of anyone believed to be engaged in terrorism.[55] The law concentrated power in the hands of the attorney general, allowing law-abiding immigrants to be certified as potential terrorists without actual charges being filed, without showing evidence, and without following due process. The PATRIOT Act turned otherwise lawful or expressive activities into grounds for deportation or indefinite detention.[56]

Under section 412 of the PATRIOT Act, noncitizens certified by the attorney general as possible "terrorists" could be held for up to seven days before criminal or immigration charges had to be filed. Detention was allowed on the attorney general's finding of "reasonable grounds to believe" that immigrants were involved in terrorism or activity that posed a danger to national security.[57] Although the law specified that immigration or criminal charges must be filed within seven days, it did not require that these charges have anything to do with terrorism; they could be minor visa violations. The type of violations that enabled detention carried no such liabilities prior to 2001. For example, foreign students who failed to register for a full load of classes during a single semester were deemed sufficiently suspicious to fall under the purview of this act. According to provisions in the act, the attorney general was required to review these "terror-suspect" certifications and report to the judiciary committees in Congress for oversight and accountability. DOJ records indicate, however, that the department did not comply with these provisions, regularly failing to submit necessary reports and often detaining immigrants for weeks and months without filing charges—far beyond the seven-day limit specified in the act.[58]

Under section 203 of the PATRIOT Act, immigrants who were detained and certified as "terrorists" or threats to national security (with merely the weight of reasonable suspicion articulated by the attorney general) were deportable without trials or hearings in which the government had to prove the terrorism allegations. The attorney general was allowed to act as both prosecutor and judge, sentencing immigrants to deportation on the basis of "reasonable" suspicion.

Despite the alleged threat posed by immigrants, the new law did not require that those who were detained indefinitely as suspected terrorists be removed from the United States. Noncitizens could be imprisoned indefinitely without ever being charged with a crime. If an immigrant were charged with engaging in terrorist activity, indefinite detention could result from the attorney general's determination that the individual threatened national security, the safety of the community, or any person. Noncitizens ordered removed on charges of terrorism could be indefinitely detained if they were determined to be stateless, their countries of origin refused to accept them, or they were granted relief from deportation because they would be tortured if they were returned to their countries of origin.[59] Thus, immigrants who were designated as terrorists risked not only incarceration but also the real possibility of permanent detention by virtue of this new legislation.

Under the PATRIOT Act, those immigrants who were ordered removed but could not be deported within the reasonably foreseeable future were entitled to reviews, at minimum every six months, to determine whether they continued to pose a danger to the government. There were no requirements that indefinite detainees ever be given trials or hearings in which the government had to prove its case; nor did other important procedural protections apply, such as "proof beyond a reasonable doubt" (in criminal proceedings) or proof by "clear, convincing, and unequivocal evident" (federal standard in deportation proceedings). Instead, indefinite detention could be ordered merely on the basis of vague and unspecified allegations of threats to national security.

The PATRIOT Act radically strengthened the power of the attorney general to review and designate immigrants as threats to the country, stripping them of habeas corpus and other due process rights and subjecting them to extreme forms of incarceration and abuse. The PATRIOT Act also restricted immigrant rights by threatening deportation of those who challenged the state by engaging in expressive activity. For example, the act permitted the detention and deportation of noncitizens who provided assistance for lawful activities of a group the government claimed was a terrorist organization, even when the group was never officially certified or designated as such. According to this provision, immigrants could "engage in terrorist activity" if they solicited funds for, became members of, or provided material support to an organization the government deemed to be "terrorist," even when that organization had legitimate humanitarian ends and the support was aimed at those ends.[60]

The secretary of state could designate groups as terrorist or nonterrorist under section 219 of the existing Immigration and Nationality Act (INA) or under a new provision created by section 411 of the USA PATRIOT Act. Under this new power, the secretary of state could designate any group that had *ever* engaged in violent activity as a "terrorist organization," even when the group no longer participated in violence or had repudiated its former activities. Under the PATRIOT Act, the "terrorist" designation no longer applied only to groups that had been designated as such and listed in the Federal Register.[61] Thus groups could be designated as terrorist organizations in secret without any official acknowledgment by the U.S. government.

When a group was designated as "terrorist," noncitizen members were deemed inadmissible to the United States, which made payment of membership dues a deportable offense. Under the PATRIOT Act, individuals could be deported even when they had no knowledge of a group's designation and when their assistance had nothing to do with the group's alleged terrorist activity. As Nancy Chang describes it, "In situations in which a non-citizen has solicited funds for, solicited membership for, or provided material support to a designated 'terrorist organization,' Section 411 saddles him with the difficult if not impossible burden of 'demonstrating that he did not know, and should not reasonably have known, that the act would further the organization's terrorist activity.'"[62]

The heightened restrictions on immigrants made possible through the PATRIOT Act were not limited to the formal changes specified in the legislation. In October 2001, as Congress debated the legislation, Attorney General John Ashcroft requested authorization to indefinitely detain immigrant terror suspects without finding reasonable suspicion or probable cause and without submitting to due process. Although this language was eliminated from the act itself, shortly after its passage, Attorney General Ashcroft wrote DOJ administrative guidelines that incorporated all the deleted PATRIOT Act detention powers. Mere days after 9/11, he changed the rules concerning the length of time an immigrant could be held before being charged from twenty-four hours to forty-eight hours, plus additional "reasonable time" was allowed in the event of an emergency situation. Additional policy changes Ashcroft put in place without review from Congress included "giving the [DOJ] an automatic override of an immigration judge's order to release an alien (regardless of the judge's findings, immigrants may now remain incarcerated at the discretion of their prosecutors)"; "closing immigration hearings for all 9/11 detainees and sealing all records about their cases"; and "forbidding nonfederal institutions from releasing information on INS detainees."[63]

The attorney general was not alone in pursuing changes that suspended due-process rights. Changes to the language and execution of immigration policy were supported by agency directives and court orders, such as the September 21, 2001, directive from Chief Immigration Judge Michael Creppy ordering that all immigration hearings pertaining to special-interest detainees (those deemed not cleared of connections to terrorism) be held in closed court sessions. This directive effectively banned the public, the press, and detainees' families from attending the hearings and prevented the hearings from being published on court dockets. On April 17, 2002, INS Commissioner James Ziglar issued an interim rule that forbade nonfederal facilities holding INS detainees from releasing any information about them, including names, countries of origin, or reasons for detention. Although the Third Circuit Court struck down both of these measures, it did so only after more than a year of implementation. The effects of these legislative changes reached far beyond the specific language of the law and often rested on its execution—a process discussed in greater detail in the next two chapters.[64] Although the PATRIOT Act was directed principally at Muslim, Arab, and Southeast Asian men and women—populations initially targeted by security and enforcement teams after 9/11—the securitization of immigration enabled through the act introduced fundamental shifts in immigration politics that had the potential to affect all immigrants.

2002 Homeland Security Act

Shortly after enacting the USA PATRIOT Act, Congress dramatically restructured the administration of immigration policy and services with passage of the 2002 Homeland Security Act. Under the terms of this act, virtually all immigration powers and procedures were transferred from the Departments of Justice, Treasury, and Agriculture to the newly created Department of Homeland Security (DHS). The Immigration and Naturalization Service (INS), which had administered immigration policy, was dismantled. With the creation of the DHS as a centerpiece of the war on terrorism and the consolidation of immigration policy under this new rubric, immigrants and immigration were formally institutionalized within the leading security arm of the federal government. The Homeland Security Act restructured immigration politics by establishing new bureaus, agencies, and departments; shifting duties among departments at the federal level; and redefining immigrants as threats to the country.

Prior to 2002, immigration policy was divided primarily among three federal agencies: the INS (under the DOJ), the U.S. Customs Service (under the Department of the Treasury), and Animal and Plant Health Inspection Services (under the Department of Agriculture). The largest of these operations was managed by the INS, whose duties included processing applications for visas, asylum, citizenship, and all other petitions for changes in status along with border patrol and enforcement. With the passage of the 2002 Homeland Security Act and its implementation on March 1, 2003, most immigration duties previously handled by these departments were transferred to the DHS and redistributed across several smaller bureaus. The 2002 Homeland Security Act created two new bureaus—the Bureau of Border Security[65] and the Bureau of Citizenship and Immigration Services.[66]

It transferred the U.S. Customs Service (of the Department of the Treasury), the Transportation Security Administration (of the Department of Transportation), the Federal Protective Service (of the General Services Administration), the Federal Law Enforcement Training Center (of the Department of the Treasury), and the Office for Domestic Preparedness (of the Office of Justice Programs) to the Directorate of Border and Transportation Security, headed by an undersecretary.[67] In so doing, law enforcement was severed from citizenship and immigration services.

The separation of enforcement functions from immigration services seemed to construct a clear wall between the management of applications for admission to the country and the incorporation of immigrants via naturalization from national security. The U.S. Citizenship and Immigration Services (CIS), which emerged from the former INS system, was charged with overseeing applications for citizenship, asylum, permanent residency, employment authorization, refugee status, and foreign student authorization as well as any adjustments to a person's immigration status.[68] In creating this new agency, Congress sought to improve the quality and efficiency of these services by establishing them as an independent component of the DHS.[69] A consequence of severing enforcement initiatives from citizenship and immigration services, however, was the rapid expansion and enhancement of the enforcement side of immigration politics.

As enforcement and services were separated into two bureaus under the 2002 Homeland Security Act, three new agencies emerged—two of which were dedicated to enforcement, especially as a vehicle for preventing terrorism. U.S. Customs and Border Protection (CBP) was established and charged with securing national borders, facilitating trade and travel, collecting import duties, and enforcing U.S. regulations pertaining to customs, immigration, and drugs. With a workforce of more than forty-five thousand agents and officers, and an increase in the number of Border Patrol agents from nine thousand in 2001 to more than eighteen thousand by the end of 2008, CBP became the largest law-enforcement agency in the United States.[70]

The U.S. Immigration and Customs Enforcement (ICE) agency, which served as the principal criminal investigative arm of the DHS, charged with investigation and enforcement of federal law governing border control, customs, trade, and immigration, added to the growth in enforcement efforts. Much like CBP, ICE expanded rapidly after 2001 to become the second-largest investigative agency in the federal government, with more than twenty thousand employees and field offices in forty-seven foreign countries.[71]

As CBP took over duties related to border patrol, customs, and review of traffic at ports of entry, ICE became the agency primarily charged with interior enforcement of immigration laws. Staff and offices of both agencies overlapped, however, with ICE agents working within and across the border and CBP's work expanding far beyond the initial entry points. Under this new system, investigations within the United States surged, expanding from immigrant homes to sites of employment. Large-scale raids and roundups resulted disproportionately in the apprehension of Latina/o immigrants. The details of this surge are examined in the next chapter, but it is important to note here that ICE defined its strategic goals as linking immigration and national security, conflating immigrants with potential terrorists. According to ICE, its primary work is

> to prevent terrorist attacks against the United States and to dismantle threats to homeland security before they materialize. This includes preventing the entry of people and materials that pose a threat to national security; investigating and removing suspected terrorists or their supporters; and preventing the export of weapons and sensitive technologies that could be used to harm the United States (2).[72]

Building upon existing immigration laws and public discourse that demonized immigrants, the 2002 Homeland Security Act contributed powerfully to the restructuring and redefinition of U.S. immigration policy. Even as the language of immigration enforcement softened in subsequent years (see Chapter 7), the infrastructure disproportionately dedicated to enforcement remained.

Emergency Supplemental Appropriations Act for Defense, the Global War on Terror and Tsunami Relief, 2005

During the height of the war on terror, Congress included provisions that imposed restrictions on immigrants in the Emergency Supplemental Appropriations Act for Defense, the Global War on Terror, and Tsunami Relief, which was principally focused on expanding resources for the war and providing relief to victims of a natural disaster abroad. Although this bill seemed far removed from issues pertaining to immigrants, amendments added to it substantially altered the identification process for all Americans. For example, provisions in the bill expanded grounds for inadmissibility and the deportation of immigrants to include noncitizens who were "representatives of terrorist organizations or political, social or other groups that endorse or espouse terrorist activity" and/or "endorse or espouse terrorist activity or persuade others to do so."[73] These broadly defined forms of terrorist association permitted the exclusion or removal of persons on the basis of loose and indirect relationships to other groups and persons who had the potential to cause harm. By declaring "suspect" persons loosely affiliated with organizations that the government designated as terrorist, Congress again extended the presumption that immigrants were threats. This act limited the judicial relief available to immigrants, barring anyone who fell under the purview of the act from appealing removal and denying access to discretionary relief provided by habeas corpus, mandamus, and other extraordinary petitions.[74]

The 2005 supplemental appropriations act also altered securitization practices along the southern U.S. border. Sections of the legislation expedited the expansion of barriers and construction of roads for use in immigration enforcement along the U.S.-Mexico border.[75] To enhance U.S. border security, it also authorized implementation of pilot programs designed to expand the use of ground-surveillance technologies, including video cameras, sensors, and motion-detection devices.[76]

Consistent with a great deal of post-9/11 legislation, this act extended collaboration among local, state, and tribal law enforcement and federal immigration enforcement. In this iteration, the DHS secretary was required to develop and implement a plan to facilitate integrated communications and information sharing on border security among federal agencies, state and local government agencies, and Indian tribes.[77]

The supplemental appropriations bill also imposed new burdens on persons seeking political asylum in the United States. The act established stringent criteria for determining eligibility for asylum. Intake officers were accorded increased discretion to make judgments about a petitioner's demeanor, candor, plausibility, and consistency—judgments that are particularly difficult if the officers lack linguistic competence in the applicant's native language.[78] For immigrants escaping violence and harm in their countries of origin, these provisions subjected them to heightened suspicion, imposed additional burdens of proof on them, and made the process of seeking relief far more difficult.

The REAL ID Act, which was included as an amendment to the appropriations legislation, created uniform standards for the issuance of driver's licenses, which made it impossible to secure a license without proof of lawful residency. President Bush had advocated for the measure as an essential part of his war on terror. The National Strategy for Homeland Security released by the Office of Homeland Security (the precursor to the DHS) in July 2002 had recommended adoption of such uniform standards. Because uniform standards would encroach on state jurisdiction, the National Intelligence Reform Act of 2004 had attempted to establish a negotiated rule-making process to define minimum standards for state-issued driver's licenses and identification cards. The amendment to the supplemental appropriations bill established these standards by federal fiat.

The REAL ID Act of 2005 required that all driver's licenses and identification cards issued by states had to conform to federal standards within a prescribed period of time. The new uniform standards included documentation of the person's date of birth, proof of the authenticity of the person's social security number (or verification that the person was not eligible for a social security number), and evidence of lawful status, including determination that the person was either a citizen, a lawful permanent or temporary resident, a refugee, or a valid visa holder. Under the terms of the Real ID Act, states were required to enter an MOU with the DHS secretary to routinely utilize the Systematic Alien Verification for Entitlements (SAVE) database to verify the legal status of a person applying for a driver's license or identification card.[79]

These provisions did far more than ask or encourage states to become immigration agents—they required states to regularly scrutinize the identification and status of their own residents, thereby extending the reach of federal enforcement. By bringing questions of state-issued IDs within the orbit of the war on terrorism, Congress linked immigration to national security and made it more difficult for immigrants to function in the United States. Requiring proof of an applicant's date of birth for a driver's license, for example, presupposed that the applicant possessed a state-issued birth certificate, a condition that was impossible for many immigrants to meet. By targeting driver's licenses and state-issued IDs, this legislation had a disproportionate impact on Latina/o immigrants, many of whom used such IDs as fundamental forms of documentation to open bank accounts, cash checks, or simply get work.

Conclusion

Despite recurrent charges of inactivity and impasse from political pundits on both the right and the left, Congress was indeed active in creating new laws and amending existing laws to restructure and reform immigration law and policy in the United States in the years immediately after 9/11. The war on terrorism and the rise of the national security state were intricately linked to the passage of legislation that racialized immigrants as foreign threats to the security of the homeland. Arab and Muslim men felt the full force of this gendered racialization, but so too did Latina/o immigrants. Continuing the long-standing racialization of Latinas/os, Congress blurred the boundaries between citizens and immigrants, documented and undocumented immigrants, and immigrants and terrorists. Within the new national security regime, all Latinas/os were subjected to enhanced technologies of surveillance, identification, and control.

Subjected to increased scrutiny; heightened possibilities of detention, arrest, and/or deportation; and denial of federal and state benefits, Latinas/os experienced systemic changes in daily life within the United States. With increasing militarization of the border region and growing collaboration among local, state, tribal, and federal law-enforcement agencies, Latinas/os were cast under suspicion. Whether citizens or immigrants, they could fall prey to investigation, arrest, detention, or deportation. These changes later solidified an important facet in the transformation of immigration politics, further enabling the construction of immigrants as threats at every level of law enforcement and extending the state's capacity to execute new restrictions.

Congress took advantage of multiple legislative opportunities to forge the links between immigrant and terrorist suspect. In addition to the 2001 USA PATRIOT Act and the 2002 Homeland Security Act, Congress used the 2005 reauthorization of the VAWA, the 2003 TVPRA, and the 2005 Emergency Supplemental Appropriations Act for Defense, the Global War on Terror, and Tsunami Relief to securitize immigration processes. To protect women from domestic violence, sexual assault, and sexual trafficking, Congress empowered networks of NGOs, law-enforcement officers, and federal authorities to carry out restrictive raids against immigrant communities. The coordinated response teams that were the hallmark of the VAWA's initial success and the model for the TVPRA became vehicles to facilitate the additional scrutiny, harassment, and apprehension of immigrants during the war on terror. Present in both acts was a problematic blurring of conceptual boundaries between antiviolence/anti-trafficking legislation intended to support and expand women's rights and securitization and anti-terror initiatives targeting immigrants and constructing them as potential threats to the homeland.

By positioning law-abiding immigrants as potential terrorists, Congress launched comprehensive surveillance of virtually all aspects of immigrant life through an expansion of funds, information, personnel, databases, and technologies and the sharing of these resources across departments, agencies, and law-enforcement jurisdictions. Heightened scrutiny generated increasing numbers of detainees, indefinite detentions, deportations, raids in immigrant communities, criminalization of legitimate expressive activity, denial of basic services, rising fees, and persistent harassment at the hands of multiple law-enforcement agencies, with few if any sources of support or respite. The securitization of immigration heightened levels of vulnerability, fear, and anxiety within Latina/o immigrant and citizen communities alike, as suspicion overrode legal statuses, rights were suspended, and threats of detention and deportation loomed large.

Altogether, this chapter documents a remarkable increase in the types of restrictions aimed at immigrants and how these restrictions built upon and extended the racialization of Latina/o immigrants. Collectively, these shifts in legislation constructed Latina/o immigrants as threatening and restructured the administration of immigration law and policy. In the next chapter, I examine how the laws of the new national security regime engendered trends in enforcement practices that disproportionately affected Latina/o immigrants, as large-scale raids and roundups became routine.

5

Terrorizing Immigrants

The Return of Large-Scale Raids and Roundups
and Their Impact on Latina/o Communities

> *In this new war on terrorism our enemy's platoons infiltrate*
> *our borders. . . . [T]heir tactics rely on evading recognition at*
> *the border and escaping detection within the United States.*
> —ATTORNEY GENERAL JOHN ASHCROFT, 2002, as quoted in
> Eunice Hyunhye Cho, "The New War against Immigrants," in
> American Friends Service Committee, *Militarized Zones*

In June 1998, Heidi Fortin left her home in Tegucigalpa, Honduras, shortly after Hurricane Mitch devastated much of the country and became known as one of the worst natural disasters in the region. Fortin left behind her infant daughter and set out for the United States with $50 and no entry or work visas. She crossed the border into Guatemala and subsequently into Mexico, where she stayed for five months earning money by harvesting crops, cleaning houses, and cooking. Despite being deported from Mexico twice and robbed by local Mexican police, she eventually crossed the U.S.-Mexico border in 1999 through a hole in the fence bordering Tijuana and was quickly apprehended by U.S. Border Patrol agents operating under the Immigration and Naturalization Service (INS). However, Fortin was allowed to stay in the United States and received a temporary work permit under the terms of a special federal order granting asylum to Hondurans (and other Central Americans) impacted by Hurricane Mitch. Shortly thereafter, Fortin moved in with family in Boston and found work in various service capacities at Logan International Airport. Yet despite the existence of a legitimate work permit, Fortin and eighteen other Latina/o immigrants employed there were arrested in 2002 in conjunction with the anti-terrorism campaign Operation Tarmac.[1]

This campaign, targeting persons of "unknown origin" working in more than one hundred airports and other secured facilities throughout the country, led to the arrest of more than seven hundred documented and undocumented Mexican and Central American immigrants by December

2003.[2] Like Fortin, most of the immigrants were apprehended while working as janitors, gardeners, cooks, and service personnel in these facilities. In addition, most were charged with federal felonies associated with the use of fraudulent documents—charges that carried penalties ranging from two to five years in prison, fines as high as $250,000, and/or deportation. Ultimately, despite the operation's significance in the domestic war on terrorism, the process failed to identify any suspects linked to terrorism, succeeding only in terrorizing hundreds of immigrant and their families.[3]

This is but one of many scenarios that have played out thousands of times among immigrants throughout the country since 9/11. Amid the clamor over security and the rush to detain potential terrorist threats, immigrants have been routinely detained without cause and without bonds, denied access to lawyers, deported without appeals, and assessed harsh punishments for minor infractions that far exceed the boundaries of reasonable execution of the law. Even judges who would normally grant some degree of flexibility or exception have been bound by changes in the law that preclude such discretion.

As a result, deportations of immigrants increased rapidly in the aftermath of 9/11. Between 1999 and 2007, deportations increased by 78 percent. In addition, much like Fortin's case, many of those deported committed no actual crimes or only minor infractions that were elevated to deportable offenses within the securitization process. In a period of economic decline, immigrant detention centers expanded rapidly, with detainees regularly being required to sleep on floors.[4] Moreover, while much of the attention regarding immigrants after 9/11 centered on the cases of high-profile Arabs, Muslims, and Southeast Asians, the vast majority of those detained, arrested, and/or deported in conjunction with large-scale raids executed as part of the war on terrorism were Latinas/os.

The targeting of Latina/o immigrants via Operation Tarmac and similar federal initiatives occurred through the same logics of racialized demonization, masculinized protectionism, and securitization articulated in previous chapters. In particular, this chapter extends the analysis to examine how the construction of immigrants as terrorist threats, which manifested in security discourse and congressional legislation, animated the initiation and execution of large-scale raids and roundups post-9/11, detailing their concentration within three main geographic locations: "sensitive" federally secured locations (including airports, military bases, nuclear power plants, chemical plants, defense facilities, and seaports), private residences, and commercial employment sites.

While the use of raids for large-scale immigrant removal is not new, they resumed as the preferred strategy for interior immigration enforcement after 9/11 and were executed with alarming frequency and ferocity, generating widespread fear among Latinas/os across the United States. The terrorization of entire communities became so prevalent that by 2007, the Pew Hispanic Center found that that more than half of all Latina/o adults (and two-thirds of all foreign-born Latinas/os) in the United States worried that they, a family member, or a close friend could be deported.[5]

Capitalizing on the institutional coalescing between local law enforcement and immigration authorities, the raids were led by federal agents but frequently executed via joint operating agreements between federal and local officials, such as the 287(g) agreements enabled with the passage of the 1996 Illegal Immigration Reform and Immigrant Responsibility Act (IIRIRA).[6]

As noted previously, these joint agreements drew broad criticisms from the Department of Homeland Security's (DHS's) inspector general, the General Accounting Office, and independent investigators. Collectively, these critiques alleged widespread racial profiling, insufficient oversight from the federal government, inadequate training, and incidents of abuse.

Related to these concerns was the lack of documentation and record keeping regarding the multiple raids and operations conducted through the joint agreements, specifically between 2001 and 2008. In particular, neither the DHS nor local departments maintained public records on the scope and scale of the raids or on those apprehended, detained, or deported. Moreover, efforts to recover documents and data from the DHS through direct appeals or Freedom of Information Act (FOIA) requests were met with delays, rejections, and obstacles. For example, in 2007, the Seton Hall School of Law Center for Social Justice and *Brazilian Voice,* a Brazilian community newspaper in the Northeast, filed a FOIA request with the DHS for all records (including "guidelines, instructions, memoranda, protocols, or training materials") related to operations to "identify, locate or arrest suspected fugitives in the state of New Jersey."[7] The petition noted, "There is almost no information in the public domain (aside from individual anecdotes) about the manner in which residential searches and arrests are being conducted, and the government's bases for those searches and arrests."[8] However, the FOIA request was denied by the DHS with the argument that the matter lacked public interest, because "a preliminary search of the internet does not indicate that there is substantial news interest concerning this topic."[9]

Given the scarcity of available primary sources documenting these raids from the DHS, Immigration and Customs Enforcement (ICE), or Citizenship and Immigration Services (CIS), information for this chapter draws primarily from a systematic search of newspaper articles and cataloguing of news stories between September 11, 2001, and July 2010.[10] Utilizing LexisNexis and all major newspapers for stories of immigration raids from 2001 to 2010, this research produced thousands of stories that were subsequently analyzed and grouped, yielding the three most common types of raids outlined above.

The use of newspaper accounts as a surrogate for primary documents from the federal government was admittedly an imperfect measure; however, as the evidence in this chapter demonstrates, this method still produced substantive information about the nature and extent of these raids while providing important nuances regarding the impact on Latina/o communities that might have been lost in government documents. Moreover, this method also served as a test of the DHS's allegation that a substantial body of news stories on immigration raids did not exist.

Ultimately, the terrorization of immigrants as part of the new security regime manifested in dozens of ways, from the creation of restrictive legislation to court opinions providing for the enhanced scrutiny of immigrants' daily interactions. A full accounting of each of these manifestations is virtually impossible, but the increase in large-scale raids and roundups deserves specialized attention for at least two reasons. First, the raids were public spectacles carried out by a heavily militarized team of enforcement agents who descended en masse to their targeted locations and captured the attention of local and national media. As such, the raids were especially terrifying and intimidating forms of immigration enforcement that affected broad numbers of people—often dozens of additional victims beyond those named in search warrants or subpoenas. As Joanna Dreby from the Center for American Progress notes, raids and deportations "break families up and have a wider effect on the community as a whole."[11]

Second, because of the ferocity and publicity of these campaigns, they also served as disciplining mechanisms, pointing to those apprehended as causes for concern and reminding all others of the state's role in defending the legitimate American public. In this way, as masculinized protection expanded, the Departments of Justice, Homeland Security, and Defense ended up serving dual roles of representing the state as the main security arms of the federal government and as militarized gatekeepers policing the literal and symbolic boundaries of the national body. Thus, the raids and roundups examined here, coupled with the legislation discussed in previous chapters, provide important indicators about shifts in immigration occurring through the war on terror as well as changes in American identity, belonging, and incorporation.

A History of Large-Scale Immigrant Raids and Removals

Raids on immigrants resulting in large-scale deportations and removals have been common throughout much of U.S. history. Along with border enforcement, raids on immigrant workplaces and communities became a tool of choice for immigration authorities in the last half of the twentieth century. Fueled by racial fears, the raids often satisfied a public appetite for blame, particularly during periods of economic downturn. Mexican immigrants have long been the target of these raids, including the large-scale deportations that took place in 1913 and 1921 and are detailed in Chapter 3. Moreover, the imprimatur of Operation Wetback, which led to the forced removal of more than a million Mexicans and cost more than $3 million, endures among Latina/o communities in the United States today. However, the targeting of immigrants for large-scale removal did not begin with Mexican or Latina/o immigrants.[12]

The first raids on immigrants resulting in removal by federal immigration authorities targeted Chinese immigrants who entered the country in violation of Chinese exclusion laws enacted in 1882.[13] These raids rounded up Chinese laborers in private homes, restaurants, and businesses primarily on the West Coast and in response to racialized hysteria that pinpointed Chinese as threats in a weakened economy. Chinese immigrants were rounded up again in the 1950s, this time because federal authorities sought to capture and deport supporters of the new communist regime in China.[14]

The ascendance of biological determinism and the effort to limit non-assimilable immigrants from Eastern and Southern Europe inspired most of the immigration raids between 1918 and 1920. On the heels of the 1907 Dillingham Commission's recommendation to limit the number of undesirable immigrants as well as the 1917 Immigration Act limiting Asian immigration, authorities initiated large-scale raids of supporters of the 1917 Russian Revolution, particularly anarchists, labor organizers, communists, and prominent left-wing organizers, such as Emma Goldman. Included in this effort were the Palmer raids, led by Attorney General Mitchell Palmer between 1919 and 1920, which targeted union workers suspected of radical activity aimed at the federal government in more than seventy cities. Ultimately, the Palmer raids led to the apprehension of more than six thousand individuals as well as a litany of legal challenges.[15]

The growing fear of political subversives intersected strongly with the desire of nativists to limit and remove nonwhite immigrants during World War II in the internment of persons of Japanese origin in the United States. Through the administration of executive order 9066, and pursuant to Proclamations 2525 and 2655, President Franklin Roosevelt ordered the internment of more than 110,000 persons of Japanese ancestry and the subsequent removal of all Japanese immigrants suspected of being threats to the country. Of those incarcerated, more than 40,000 were noncitizens, yet all Japanese residents were "raced as foreign and threatening" by virtue of the president's designation.[16]

A similar, albeit much smaller, level of ethnic-specific targeting wrapped up with mounting securitization was evident in the removal of Iranian students in 1979 subsequent to the Iranian invasion of the U.S. embassy in Tehran. During these efforts, immigration authorities targeted Iranian students in the United States, who at the time constituted the largest population of foreign-born students. The INS scrutinized their student visas and ordered all postsecondary Iranian students to voluntarily report to INS offices for review, resulting in the eventual deportation or forced removal of thousands of people.

As the number of authorized and unauthorized Mexican immigrants increased, particularly in response to shifts in the Mexican economy, the termination of the Bracero Program, the failure of border industrialization programs, and the continual draw of agricultural and manufacturing industries in the Southwest, immigration raids became focused on limiting and controlling this population. By the early 1970s, raids on worksites, particularly those with large numbers of Latinas/os, became common occurrences. Many of these raids were conducted without search or arrest warrants, and at times even without consent from employers. In 1974, INS agents executed a series of such raids in Illinois against employers believed to be hiring large numbers of unauthorized Mexican laborers. Agents conducted sweeps of workplaces as well as local hotels, apartment complexes, boardinghouses, and private homes, looking for undocumented immigrants. Characteristic of the racialization at work in the raids, agents were indiscriminate in rounding up persons who simply looked Latina/o, releasing them only when they could provide the proper documentation.[17]

A similar initiative took place in the early 1980s with Operation Jobs, a joint operation between the INS and Border Patrol targeting dozens of workplaces believed to be employing high concentrations of unauthorized Mexican laborers. Common to these raids was the agents' dubious use of search warrants and due process. For instance, agents regularly arrived at the location with "warrants of inspection" authorizing them to search non-public areas of the targeted workplace and giving the INS broad latitude to seize persons suspected of being undocumented immigrants working at the sites. Operation Jobs resulted in approximately five thousand arrests of mostly Latina/o immigrants in nine cities. Additional raids occurred with the support of local law enforcement, such as the 1984 INS sweep in Sanger, California, in which local and federal agents scoured the entire downtown area searching for anyone who looked Mexican. The raid resulted in the arrest and deportation of 255 undocumented immigrants.[18]

By the early 1990s, the use of large-scale immigration raids had become a common tool of law enforcement and immigration officials looking to quell anti-immigrant sentiments by targeting primarily Mexican laborers. While there was some variation in the execution of these roundups, most followed a similar pattern: militarized enforcement teams that descended in swift and severe fashion, generating panic and shock in their targeted communities.

These raids were conducted without the need for additional legislation or appropriations, often not even following the guidelines of search and seizure or due process. By and large, these raids resulted in the immediate apprehension and deportation of large numbers of vulnerable Latina/o immigrants who were disproportionately poor and lacking in the social and political capital of other immigrant groups. Ultimately, regarding shifts in immigration politics post-9/11, one of the more troubling manifestations has been the return of large-scale operations, which have the effect of once again targeting large numbers of highly vulnerable immigrants in public spectacles meant to legitimate a masculinized state authority. Moreover, newspaper reports and stories from individuals apprehended in these raids suggest that they were often conducted without proper warrants and in a fashion that left entire communities terrorized.[19]

Raids and Roundups Post-9/11

While large-scale raids and aggressive military-style roundups had abated by the late 1990s, reflecting a movement toward liberalizing immigration enforcement, they resurfaced forcefully after September 11.[20] Much has been made of the raids on employment facilities; however, federally coordinated raids most often took one of three forms: raids aimed at airports, military bases, federally secured buildings, and "sensitive areas";[21] raids aimed at private worksites; and raids targeting "criminal aliens and fugitive absconders," most frequently carried out in homes and private residences. All raids were conducted under the auspices of rooting out potential terrorists and protecting homeland security, yet none of the raids conducted between 2001 and 2008 yielded evidence of any terrorist activity, nor were any terrorists apprehended in the process. On the contrary, the vast majority of those detained, arrested, and/or deported in conjunction with the raids conducted in support of the war on terror were Latinas/os working in multiple service capacities, including janitors, gardeners, cooks, maids, cleaners, meatpackers, and sewers.

Finally, the raids were typically executed via joint agreements between federal and local officials, if not explicitly as a function of the 287(g) agreements described previously. While the 287(g) programs were created with the 1996 IIRIRA, they remained inactive until 2002, when the first agreement was signed with Florida. After that initial agreement was executed, joint operations proliferated, and more than seventy agreements were signed with local police, sheriff, and law-enforcement units in more than two dozen states by 2008. The reliance on these joint operations further underscores the shifts in immigration politics after September 11, 2001, as restrictive policies and laws enacted in the previous decade were given new life with the racialization of immigrants as security threats and the mobilization of public fear.

TABLE 5.1. ESTIMATED NUMBER OF RAIDS AND INDIVIDUAL APPREHENSIONS AT FEDERALLY SECURED FACILITIES, WORKSITES, AND RESIDENTIAL NEIGHBORHOODS, 2001–2008		
	Estimated Number of Raids	*Estimated Number of Apprehensions*
Raids conducted at federally secured facilities	44	1,056
Raids conducted at worksites	191	9,216
Raids conducted in residential neighborhoods (targeting immigrant fugitives)	153	5,918

Table 5.1 provides the estimated number of raids and apprehensions that occurred between 2001 and 2008.[22]

While the number of reported raids accelerated from 2002 to 2008, they reached a fever pitch by 2006, particularly after the launch of Operation Return to Sender and the Secure Communities Program.[23] Moreover, the raids proliferated at the same time that comprehensive immigration reform was debated in both the House and the Senate, and in the context of a heavily contested midterm election that resulted in the Democratic Party's taking control of the House of Representatives, the Senate, and a majority of the thirty-six governor seats in the race. The proliferation of raids and apprehensions also peaked in the same year that the Republican Party experimented with roving committee meetings on immigration enforcement held in locations that were all home to the most competitive House, Senate, state legislative, and governor seats.

As the raids became larger and more coordinated, more immigrants were apprehended, and an even broader reach of individuals were affected. For example, while fewer workplace raids than residential raids were conducted between 2001 and 2008, two raids conducted at private worksites in 2006 yielded more than 2,400 apprehensions. As such, the largest number of raids took place in residential neighborhoods; however, the largest number of apprehensions occurred as a result of raids happening at private worksites.

Raids Targeting Airports, Military Bases, and Other Federally Secured Facilities

Raids centered on airports, military bases, and other federally secured and/or sensitive locations were most common between 2001 and 2005, but newspaper accounts indicate they were still taking place in November 2007. In particular, with the 2006 creation of Operation Return to Sender, the raids became increasingly centered on private employment sites and residential locations; however, a number of raids still took place in areas described as "critical infrastructure" locations, including airports, nuclear power plants, chemical plants, military bases, defense facilities, seaports, and construction zones near military bases. Reflecting the militarization of these campaigns, they were conducted under such names as Operation Tarmac, Operation Safe Travels, Operation Joint Venture, Operation Access Denied, Operation Fly Trap, Operation Safe Sky, and Operation Plane View.[24] Moreover, in many locations, these raids were extended to hotels, gardens, and restaurants adjacent to the main facilities.[25] They were typically presented in language that was facially neutral—that is, language that emphasized the collective benefit of "securing the nation" for all Americans without invoking a specific ethnic or racial target, even while they disproportionately impacted Latina/o immigrants with no apparent connection to terrorist activity.

As mentioned previously, the raids were often conducted via joint operating agreements that were either established prior to 9/11 or that modeled those arrangements. These joint operations involved several federal agencies convened to conduct audits of individuals and contractors working at airports, federal buildings, and military posts and to determine the immigration status of employees with access to secure areas across the country.[26] The agencies involved were numerous and included major departments (Defense, Justice, Homeland Security, Transportation, Labor, Agriculture) as well as a myriad of agencies and bureaus within them (e.g., the INS, the Federal Bureau of Investigation [FBI], the Social Security Administration Office of the Inspector General, the Transportation Security Administration [TSA], the U.S. Marshals Service, the U.S. Attorneys Office, the Federal Aviation Administration [FAA], the Civil Aviation Security Field Office, and U.S. Customs). By late 2007, raids associated with these enforcement teams had been conducted on more than one hundred airports, scrutinizing the employment and authorization records of more than 750,000 airport workers.[27]

As a result of the raids on airports alone, more than 1,250 individuals were indicted and/or charged, and more than 800 were arrested. Many of those detained or arrested were charged with presenting false information regarding their immigration statuses, using false documentation to obtain employment, or overstaying visas.[28] These charges typically carried penalties ranging from two to ten years in prison, fines as high as $250,000, and deportation.

Despite the high profile of these operations and their role in the domestic war on terrorism, no evidence was presented linking anyone detained in these raids with any terrorist organizations or terrorist activities. On the contrary, those arrested included pilots, construction workers, airline mechanics, baggage carriers, security personnel, ramp agents, and trans-portation workers. The preponderance of persons detained were janitors, members of cleaning crews, and food-service workers (those working in food service at the airport and those preparing in-flight meals), and virtually all of those arrested were Latina/o. In fact, the largest airport raid took place in Houston on September 9, 2002, in which 143 employees were ultimate-ly indicted, all of whom were Latina/o.[29] In short, the operations targeted "persons of unknown origin"—terminology that became synonymous with undocumented Latina/o immigrants.

In many respects, these raids were the first indication that the domes-tic war on terrorism would far exceed its charge of protecting Americans against potential terrorists and serve as a cover to police immigrant com-munities. With initial detentions in Salt Lake City, Utah, and their extension to other locations came language that increasingly positioned those immi-grants apprehended as potential terrorists. Thus, U.S. Attorney Daniel G. Bogden stated in conjunction with a raid in Nevada:

> The federal government is committed to doing everything possible to ensure the safety of the traveling public. The employment of persons at our airports who have provided false identities and false back-ground information represents a danger to the community and to the persons using the airports. I feel that this operation, in which thousands of records were reviewed, has gone a long way to protect the airports in Nevada.[30]

A parallel depiction of the immigrants as dangerous threats was echoed in the statements of other U.S. attorneys overseeing raids in such states as Colorado and Virginia. Thus, Colorado U.S. Attorney John Suthers stated:

> To ensure air travel safety, we are subjecting the traveling public to searches and other inconveniences. It is only logical that we also must ensure that we know the identities and backgrounds of all those who work at our airports and have access to restricted areas. If we are serious about airport security, we cannot tolerate people fraudulently obtaining security credentials.[31]

In addition, U.S. Attorney for Northern Virginia Paul McNulty (whose office coordinated the task force to carry out the operations in the D.C. area) commented:

> Today's action enhances our homeland security by cracking down on those with access to the secure areas in our airports.[32]

Descriptions of immigrants as imminent threats were reinforced by statements from allied federal agencies. Thus, Deiter H. Harper, special agent in charge of the Chicago Office of the U.S. Department of Transportation's Office of the Inspector General, stated:

> Our audit and investigative activities over the years have shown that people who lie about their background on their application for airport security clearances pose a potential threat to public safety.[33]

Moreover, while the language remained largely race-neutral, there was little question that the threat being constructed in this discourse referred to Latinas/o immigrants generally and Mexican immigrants specifically. This focus was evident in the reaction of Representative Walter Jones to the arrest of immigrants at the Seymour Johnson Air Force Base in Goldsboro, North Carolina:

> These arrests illustrate the extent to which illegal immigration threatens America's security. We know that over 16,000 illegal aliens stream across our southern border each week. We now also know that illegal aliens have successfully infiltrated our military bases, nuclear facilities and airports. The Administration and members of Congress on both sides of the aisle have got to get serious about cutting off the flow of illegal immigrants coming into our country. The longer we wait to address this problem, the greater the risk to American lives and security.[34]

In much the same way that the deployment of military troops to Afghanistan and Iraq was presented as a benevolent gesture intended to protect law-abiding Americans (and women and children in need), masculine protectionism emerged in the discourse defending these aggressive military-style raids. Thus, INS Acting Denver District Director Michael M. Comfort said in 2002:

> The INS began laying the groundwork for this initiative [Operation Tarmac] shortly after the terrorist attacks against our nation. The goal here was and is to work with federal, state and local agencies in shoring up our nation's homeland security in a post 9-11 environment. *A key element to the national security infrastructure is the safety of the traveling public. The American public deserves nothing less than the highest priority of protection.* (Emphasis added)[35]

Similarly, U.S. Attorney General John Ashcroft said:

The American people are being asked to put up with long lines and intrusive searches. Americans deserve the confidence of knowing that individuals working in our airports are worthy of our trust.[36]

U.S. Attorney Michael Selby, of the Texas Division, was most succinct when he stated:

Our mission since my arrival is to do whatever that's necessary to protect the public so that when people look up in the sky [they] won't have to wonder if that's an airplane or a missile.[37]

Here, not only are immigrants proffered as the external enemy waiting to disrupt the daily life of legitimate American travelers; the state becomes the arbiter of masculinized protection—determining who is worthy of protection, how they will be protected, and even reminding the dutiful protected public why they should be grateful for such services.

Finally, a perverted version of this protectionism appeared regularly in public statements from U.S. attorneys and other federal actors looking to put a benevolent spin on the raids. In this version of events, the federal government was depicted again as a benevolent authority figure aiding those unauthorized workers it apprehended and shielding them from becoming unwitting accomplices to more nefarious forces. Thus, as U.S. Attorney Michael Selby stated:

Undocumented employees place themselves in a compromised position where terrorists could gain access to secure areas by threatening to notify immigration officials if workers did not comply.[38]

Similarly, DHS Assistant Secretary Michael J. Garcia stated:

The aliens arrested in this operation had access to sensitive critical infrastructure locations and therefore pose a serious homeland security threat. Not only are their identities in question, but given their illegal status, these individuals are vulnerable to potential exploitation by terrorist and other criminal organizations.[39]

In this iteration of masculine protectionism, the aggressive military-style raids resulting in large-scale detentions, arrests, and often deportation in addition to fines, penalties, and disruptions of families were justified as necessary for the immigrants' *own* protection.

Despite the significant number of individuals detained and arrested in conjunction with the operations, few employers faced civil or criminal penalties. Such raids as the one conducted in San Diego, California, in September 2004 resulted in the apprehension of fourteen employees of the Golden State Fence Company, a contractor that also supplied laborers to the North Island Naval Air Station. However, while the employees and their families faced fines, deportation, and a frightening disruption of their lives, the company escaped all fines and penalties, demonstrating the lopsided application of the war on terrorism.[40]

Raids Targeting Worksites

By 2005, raids of private worksites increased as raids of airports began to wane.[41] In particular, while the number of undocumented immigrants arrested at workplaces increased from 510 to 845 between 2002 and 2004, these figures rapidly escalated between 2005 and 2008, resulting in more than 6,200 arrests in 2008.[42] Publicly, these raids were part of an enhanced worksite enforcement strategy launched by the DHS.[43] Politically, they appeased a conservative section of the Republican Party unnerved by renewed talks of immigration reform and especially President Bush's support for a guest-worker program.[44] These raids generated even bigger public spectacles and netted larger numbers of immigrants, allowing the executive branch to reinforce its masculine protector image while simultaneously shifting the burden for immigration reform to Congress.

The largest raid conducted at a single worksite after 9/11 took place on December 12, 2006, and targeted Swift and Company meat-packing plants in six states.[45] As part of the raid, dubbed Operation Wagon Train, more than 1,000 federal agents working in conjunction with local police and sheriffs executed simultaneous raids at plants in Greeley, Colorado; Grand Island, Nebraska; Cactus, Texas; Hyrum, Utah; Marshalltown, Iowa; and Worthington, Minnesota. As a result, 1,297 immigrants were arrested on administrative charges, with the preponderance coming from Latin America—specifically, Mexico, Guatemala, Honduras, El Salvador, and Peru.[46]

Like the raids on airports and military bases, Operation Wagon Train united multiple federal departments (Homeland Security, Agriculture, Justice, Labor, the Federal Trade Commission, and the Social Security Administration) in collaboration with local law enforcement. Investigations leading to the raid began with information provided by local police under the DHS/ICE's Criminal Alien Program (CAP). Under this program, local police would notify the DHS when an immigrant was incarcerated, and ICE agents would process that immigrant for removal following completion of his or her sentence. In the case of Operation Wagon Train, ICE agents conducting

CAP interviews found multiple cases of individuals working at Swift. This information was combined with local law-enforcement referrals as well as anonymous hotline tips.[47]

Cooperation with local law enforcement was also facilitated through the work of the Federal Trade Commission, which runs the National Identity Theft Data Clearinghouse. As a function of the clearinghouse, the DHS amasses consumer complaints about specific crimes that are then shared with more than 1,400 law-enforcement agencies across the country. In the case of Operation Wagon Train, the clearinghouse database was used to detect the criminal use of thousands of social security numbers for credit-card fraud, student-loan fraud, and tax evasion, among other crimes.[48]

Finally, Swift became the focus of this raid because it was one of the few employers nationally that had been using the Basic Pilot Employment Verification Program (which later became known as E-Verify) initiated in the 1996 legislation discussed in Chapter 3. Swift had utilized the program to verify its employees' social security numbers since 1997, a factor that proved significant in shielding the company from liability and charges associated with hiring unauthorized workers.[49]

Much like the arguments offered in defense of Operation Tarmac, the state's defense of worksite raids traded on the suspicion of immigrants as criminal agents whose potential harm extended to acts of terrorism. In the case of Operation Wagon Train, DHS Secretary Michael Chertoff defended the scale of the operation as necessary to root out an "identity theft ring" that was allegedly bringing harm to Americans through the use of fraudulent work documents:

> Now, this is not only a case about illegal immigration, which is bad enough. It's a case about identity theft in *violation of the privacy rights and the economic rights of innocent Americans.* I will tell you that the people whose identities were stolen—and we believe, based on reporting we got at the federal Trade Commission (FTC)—that these number at least in the hundreds. These individuals suffered very real consequences in their lives. These were not victimless crimes. (Emphasis added)[50]

The establishment of Americans as "innocent victims" necessitated the DHS's role as defender and protector, even as it carried out this role with aggressive and violent tactics that terrorized immigrant families. But this depiction of immigrants as harmful to the protected stock of legitimate Americans was insufficient, so Chertoff again invoked national security concerns as justification for the worksite raids:

We've stepped up our targeting of criminal organizations and enterprises that support illegal migration by trafficking in false and stolen documents, including Social Security numbers and driver's licenses. This is a serious problem not only with respect to illegal immigration, *but with respect to national security.* And that's precisely the point made by the 9/11 Commission a couple of years ago, because illegal documents are not only used by illegal migrants, but they are used by terrorists who want to get on airplanes, or criminals who want to prey on our citizens. (Emphasis added)[51]

In this depiction, undocumented Latina/o laborers using false identification cards to secure work were once again conflated with terrorists, thereby justifying the masculine protector in the form of the DHS to take aggressive action to shield its protected citizenry—this despite the absence of any evidence linking Latina/o immigrants in the United States to terrorist organizations or any evidence of terrorist activity occurring around the U.S.-Mexico border.

Finally, while the raids on Swift and Company were not the first executed upon private employers after 9/11, Chertoff used the event to signal a new era of similar targeting, noting to reporters covering the operation, "I'm pretty much going to guarantee we're going to keep bringing these cases."[52]

Raids Targeting Fugitive Absconders

The third category of raids emerged as a product of the proliferation of fugitive operation teams after 9/11 whose congressional mandate was to locate and remove dangerous absconders or individuals with existing removal orders. Much like other changes in immigration politics and enforcement in the past decade, the initial operations began in 1995 (with congressional funding authorized in 1996) in the context of other sweeping changes in immigration enforcement outlined previously. What began as an effort to focus INS resources on removing "criminal aliens" became a vehicle for targeting fugitives who purportedly posed a threat to the nation after 9/11. Thus, out of the initial programs in 1995 came the National Fugitive Operations Program (NFOP) in 2002, a federal initiative targeting "dangerous individuals with existing removal orders" conducted by the Office of Detention and Removal Operations (DRO), a division of ICE within the DHS.

While other federal initiatives resulted in the apprehension and removal of deportable immigrants, the NFOP expanded rapidly to more than one hundred teams, with a 1,300 percent growth in personnel, during the war on terrorism.[53] The Migration Policy Institute notes that in its 2003 strategic plan, the DHS presented the work of these fugitive operations teams as key to national security:

> Moving toward a 100 percent rate of removal for all removable aliens is critical to allow ICE to provide the level of immigration enforcement necessary to keep America secure. Without this final step in the process, apprehensions made by other DHS programs cannot truly contribute to national security.[54]

As immigrants, particularly those with existing criminal records or deportation orders, were ensconced in the war on terrorism, the work of the fugitive operations teams escalated, with more than ninety-six thousand apprehensions by 2008. Ironically, despite the vast expansion of arrests made as a result of the NFOP and the number of immigrants who were apprehended en masse in the course of these operations, ICE insisted that "Fugitive Operation Teams do not conduct 'raids.'"[55]

Of particular note in these operations is the number of noncriminal immigrants apprehended in conjunction with the NFOP. In their 2009 report, Margot Mendelson, Shayna Strom, and Michael Wishni note that in 2003, 32 percent of those persons apprehended and arrested by the teams had criminal convictions, a number that had dropped to 17 percent in 2006 and 9 percent by 2007. In other words, by 2007, the preponderance of immigrants apprehended by the Fugitive Operations Teams as part of the war on terrorism had no connection to terrorism *and* no criminal convictions in their records. In fact, most were "ordinary status violators—those who have never been charged before an immigration judge, but whom ICE arrests on the belief that they are unlawfully present in the country," leading the authors to conclude that the "NFOP has failed to focus its resources on the priorities Congress intended. . . . In effect, NFOP has succeeded in apprehending the easiest targets, not the most dangerous fugitives. Furthermore, the program's structure and design appear to encourage officers to jeopardize their own safety, alienate communities, and misdirect expensive personnel resources."[56]

In addition to the problematic apprehension of large numbers of immigrants who posed no threat to homeland security and had no criminal convictions, the actual conduct of the raids added another dimension to the terrorization of residential neighborhoods. Following the pattern of previous raids executed in the 1980s and early 1990s, multiple sources allege that agents entered homes without required warrants; bullied occupants, including children; and prevented apprehended immigrants from exercising their legal rights.[57] In this way, the creation of the Fugitive Operation Teams under the auspice of the DHS, the rapid escalation of the apprehension and arrest of immigrants (most of whom had no prior criminal convictions or showed no evidence of security threats), and the execution of the teams' raids worked to implement the notions of securitization and racialized demonization on the bodies of immigrants and their families.

Working in conjunction with the expansion of these operations was the collection and concentration of information on immigrants in the National Crime Information Center (NCIC) database—the primary FBI database accessible to law-enforcement agencies around the country. In December 2001, the INS announced it would drastically expand the database by adding intelligence on more than 310,000 "alien absconders" to the NCIC and sharing this information, despite inaccuracies in the data. Utilizing the expanded NCIC database, the Department of Justice (DOJ) launched the Alien Absconder Initiative in January 2002, targeting noncitizens with outstanding removal orders for apprehension and deportation. Moreover, the DOJ announced it would prioritize noncitizens from countries with a notable Al Qaeda presence; however, as David Cole notes, the program failed to include Spain, Germany, and other European countries among these calculations, despite the active presence of Al Qaeda there.[58]

By 2003, the NFOP had been established as an independent unit within ICE and was highlighted as part of the newly developed Secure Border Initiative (SBI). This initiative concentrated DHS efforts on reducing the flow of unauthorized immigrants and fortifying the U.S.-Mexico border. Emerging from the securitization discourse, this renewed targeting of undocumented immigrants was firmly grounded in the war on terrorism and as such facilitated the perception of Mexican immigrants as potential terrorists. The initiative included an increase in Border Patrol agents, expanded detention and removal capabilities, systematic upgrades in border control technology (e.g., increased manned and unmanned aerial vehicles), and increased investment in fortifying the border fence. The SBI also set out to "greatly increase interior enforcement of our immigration laws—including more robust worksite enforcement."[59] Thus, the NFOP not only was responsible for the increased raids in residential neighborhoods but also was tied to the increase of raids in worksites across the country.

Apprehending and deporting violent gang members became a key segment of the NFOP's work during the war on terrorism. Among the dozens of raids conducted in neighborhoods across the country, high-profile campaigns targeted criminal gang members, including Operation Return to Sender and Operation Community Shield.[60] In addition, DHS guidelines for the teams increasingly put pressure on agents to apprehend more immigrants and to prioritize those who were considered most dangerous, posing a threat to the nation and to the communities in which they resided. By January 2006, revised guidelines directed officers operating under the NFOP to apprehend "at least 1,000 fugitive aliens a year."[61] As pressure to apprehend more noncitizens increased, ICE agents working with other federal agents and local officials conducted more and more residential raids and arrested more individuals. However, as the number of arrests increased, the numbers of fugitives with criminal convictions actually decreased. Despite the mandate to arrest dangerous immigrants, and despite the positioning of these operations as central to homeland security, between 2003 and 2008, approximately three-fourths of those apprehended had no criminal convictions, and not one of the immigrants apprehended posed a threat to the nation.[62] At the same time, the number of arrests of "ordinary status violators"—those immigrants who had never been charged before an immigration judge but whom ICE arrested, believing they were unlawfully present in the country—grew from approximately 22 percent to 40 percent of all NFOP arrests.[63]

The pressure to make more and more arrests and to prioritize "dangerous aliens" led to larger-scale raids, many of which targeted gang members in Latina/o neighborhoods. Under Operation Community Shield, ICE agents, the DOJ, and local police departments led a crackdown on street gangs—particularly immigrant youth associated with *Mara Salvatrucha*, or MS-13. MS-13 originally began as a gang of largely Salvadoran refugees in the 1980s but evolved over the years into a broad association of Guatemalan, Honduran, Ecuadorian, and Mexican youth. The NFOP was eventually expanded to target all street and prison gangs with foreign-born members, and by October 2007, more than five thousand gang members had been arrested.

In March 2005, under Operation Community Shield, the DHS declared these youth to be not merely criminals but "homeland security risks," invoking an image of terrorism despite the absence of any evidence of their involvement with known terrorist groups or terrorist activity. As part of the operation, ICE and local police targeted more than three hundred undocumented youth in these gangs in Washington, D.C., Baltimore, New York, Miami, and Newark, virtually all of whom were Latino and were subsequently tried or deported.

Following the security discourse, state-level authorities prosecuting gang members apprehended in these raids also constructed these immigrant youth as potential terrorists. In one case in New York, nineteen Latino gang members associated with the St. James boys' street gang were apprehended and charged with violating the state's terrorism law. According to the district attorney prosecuting the case, "The terror perpetrated by gangs, which all too often occurs on the streets of New York, also fits squarely within the scope of this [anti-terrorism] statute." Similarly Police Commissioner Raymond Kelly said that the gang had "terrorized" the community surrounding St. James Park in New York.[64] In this way, the Latinas/os apprehended in association with these raids not only were equated with terrorism in popular political discourse; they were actually constituted as terrorists via the application of state law.

In this way, the raids conducted by these NFOP teams followed a similar pattern to the raids conducted in federally secured areas as well as worksite raids. Ultimately, while the raids on federally secured facilities, worksites, and residences had abated by 2008, they did not cease. An examination of how the raids shifted after 2009, and particularly within the Obama administration, is included in the final chapter.

Intersections of Race and Gender in the Bodies of Latina Immigrants

In addition to the convergence of racialization, securitization, and gendering discourse in the raids outlined above, the intersecting modes of subordination effected by race and gender also figure into my analysis of the raids, as more women became targets. In other words, the bodies of immigrant Latinas became central to contemporary enforcement initiatives as increasing numbers of women and children were apprehended in the surge of raids and roundups. While the image of detainees cultivated in raids and roundups was often that of Latino and Arab men, Latinas were apprehended with greater frequency as the raids expanded, and reports of gendered violence increased as these women were held in or transferred to immigration detention centers. Moreover, the increased impact on children affected gender dynamics, as parental and financial roles and family relationships were reconfigured, and an increasing number of immigrant women shouldered responsibilities as primary breadwinners and single parents. Ultimately, by examining the impact of the raids on Latinas, another dimension of race and gender intersectionality appears—namely, how the raids affected particular raced and gendered subjects, how their bodies became the site upon which the raids were executed, and how their own roles and relationships shifted as a consequence of the raids.

While the DHS does not release data on the racial and gendered makeup of persons apprehended in the raids, data from independent investigations indicate that initial detainees were disproportionately Latino men.[65] However, given the broad reach of the raids as well as the move from secured and sensitive facilities to commercial employment and residential raids, an increasing number of women and children were affected beginning in 2006. For example, in a 2008 raid of the Agriprocessor meat-packing plant in Pottsville, Iowa, of the 390 undocumented immigrants arrested, 76 were women. Similarly, reports from a 2007 raid on a textile manufacturing plant that produced backpacks for the U.S. military in New Bedford, Massachusetts, indicate that the preponderance of the 361 undocumented immigrants arrested were women.[66] Moreover, these apprehensions were not isolated incidents, and the analysis of newspaper accounts suggests that more women and parents with children were apprehended as the scale of immigration raids expanded, particularly after the inauguration of the Secure Communities Program.

As the number of apprehensions and detentions escalated, and particularly as more women were held in detention facilities for processing and deportation, reports of physical, mental, emotional, and sexual abuse in these facilities also increased.[67] The American Civil Liberties Union (ACLU) documented close to two hundred allegations of sexual abuse of immigrants between 2007 and 2010, including sexual assaults by officers working in the detention facilities. These incidents were reported at virtually each of the eighty-five detention facilities across the country, with fifty-six emanating from Texas facilities alone. Immigrant women, already marginalized by race, gender, and class, faced legal and political constraints, coupled with fear and intimidation, making them vulnerable targets for such abuse and offering them little remedy from a country that already constituted them as threats. As such, their bodies became the locus upon which law-enforcement initiatives were executed, and their position as marginalized "aliens" left them with few means of protection, rights, or opportunities to challenge these operations.

Testimony from "Raquel," one of three female litigants involved in a lawsuit against the DHS who suffered sexual abuse while being held in the T. Don Hutto Residential Center in Texas, highlights the particular problem experienced by the growing number of immigrant Latinas in detention. She was being transported to the airport after being bonded and released when she experienced the following at the hands of an ICE officer:

> We started driving. . . . After a while the driver pulled off the road and stopped. He opened the door and unlocked the cage and gestured for me to get out. He told me to raise my hands and I did. Then he started touching me all over. He pulled up my bra, fondled my breasts, and put his hand down my pants. He was talking in English and touching himself. I asked him why he was doing this to me. . . . Then he continued to touch me.
>
> He hurriedly shoved anything that was on the floor of the front area of the van and motioned for me to lay down on my back. I refused. When he saw that I wasn't going to cooperate, he went to the back of the van. He pushed my things off the seat in the cage inside the van and gestured for me to get back in. I complied. He followed me into the van. I told him I would report him if he continued to touch me and he pushed me into the van. I was crying and I thought

it was the end of my life. I thought he was going to kill me. I thought I should have stayed in my home country if my life was going to end like this because at least I would have had more time with my children. He got in the cage with me and started unzipping his pants and pulling off my clothes. He exposed himself to me. He was angry that I would not take off my clothes. I kept yelling, saying that if he didn't stop I would tell someone.[68]

Raquel eventually reached the airport but only after surviving terrifying abuse that left her traumatized. She recalls, "I left one problem in my home country and encountered another one here. I felt afraid of every one on the street, men and women, especially if they came near me or touched me. I was very afraid that the man who hurt me had bad friends and they were going to find me and hurt me. I cried at night and had a hard time falling asleep. Every time I closed my eyes, I saw him. I also felt dirty all the time, because his hands had been on my body."[69] Raquel's experiences point to the increased vulnerability, and especially the increased risk of sexualized violence, immigrant women faced as a consequence of their already marginalized status and their increased levels of detention.

In addition to the specific forms of racial and gender discrimination at work in these cases, the proliferation of raids and rapid deportation of adults with children reconfigured entire Latina/o families. As parents were incarcerated or deported, families were separated, while parental and financial roles and responsibilities were redefined. In particular, within the first wave of apprehensions, many women were rendered single parents as a disproportionate number of men were apprehended and deported.[70] Single mothers were left to provide for their families with limited economic opportunities while simultaneously negotiating complex and hostile immigration rules in the hopes of reunification with their partners. The tenuous legal status of many women meant they were also subject to constant scrutiny and generally could not rely on state-sponsored support or services to ameliorate their situations. In short, the "enforcement policies left women—more so than men—in extremely vulnerable situations."[71]

Latina/o children were not shielded from the effects of the raids, particularly as they witnessed family members deported with little hopes of reunification and lived with persistent fear of reprisal. A 2007 study by the Urban Institute documented the heavy burden on children and families borne out through the raids. In its examination of three raids conducted in 2006—in Greeley, Colorado; Grand Island, Nebraska; and New Bedford, Massachusetts—it found that in addition to the 912 adults arrested, more than 506 children were affected. Moreover, a large majority of the children impacted were U.S. citizens, and many were among the youngest of children—namely infants, toddlers, and preschoolers. After these raids, several children showed overt signs of trauma and psychological duress, including depression, separation anxiety disorders, posttraumatic stress, and suicidal thoughts.[72]

Even in cases where the children were natural-born citizens or deportations had not occurred, children still lived in constant fear of separation from family members whose status was not secured as a result of the indiscriminate methods by which the raids were executed. Given the preponderance of local police and sheriff's officers employed in the course of the raids, several children reported being fearful of all law-enforcement officials, while others associated all immigrants with illegal status and sought to disassociate themselves from an immigrant identity.[73] Finally, still more children were incarcerated as they were held with their parents in detention facilities, while hundreds of unaccompanied minors were held for weeks and even months in adult detention facilities.[74]

An alarming number of children were also placed in foster care after their parents were detained or deported. In some of the most tragic cases, after months of detention or deportation and lengthy struggles, some immigrant parents had their parental rights severed, and their children were put up for adoption. The families most likely to be separated were those living in states and localities where local law enforcement was most closely linked to federal immigration enforcement initiatives.[75]

Focusing on the race and gender of those apprehended in the course of the raids brings to the forefront the significant obstacles encountered by immigrant Latinas and children in these enforcement initiatives and the degree to which enforcement, scrutiny, intimidation, and fear reconfigured race and gender identities, roles, and vulnerabilities. Examining the intersectional experiences of those apprehended also challenges the presumption of uniformity within the raids, as Latino bodies become the de facto face of enforcement. Thus, the bodies of Latina/o adults and children became the sites upon which the enforcement initiatives came to life; however, the experiences of these subjects were mediated by their race and gender. That is, these enforcement initiatives exacted a particularly harsh gendered consequence, as women and children faced apprehension and their status as marginalized subjects made them vulnerable to additional violence and abuse. Immigrant women not only were demonized as terrorist threats; they also faced additional harm in the form of physical and psychological abuse as the raids proliferated.

Comparing Historic and Contemporary Raids

As evident through reviewing past immigration practices, the use of raids and roundups for large-scale immigrant removal has been a recurrent strategy of immigration officials, particularly throughout the twentieth century. In this way, the raids conducted after 9/11 and under the auspice of the war on terrorism followed the pattern of a larger history. Moreover, these raids made use of similar practices, including highly militarized public spectacles intended to intimidate entire communities, raids conducted in residential homes without proper search warrants or with no search warrants at all, and even raids using "sting operation" tactics.[76] However, the raids conducted as part of the war on terrorism were distinct from previous raids among Latinas/os in a number of ways.

First, the raids examined here were formally presented as race-neutral and justified through the logic of securitization, an appeal to protecting homeland security. For example, in the case of raids on federally secured facilities, agents targeted "persons of unknown origins." Similarly, in the case of worksite raids, ICE agents targeted immigrants using fraudulent identification documents. Finally, in the case of the NFOP, agents targeted "dangerous criminal aliens." In other words, unlike previous raids aimed at large-scale detention, such as Operation Wetback, the formal charge of these operations excluded any specific ethnic targeting, even while key proponents (and even spokespersons) revealed more nuanced racialized demonization in their justifications for the programs.

Despite the absence of overt racial targeting in the operations' missions, each of these programs had a racialized effect—namely, they disproportionately apprehended Latina/o immigrants and constituted these persons as foreign, dangerous, and menacing, despite the lack of evidence linking any one of them to actual terrorist organizations. As such, these operations diverged sharply from the language of such raids as Operation Wetback, which invoked overtly racist language, and instead maintained that the targeting was "not about ethnic background or race."[77] In contrast, these contemporary raids were ensconced within language of masculine protectionism and homeland security that constituted immigrants as terrorist threats, justifying the need for the state's overreaching and abusive power.

Second, these later raids were part of joint operations that united multiple federal departments and agencies with local law enforcement in unprecedented extensions of immigration review. In this process, local officials became deputized as immigration agents, radically extending the surveillance powers of federal immigration authorities and the policing of immigrant bodies. Extension of immigration authority to local law enforcement also empowered local officials to exercise power over immigrants in unprecedented ways, such as initiating multiagency taskforces independent of the federal authorities. This was the case in a countywide raid in Santa Rosa County, California, where Sheriff Wendell Hall reportedly formed a multi-county immigration taskforce without first contacting ICE authorities. This task force was subsequently responsible for launching a raid that resulted in the arrest of more than a dozen men and women. According to the report on the raid, the sheriff "seemed proud to have found a way around rules allowing only the federal government to enforce immigration laws."[78]

Finally, these raids reflected an escalation of state authority premised on a gendered logic of masculine protectionism coupled with a racialization of immigrants as threatening foreigners. While the authority for the raids typically rested on laws that predated the 9/11 attacks, in particular the expansion of restrictive immigration policies in the 1990s, these programs were executed with greater frequency and ferocity between 2001 and 2008. Thus, as the security state expanded as a consequence of the war on terrorism, so too did the scrutiny, apprehension, arrest, and deportation of immigrants.

Conclusion

Among the changes in immigration politics after 9/11, one of the most troubling aspects is the return to large-scale raids and roundups as vehicles for implementing and enforcing immigration policy. Distinct from border enforcement and individual arrests, these raids disproportionately affected Latina/o communities through the use of swift, severe, and coordinated operations that were concentrated in federally secured areas and critical infrastructures, private worksites, and residential neighborhoods. The raids not only impacted Latina/o immigrants; the terrorizing effect was also felt among the friends and families of those apprehended, including permanent residents and citizens. It is also important to note that the raids were not conducted in high-income neighborhoods or at professional office complexes (despite the proliferation of professional foreign laborers), and they left employers largely unscathed. Instead, the execution of the raids served to intimidate, harass, and terrorize a population already marginalized by age, status, race, ethnicity, and income.

The raids had a particular effect on Latina women and children, as revealed through an analysis cultivated here attentive to the racializing and gendering processes and intersecting modes of subordination at work in the raids. In particular, Latina immigrants were apprehended with greater frequency, especially as the raids expanded after 2006, challenging the tacit or explicit presumption that shifts in enforcement were targeted exclusively at men. More importantly, women already marginalized in relation to racist and sexist law-enforcement institutions that regarded them as expendable "aliens" were further marginalized, as sexual harassment and sexualized violence against them proliferated. Finally, the gendered roles of Latinas, in particular their disproportionate responsibilities as caretakers within the home, were challenged and reconfigured as Latina/o children were traumatized, separated from, and dislocated from families, and women were forced to become primary (or sole) financial providers and single parents in a hostile environment that also denied them most forms of state-sponsored support.

While the previous two chapters focused on the legislative changes that occurred in immigration politics after 9/11 and how implementation of those changes affected Latina/o immigrants, the next chapter traces the extension of masculine protectionism, racialized demonization, and de-Americanization to natural-born citizens. In this way, the effects documented here are important for gaining a better understanding of the state's treatment of immigrants generally and Latina/o immigrants specifically, but they also establish a logic and course of action that undermine fundamental democratic principles for all persons.

6

Security and Citizenship

*"Enemy Combatants" and the Cases of John Walker Lindh,
Yaser Hamdi, and José Padilla*

On May 8, 2002, José Padilla was apprehended by federal law enforcement as he disembarked a plane traveling from Pakistan to Chicago's O'Hare International Airport. At the time of his apprehension, Padilla was considered a potential terrorist by federal authorities and was detained by marshals working in conjunction with the Federal Bureau of Investigation (FBI) and local police, who alleged he was conspiring to detonate a "dirty bomb" in a major metropolitan city. Padilla spent the next two and a half years incarcerated and incommunicado—without access to an attorney, without access to his family, in solitary confinement for twenty-three hours a day— all while being subjected to continual interrogations.[1] During those two and a half years, he was never charged with conspiracy, domestic terrorism, or any act of criminality; in fact, in the course of those years, he was never formally charged *at all* but was held in a military brig on the unilateral designation of President George W. Bush that he constituted an "enemy combatant," a designation up to this point used exclusively for noncitizens. In short, regardless of the fact that he was never charged or convicted as a terrorist, Padilla was constructed as one by executive order and federal agents working to implement the order. In the end, his circumstances mirrored those of millions of Latinas/os generally and Latina/o immigrants specifically who were symbolically and legally designated as enemy outsiders.

However, Padilla was not a prisoner apprehended on a foreign battlefield, a soldier captured in the course of combat, or even an immigrant with suspicious associations with home-country organizations. Padilla was, and continues to be, a natural-born U.S. citizen who spent most of his life on U.S. soil and was apprehended in the United States. In fact, Padilla was born in New York and raised in working-class barrios in Brooklyn and Chicago. Growing up in these environments, Padilla lived a life similar to that of other Latino urban youth: attending public schools; living in substandard subsidized housing, where he was exposed to gangs; witnessing high levels of criminal activity; and ultimately becoming affiliated with local gangs. In 1983, he was convicted of murder charges and was incarcerated until his eighteenth birthday. He was subsequently convicted of a handgun charge in Florida and sent to prison, where he converted to Islam and went by the names of Ibrahim Padilla and Abdullah al Muhajir.[2] Upon his release from prison, Padilla moved to Egypt and ultimately traveled to Afghanistan and Pakistan on a religious pilgrimage.[3]

It was on a trip back to the United States from Pakistan in 2002 that Padilla was taken into custody and held initially in a civilian correctional facility in New York. When the Department of Justice (DOJ) failed to marshal the necessary evidence to charge him with conspiracy, it asserted various legal prerogatives to justify his continued incarceration, including detention as a material witness before a grand jury trial. While this initial detention appeared cumbersome if not extreme, what distinguished the actions of federal agents in the initial phases of this case (as compared to their later treatment of Padilla and other citizens) was their outward performance of constitutionality. That is, they grounded Padilla's detention within a standard of due process, which provided a reasonable legal prerogative for imprisoning a U.S. citizen, one that maintained their status as purveyors of democracy even as the expansion of the security state and the subsequent terrorization of entire communities called this status into question.

By contrast, in June 2002, the executive office abandoned any semblance of constitutionality with its unilateral designation of Padilla as an "enemy combatant."[4] Specifically, on June 9, 2002, President Bush signed an order in which he borrowed language that had been used exclusively in the racialization of immigrants as terrorist threats. That is, he asserted that Padilla represented "a continuing, present and grave danger to the national security of the United States, and detention of Mr. Padilla is necessary to prevent him from aiding al Qaeda in its efforts to attack the United States or its armed forces, other governmental personnel or citizens."[5] This order politically constituted Padilla as a threat to national security and legally enabled his indefinite detention with the possibility of trial through a military tribunal. Following this designation, Padilla was transported from the civilian correctional facility in New York to a naval brig in South Carolina, where he was held until November 22, 2005.

This chapter extends the analysis developed in previous chapters to consider how fundamental rights, values, and conceptions of citizenship were sacrificed in the context of mounting securitization. With growing frequency, the terrorizing restrictions applied to immigrants in the years after 9/11 were applied to the most protected class of persons in the United States—namely, natural-born citizens. Moreover, this slippage from constructing immigrants as terrorists to terrorizing citizens was not accidental; rather, the national security state engaged in a parallel process of racial demonization and de-Americanization, ultimately stripping Padilla and other detainees of legal protection and political agency while publicly appealing to a masculinized discourse of protection.

Thus, this chapter examines fundamental shifts in the rights, statuses, and meanings of citizenship that occurred during the height of the war on terror as demonstrated in the cases of three natural-born U.S. citizens: John Walker Lindh, Yaser Hamdi, and José Padilla. In particular, this analysis points to a systematic erosion of due process, representation, and political agency as the efforts to expand the security state mounted while attending to shifts in meaning and construction of citizenship in the context of the discursive regimes of racialized demonization, masculinized protectionism, and securitization. Following the challenges to "value-neutrality" in law and policy spelled out in Chapter 1 and engaging in a parallel process of "denaturalization" with respect to congressional legislation as applied in Chapter 4, I explore the race-gendering process at work in the production and reconfiguration of citizenship as revealed in these cases. More to the point, I employ race-gendering as a frame of analysis to examine the cases surrounding the three detainees and the ways in which specific racialization and gendering took place that legitimized and enabled the erosion of citizenship, particularly for Hamdi and Padilla.

Moreover, I extend the argument advanced in Chapter 5 on detentions—namely, that in focusing on state policies and practices, I am reading the Departments of Justice, Homeland Security, and Defense not merely as representatives of the state but as agents "policing the national body," determining who is and who is not deserving of membership and rights.[6] In this way, I borrow from Michel Foucault to examine the "technologies of government"—specifically, the policies, laws, and practices that construct a citizen-subject and not merely the texts of the court opinions.[7] In addition, I examine the link between the logics of protectionism and fear outlined in Chapter 1 and the delineation of legitimate and deserving citizens from illegitimate and threatening citizens as a product of governmentality. The process of constructing citizenship is read here as a political process of "subjectification," one in which persons are literally subjected by particular logics and the ways in which these are ultimately challenged, rejected, modified, and negotiated through court challenges and even between judicial bodies.

Ultimately, while the chapter is focused on the responses of the national security regime in the specific cases of Lindh, Hamdi, and Padilla, it is also a wider study in the shifts in citizenship, the transference of language and limitations from immigrants to citizens, and the state's broadened definition of enemies in the war on terrorism. In other words, this chapter squarely addresses this question: Why should non-Latinas/os and especially American citizens seemingly unaffected by the war on terrorism concern themselves with shifts in immigration politics and securitization? The answer lies in a systematic degradation of citizenship drawn from the restrictions on immigrants and transferred through overt and subtle mechanisms to the most protected class of individuals: natural-born citizens.

Masculine Protectionism and Racialized Demonization

While the domestic war against terrorism was waged largely on the backs of noncitizens, the new security state has consistently demonstrated its capacity and willingness to restrict even the most venerated constitutional protections for natural-born citizens. The status of citizenship that had provided a set of legal protections assuring due process against unwarranted intrusion by the state eventually gave way to the logic of suspicion and protectionism, along with racialized demonization. In this shift, natural-born citizens were made foreign and ultimately, as in the cases of Hamdi and Padilla, became "de-Americanized"—literally constituted as enemies of the state, stripped legally and symbolically of their political rights.

As outlined in Chapter 2, the underlying logics of suspicion, protectionism, and demonization enabling this shift were themselves gendered and raced. The protectionist logic relied on the construction of an enemy "other" and the demonization of this enemy as foreign, threatening, suspicious, and ultimately terrorist. Moreover, protectionism also required dependents, and to facilitate this Americans and Afghans (particularly Afghan women and children) were cast as dependents in need of the state's chivalrous protection in exchange for their unfettered allegiance. Finally, the concept of the external enemy, initially imagined as distant foreign subjects in the form of Al Qaeda operatives, was expanded to include "terrorists" at home, particularly immigrants who were marked by race, ethnicity, religion, and political tradition as deviant.

Thus, just as President Bush and the State Department defended aggressive intervention in Afghanistan as being necessary for the protection of its "women and children" and "our way of life" at home, thereby gendering its loyal subjects and feminizing citizenship, so too did the president justify the designation of Padilla as an enemy combatant without due process as "necessary to prevent him from aiding al Qaeda in its efforts to attack the United States or its armed forces."[8] In this way, Padilla's racialized demonization legitimated at home the same application of protectionism exercised abroad; however, in this case, the target of suspicion was not an actual foreign subject but rather a natural-born citizen constituted by the state as a hostile terrorist.

As I note in this chapter, the processes of racialized demonization and de-Americanization that had been applied frequently to immigrants in the war on terror was applied to both Hamdi and Padilla. The difference was that both men were natural-born citizens whose status was supposed to have shielded them from the most restrictive conditions applied to immigrants. Thus, in much the same way that immigration policy has been racialized in the United States, imparting disproportionate burdens on Latina/o and other nonwhite immigrants, so too has citizenship become raced in this period, with Arab, Muslim, and increasingly Latina/o citizens subjected to a variety of encumbering state laws, forms of federal scrutiny, restrictions on due process, threats of removal, and indefinite detention, all with virtually no possibilities for resistance.

Demonization and Political Agency

The process of racialized demonization and its extension to de-Americanization is similar to the process of racializing immigrants described in previous chapters, both with respect to the logic of suspicion and protectionism and with respect to loss of political agency.[9] In the case of immigrants, not only were new laws invoked to target and constrain their behavior; existing statutes were also aggressively enforced, eventually resulting in large-scale detentions and deportations. In effect, as immigrants became increasingly constituted by the state as threatening, their hold on due process, representation, or any form of political agency became increasingly tenuous or disappeared entirely, as was the case among thousands of Latina/o immigrants apprehended in the escalation of raids and round-ups. A parallel loss of political agency took place with respect to citizens racialized as foreign and threatening, as their status as citizen-subjects was worn, tattered, and, in the cases of Padilla and Hamdi, suspended altogether.

A unique quality of the cases examined here that adds to the way that citizenship was reconfigured is the *absence* of—or more specifically, constraints on—political agency. In the cases of Padilla and Hamdi, they were held incommunicado for prolonged periods, making it impossible for them to assert their constitutional rights to counsel or protection from unlawful detention and erasing them as political subjects capable of action. Enabled by Padilla's and Hamdi's designations as enemy combatants, the state exercised an extreme form of isolated detention whereby little to no information about their daily rituals or behavior was revealed, while these individuals were subject to continual interrogations.

In this context, agency was expressed literally *in absentia*, as legal and political challenges were filed on their behalf and argued without their presence or even their words entering into the official record.[10] For example, in the initial attempts to secure representation for Hamdi, the public defender asserted not only that he was unable to communicate with Hamdi but also that he had no idea whether Hamdi even wanted to challenge his detention in U.S. courts. He stated, "And guess what? It's quite possible that this man could tell me, look, you're a Christian infidel, I don't want to talk to you, I don't know why you filed this petition for me, I'm not interested."[11] Similarly, in a second "next-of-friend" habeas petition filed on Hamdi's behalf, the petitioner stated, "I have no prior existing relationship with [Hamdi] and have filed the above petition out of concern for only the unlawful nature of his incarceration. As a citizen born in the United States, it is my responsibility as much as any of my fellow citizens to uphold the law not only as it is written but as it was intended by the fathers of the Constitution."[12]

In this way, Padilla and Hamdi were equated with terrorists, and their treatment paralleled that of millions of immigrants who had been apprehended and held without charge across the country. Moreover, they were erased as citizen-subjects and reconstituted as persons only by attorneys, activists, and family members acting on their behalf. As is evident in their specific cases, this marginalization was justified as necessary for the protection of national security against "unconventional and savage enem[ies]" who may use the judicial system to their interests (which are presumably opposed to U.S. interests) and even turn the "most honorable of [public defenders] into unknowing and unwitting conduits for the transmission of nefarious messages."[13] Masculine protectionism became the justification for detention, isolation, and erasure, all while racializing the suspects as foreign and threatening. This process attests to not only the erosion of constitutional guarantees for natural-born citizens but also the loss of their political agency, a practice that parallels the silencing experienced by immigrants.

Challenging this erasure, we see attempts to resist, reject, and modify the parameters of these restrictions by lawyers, defendants, friends of the petitioners, and judicial bodies.[14] This resistance was especially apparent within the courts, from the district courts all the way to the Supreme Court, as judges and judicial bodies differed on the required degrees of deference to the executive and scrutiny to military authority that would be permitted in the name of national security. Thus, despite the harm generated through masculine protectionism, racialized demonization, and the loss of political agency, important attempts to challenge and renegotiate the citizen-subject post-9/11 have appeared in unexpected forms.

Cases: Lindh, Padilla, and Hamdi

John Walker Lindh

The slippage of citizens into the category of suspected terrorists and enemy combatants occurred slowly as the war on terror and the new security state emerged. At the outset, the state's worst treatment was reserved for immigrants, while the rights of citizens were continually affirmed in law and public discourse.[15] For example, on November 13, 2001, two months before any detainees were brought to naval facilities in Guantanamo Bay, Cuba, President Bush issued a Military Order authorizing indefinite detention without due process *exclusively* for individuals who were "not United States citizens."[16] Wrapped in the language of protectionism and security, Bush declared that any noncitizen accused of terrorism could be tried not by a civilian or criminal court but by a military tribunal, without any appeal to a civilian court: "To protect the United States and its citizens, and for the effective conduct of military operations and prevention of terrorist attacks, it is necessary for individuals subject to this order . . . to be detained, and when tried, to be tried for violations of the laws of war and other applicable laws by military tribunals."[17]

This order made a point of distinguishing deserving citizens from threatening noncitizens and refining the target even further to apply to immigrants whom the executive or the Defense Department believed to be affiliated with Al Qaeda, who had harbored potential terrorists, or who had engaged in actions that "caused, threaten[ed] to cause or ha[d] as their aim to cause injury to or adverse effects on the United States, its citizens, national security, foreign policy or economy."[18] This order was an extension of the Authorization for Use of Military Force (AUMF) provided to the president by Congress in the immediate aftermath of 9/11, granting him the authorization to use "necessary and appropriate force against those nations, organizations, or persons he determine[d]" were involved in the 9/11 attacks or other acts of terrorism against the United States.[19] Moreover, the White House established a line of demarcation through this order, delineating citizens from noncitizens and upholding due-process protections for citizens while authorizing the indefinite detention of immigrants who presented a challenge to the state, including challenges to the economic order.

President Bush, Vice President Dick Cheney, and even Attorney General John Ashcroft also repeatedly affirmed the rights of citizens (and distinguished them from the limits on immigrants' rights) in statements to the press surrounding the treatment of detainees in Guantanamo Bay, Cuba, and the first post-9/11 case involving a natural-born citizen—that of John Walker Lindh. Defending the Military Order distinguishing citizen and noncitizen rights, Vice President Cheney noted, "Somebody who comes into the United States of America illegally, who conducts a terrorist operation killing thousands of innocent Americans—men, women, and children—is not a lawful combatant. . . . They don't deserve the same guarantees and safeguards that would be used for an American citizen going through the normal judicial process."[20] Similarly, Ashcroft extended the same argument when asked why Lindh was not being tried in the military tribunals created by the order. He responded, "Mr. John Walker Lindh is a U.S. citizen, and according to the military order issued by the president, it's for dealing with non-citizens of the United States."[21] Ashcroft equally underscored the logic of masculinized protection by stating:

Walker was blessed to grow up in a country that cherishes freedom of speech, religious tolerance, political democracy, and *equality between men and women*. And yet he chose to reject these values in favor of their antithesis, a regime that publicly and proudly advertised its mission to extinguish freedom, *enslave women*, and deny education. John Walker Lindh chose to fight with the Taliban, chose to train with al Qaeda, and to be led by Osama bin Laden. (Emphasis added)[22]

By contrast, when Hamdi was detained and interrogated in Afghanistan, even after his identity as a natural-born citizen was established, the Defense Department unilaterally defined him as an enemy combatant subject to incarceration in Guantanamo Bay.[23] Lindh and Hamdi were originally apprehended in the same location, by the same Northern allied forces, and detained in the same prison; however, in the case of Hamdi, national security discourse had shifted to the point that the United States relinquished any presumption of protection for citizens—a process that was later replicated in the case of Padilla.

Lindh was the first case post-9/11 involving a natural-born citizen implicated in crimes against the United States and, more specifically, acts of international terrorism—thereby serving as an initial test of the boundaries of citizenship in the war on terror.[24] Moreover, his case contrasted with the proceedings in Hamdi's and Padilla's cases (both of which overlapped in sequence with Lindh's case), especially in the escalation of the state's authority to detain and erase political agency, the administration's performance of constitutionality, and the racialization of the subjects themselves.

Lindh was apprehended shortly after the onset of U.S. military air strikes in Afghanistan in October 2001. However, Lindh was not apprehended by

U.S. military personnel but by Northern allied forces that purportedly captured him and negotiated his surrender on a battlefield in Afghanistan, after
which he was transported to a military prison there.[25] According to official
testimony, Lindh was held at the facility and questioned for several weeks
before it was confirmed that he was an American citizen.[26]

While the details surrounding Lindh's apprehension and initial detention are at best hazy, with competing narratives offered by his parents and
the Justice and Defense Departments, an important distinction in the state's
handling of his case, as opposed those of Hamdi and Padilla, is the application of due process, even inconsistently, that prevented his erasure as a
citizen-subject. In particular, unlike other detainees who were held without charges for extended periods of time, Lindh was detained, arrested, *and*
charged with a crime. Lindh was never declared an enemy combatant by
unilateral order of the executive but was formally placed under arrest and
charged with criminal conspiracy, providing material support to foreign
terrorist organizations, and engaging in transactions with the Taliban, all
federal charges under U.S. law.[27] In addition, while he was eventually held
incommunicado, upon his initial apprehension, Lindh was able to communicate a message through a Red Cross worker and was visited briefly by his
father.[28]

In 2002, Lindh was transferred from Camp Rhino in Afghanistan back
to the United States and held in a civilian prison while awaiting trial. In
prison, he was able to visit with family and his attorney, and he eventually accepted a plea agreement wherein all terrorism-related charges were
dropped.[29] In short, in keeping with the language of Bush's Military Order
and delineations between citizens and noncitizens, Lindh was afforded due
process not extended to the hundreds of other prisoners simultaneously
detained and interrogated at prisons in Afghanistan and Iraq as well as those
transferred for indefinite detention to Guantanamo Bay.

The distinctions drawn by the state between these different classes of
prisoners (citizen versus noncitizen) are best demonstrated by the treatment
of individuals held in the same time period at Abu Ghraib and other "black-
site" detention facilities in Afghanistan and Iraq.[30] In Abu Ghraib, the
actions of military officers revealed the violent and overtly dominating side
to masculine protectionism in graphic forms of gendered, racialized, and
sexualized torture. According to Major General Antonio M. Taguba, military police personnel overseeing the detention of prisoners in Abu Ghraib
engaged in "sadistic, blatant and wanton criminal abuses," including "break-
ing chemical lights and pouring the phosphoric liquid on detainees; beating
detainees with a broom handle and a chair; threatening male detainees with
rape; allowing a military police guard to stitch the wound of a detainee who
was injured after being slammed against the wall in his cell; sodomizing a

detainee with a chemical light and perhaps a broom stick; and using military working dogs to frighten and intimidate detainees with threats of attack, and in one instance actually biting a detainee."[31]

Furthermore, when investigators sought to attribute blame for these abuses, it became apparent that even lower-level military officers were acting with the support and recognition of military intelligence, Central Intelligence Agency (CIA) agents, and private contractors, and their actions were consistent with confinement practices used in military-intelligence gathering.[32] In this way, the violence perpetrated against foreign subjects in Abu Ghraib served as a political indicator of the level of entrenched dehumanization of foreigners under the war on terror, in contrast to the professed protections and assurances for American citizens.[33] Moreover, the dehumanization of foreign subjects was propelled by a rapid expansion of U.S. state authority initially legitimated as a necessary form of protection and interrogation against terrorists, which was later applied to American citizens.

The differences in treatment and status afforded Lindh yield some key conclusions about his case: Namely, while Lindh was ultimately sentenced to twenty years' imprisonment on charges that he violated an embargo regulation by working with the Taliban and that he carried a firearm in the process, the terms of imprisonment were reached not by a secretive military tribunal or an executive order from the president but via a plea agreement between Lindh's attorneys and the U.S. attorneys—in other words, via negotiations wherein Lindh was actively represented. Part of the plea-agreement negotiations, to which the U.S. attorneys conceded, included the request that Lindh's prison sentence be served at a facility "that allows Mr. Lindh access to educational opportunities, such as university distance learning programs, as well as one that is close to his family's residence in California such that he may receive the support of regular visits by his family and counsel."[34]

In addition, Lindh's plea agreement allowed him to petition for supervised release, where he could "travel out of his district of supervision, including out of the country."[35] Finally, the United States agreed to forgo any right it had to "treat the defendant as an unlawful enemy combatant."[36] In the end, Lindh was sentenced to prison in Victorville, California, where he was allowed monthly visitation; then he was moved to a supermax facility in Florence, Colorado; and finally he was moved to a medium-security facility in Terre Haute, Indiana.[37] In these proceedings, Lindh retained the rights and political agency of a citizen (albeit constrained and even restricted in the course of his detention), including representation, choice, contact with the rest of the world, outward expressions of his thoughts and desires, and even the real prospect of return to a broader civic society.

In contrast to the detention process involving Padilla and Hamdi, Lindh was actually permitted to speak to the court and presumably to a broader

American audience after accepting a plea agreement brokered between his lawyers and the U.S. attorneys. Lindh's official statement was delivered in court and entered into official proceedings, and in it he expressed a range of emotions and ideas from regret and remorse to ruminations about the future and even subtle defiance of the popular culture references labeling him "the American terrorist":

> I went to Afghanistan because I believed it was my religious duty to assist my fellow Muslim military in their jihad against the Northern Alliance. . . . I never understood jihad to mean anti-Americanism or terrorism. I condemn terrorism on every level—unequivocally. My beliefs about jihad are those of mainstream Muslims around the world. I believe that jihad ranges from striving to overcome our own personal faults, to speaking out for the truth in adverse circumstances, to military action in defense of justice. . . . I went to Afghanistan because I believed there was no way to alleviate the suffering of the Afghan people aside from military action. I did not go to fight against America, and I never did. . . . Terrorism is never justified and has proved extremely damaging to Muslims around the world. I have never supported terrorism in any form and never would. . . . I went to Afghanistan with the intention of fighting against terrorism and oppression, not to support it.[38]

In short, Lindh was not erased but was allowed to engage, to act, to speak, to even defend himself—in effect, to negotiate the terms of his apprehension and resist the charges brought against him through legal and political channels. Moreover, the picture we got of Lindh was complex and even compassionate, with statements to the court (unchallenged by U.S. attorneys) depicting him as "gentle, shy, reserved, close to his family, sensitive to the suffering of others and very bright." He was even described as having the "mind of a doctoral candidate at any top university in the world . . . highly intelligent and scholarly but needs to be mentored."[39] Thus, we not only heard Lindh himself through these proceedings and were presented with a complex and even compassionate subject; we were led to recognize similarities in his love of life and protection of innocence and our own and even to see him as a regular participant in the daily practices of Muslims in the future.

However, Lindh's case was not as simple or as succinct as a distinction between citizens and noncitizens. Allegations of abuse and coercive conduct by the Defense Department were replete through the proceedings. Lindh's case pointed toward abusive executions of state authority in the fifty-four-day period of detention after his transfer from a facility run by Northern Allied Forces in Afghanistan to the U.S. military facility Camp Rhino in southern Afghanistan. Between December 2001 and January 2002, in accordance with the Geneva Convention, Lindh was visited by the Red Cross, allowed to send his parents a notice about his location, and visit briefly with his father. However, in the motions to suppress his testimony, Lindh's lawyers maintained that he was subject to coercive government conduct, including "incommunicado detention; food, sleep, and sensory deprivation; denial of a timely presentment before a magistrate; denial of clothing and proper medical care; humiliation and failure to inform Mr. Lindh of his rights."[40] In addition, according to his attorneys, Lindh was repeatedly derided and threatened by armed soldiers, including being told he was "going to hang," having "shithead" scrawled across his blindfold, and being told he would be shot on the spot.[41] In one of the worst instances, Lindh maintained he was deprived of food and sleep, stripped naked, hand-cuffed, blindfolded, and wrapped in duct tape on a stretcher for two days, all while being subject to interrogation and suffering extreme pain from a bullet still lodged in his leg.[42]

Ultimately, Lindh's case presents an interesting contradiction in so much as the state maintained outward attention to due process and constitution-ality by formally arresting and charging him, permitting him access to a lawyer, transferring him to custody within the bounds of the United States and holding criminal proceedings on U.S. soil, recognizing his rights to appeal the ultimate sentence imposed, and even permitting Lindh regular access to family members, who in turn relayed information about his status to the media.[43] And yet Lindh's case, and particularly the indications of coer-cive conduct by the government, equally points toward a more frightening truth about the expansion of securitization, the state's hostile engagement with foreign subjects, and the degree to which those hostilities were extend-ed to natural-born citizens with impunity. The performance of constitu-tionality by the executive office, military officials, and other political agents representing the state in this case and the expressions of agency by Lindh were notable for the ways they differed from those in the cases involving Padilla and Hamdi and from treatment afforded to other prisoners of war in Afghanistan, Iraq, and Guantanamo Bay. However, the line of demarca-tion constructed through this performance proves tenuous in the face of allegations of abuse. Ultimately, the performance gives way altogether, as the state extended its authority by constructing racialized threats out of Hamdi and Padilla, justifying detentions and treatment that paralleled the circum-stances of detained immigrants in the United States and foreign prisoners at Abu Ghraib.

Yaser Esam Hamdi

Much like Lindh and Padilla, Hamdi was an American citizen, born in Baton Rouge, Louisiana, on September 26, 1980. However, unlike Lindh and Padilla, Hamdi lived most of his life in Saudi Arabia with his parents, who were also Saudi citizens.[44] Hamdi's interactions with the U.S. military had strong parallels with Lindh's case. In fact, he was apprehended in November 2001 on the same battlefields in Afghanistan as Lindh and by the same Northern Alliances forces (not by U.S. military or civilian authorities) while allegedly fighting for the Taliban.[45] As in Lindh's case, the facts of Hamdi's apprehension and detention are at best unclear. In fact, the chronology of Hamdi's capture, along with the dates and locations of his subsequent detention and other relevant details regarding his initial incarceration, are part of the central debate in the adjudication of habeas corpus petitions filed on his behalf.

From the information made available in briefings, it appears that Hamdi and other prisoners apprehended in Afghanistan were transported to Camp X-Ray in Guantanamo Bay, Cuba, in January 2002, where he was held and interrogated for several months before his identity as an American citizen was verified; at that point, he was transferred to a naval brig in Norfolk, Virginia, in April 2002.[46] What remains unclear is what actions took place in Afghanistan to warrant his initial apprehension and continued detention, what took place in those initial months of detention, and when the Defense Department first confirmed his status as an American citizen.

Hamdi was held without charge, without a trial, and without access to a lawyer until June 2002, shortly after his case entered the public record and proceedings began on his behalf to secure representation. Here, the state's performance of constitutionality, as strained as it was in Lindh's case, quickly gave way in the context of mounting securitization, as the Defense Department challenged virtually any assertion of due process as "antithetical to national security" and unnecessary "for the success of [U.S.] military objectives," instead looking to replace constitutional guarantees with the "laws of war."[47] In Hamdi's case, the state's language took a definitive turn away from asserting due process rights for U.S. citizens to conflating Hamdi with those threatening noncitizens specified in President Bush's Military Order signed in November 2001. In the course of the proceedings, Hamdi was consistently represented by the United States as an affiliate of Al Qaeda, as a threat to national security and to U.S. military objectives, and ultimately as an enemy combatant—language specifically reserved in Bush's November 2001 order exclusively for noncitizens. These proceedings demonstrated a clear slippage from protected citizen, to racialized threatening foreign subject, to noncitizen terrorist, which served as the basis for Hamdi's political erasure and detention without due process and were applied in a similar fashion to Padilla.

During the course of Hamdi's legal proceedings, three different habeas petitions were filed on his behalf: the first on May 10, 2002, by public defender Frank Dunham; the second on May 29, 2002, by non-attorney citizen Christian Peregrim; and the third on June 11, 2002, by Hamdi's father, Esam Hamdi. These petitions formed the basis of Hamdi's legal defense and indirect interaction with the courts and were ultimately consolidated under the Fourth Circuit Court.

In the proceedings surrounding these petitions and the responses from the U.S. attorneys on behalf of the Defense Department (specifically, Secretary Donald Rumsfeld and U.S. Naval Commander W. R. Paulette), the federal government presented several arguments significant to this chapter for their reliance on masculine protectionism and racialized logic. First, the state maintained that petitions for habeas corpus, for representation, or for relief in any capacity for Hamdi represented a direct, unnecessary, and harmful challenge to executive and military authority. Furthermore, the U.S. attorneys maintained that the context of war with a foreign enemy necessitated allowing the executive office and the military to act with unfettered authority. Finally, any challenge to this authority by individuals or other branches of the government was cast as distracting and facilitating further threats to the nation. Thus, in their appeal to the District Court of Virginia, U.S. attorneys argued:

> This case directly involves the President's core functions as Commander in Chief in wartime: the capture, detention, and treatment of the enemy and collection and evaluation of intelligence vital to national security. . . . Courts are normally circumspect when asked to act in disputes that touch upon . . . sensitive matters of foreign policy or national security. . . . And of particular importance here, courts have long handled challenges to the conduct of military operations with special care and . . . have concluded that numerous areas of military affairs are not amenable to judicial review at all.[48]

In this passage, Hamdi's case—and, by extension, Hamdi himself—was constructed as strictly a foreign policy matter, rendering Hamdi a foreign subject without access to the range of due process protections, such as habeas petitions. Moreover, the logic of masculine protectionism was further affirmed here in the suggestion that the aggressive actions taken by the U.S. military were for the larger benefit of the nation and that any challenge or attempt to negotiate those actions by individuals or even other branches of government aided the enemy and weakened national security. This language invoked again the state as a protective father figure whose gendered dependents (those receiving the protection) were reminded to keep quiet about any reservations or risk aiding the enemy. It also reaffirmed that authority was centralized in the hands of the U.S. military and that vestiges of an internal enemy could be found even in other branches of government, necessitating a state of hypervigilance and constant fear.

Variations of this argument appeared throughout Hamdi's proceedings. For example, following a decision by a magistrate judge to permit unmonitored access by Hamdi to a public defender, the United States filed a challenge arguing that the magistrate's order "has raised a significant risk to national security." When the district court responded, "Hamdi must be allowed to meet with this attorney because of fundamental justice provided under the Constitution of the United States. . . . [F]air play and fundamental justice require nothing less,"[49] the United States looked to invalidate any judicial review, suggesting that it amounted to an unwarranted intrusion detracting from U.S. success abroad:

> Because the Executive's determinations regarding the status of enemy forces involves a quintessential political question and one uniquely assigned to the President by the Constitution, they are not subject to second guessing by the courts. . . . It would be difficult to devise a more effective fettering of a field commander than to allow the very enemies he is ordered to reduce to submission to call him to account in his own civil courts and divert his efforts and attention from the military offensive abroad to the legal defensive at home.[50]

In this extension of masculine protectionism, the United States attempted to shield itself from scrutiny while constraining Hamdi by suggesting that an internal enemy lurked in the court itself, one distracting the state from more important matters, such as securing military victory abroad. This defiance of judicial review and the insinuation that only the military could act in the interest of the country were also reflected in the challenge to the habeas petitions consolidated in the Fourth Circuit Court:

> In a time of active conflict, a court considering a properly filed habeas action generally should accept the military's determination that a detainee is an enemy combatant. Going beyond that determination would require the courts to enter an area in which they have no competence, much less institutional expertise, intrude upon the constitutional prerogative of the Commander in Chief (and military authorities acting at his control) and possibly create a "conflict between judicial and military opinion highly comforting to enemies of the United States."[51]

To be clear, while these arguments were articulated most consistently by U.S. attorneys representing the Defense Department and the executive branch, they also resonated in the opinions of the Fourth Circuit Court, particularly in its reversal of the lower district court's order mandating unmonitored access to a public defender for Hamdi:

> The [District Court's] order arises in the context of foreign relations and national security, where a court's deference to the political branches of our national government is considerable. It is the President who wields "delicate, plenary and exclusive power" . . . as the sole organ of the federal government in the field of international relations—a power which does not require a basis for its exercise an act of Congress. . . . There is little indication in the order (or elsewhere in the record for that matter) that the court gave proper weight to national security concerns. . . . The executive is best prepared to exercise the military judgment attending to the capture of alleged combatants . . . and it is the President who has been charged to use force against those "nations, organizations or persons he determines" were responsible for the September 11 terrorist attacks. . . . Accordingly, any judicial inquiry into Hamdi's status as an alleged enemy combatant in Afghanistan must reflect a recognition that government has no more profound responsibility than the protection of Americans, both military and civilian, against additional unprovoked attack.[52]

This deference from the Fourth Circuit Court, genuflecting to the assertions of executive military authority and national security and juxtaposed against the defiance expressed by the lower court, reflects the difference in makeup of the two courts as well as the kind of internal dissension anticipated in the notions of governmentality.

The question of deference and specifically the degree of executive authority permitted by the courts, especially against a natural-born citizen, thus became a central source of contention between the district court and the Fourth Circuit Court of Appeals. While the Fourth Circuit judges issued opinions favorable to the broad expansion of executive authority and national security, the district court repeatedly resisted, as in its order on August 16, 2002:

> While it is clear that the Executive is entitled to deference regarding military designations of individuals, it is equally clear that the judiciary is entitled to a meaningful judicial review of those designations when they substantially infringe on the individual liberties, guaran-

teed by the United States Constitution, of American citizens. . . . The standard of judicial inquiry must also recognize that the "concept of national defense" cannot be deemed an end in itself, justifying any exercise of [Executive] power designed to promote such a goal. Implicit in the term "national defense" is the notion of defending those values and ideals which sets this Nation apart. . . . It would indeed be ironic if, in the name of national defense, we would "sanction the subversion of those liberties." . . . While the Executive may very well be correct that Hamdi is an enemy combatant whose rights have not been violated, the Court is unwilling, on the sparse facts before it, to find so at this time.[53]

This conflict between the courts was replicated in Padilla's case, resulting in two rulings at odds with each other. In the Second Circuit Court, the majority of the court decided that the president lacked both constitutional and statutory authority to detain "citizens on American soil outside a zone of combat";[54] however, the Fourth Circuit Court ruled that the detention of enemy combatants was lawful and that Padilla clearly qualified as one.[55]

More importantly, in both Hamdi's and Padilla's cases, the conflict over deference to an expanded security state was highlighted in the debates about whether these men were actually enemy combatants and, if so, on which basis that designation could be applied. In both cases, the position offered by the U.S. attorneys rested largely on a document referred to as the "Mobbs Declaration," a brief memo (two pages in the Hamdi case, six pages in the Padilla case) by Michael Mobbs, a "Special Advisor" to the undersecretary of Defense for policy. These memos were cryptic and incomplete at best, but their submission by the U.S. attorneys represented a powerful symbol of the degree to which citizenship, especially as manifested in questions of constitutionality and due process, was deeply eroded in the course of these proceedings. I deal more directly with the Mobbs Declarations in my review of Padilla's case.

In a subsequent argument invoking the logic of masculine protectionism in Hamdi's case, the state suggested that the court's willingness to grant Hamdi access to a public defender threatened national security by unwittingly making the attorney a conduit for terrorist activity. Here, the protectionist logic deviated slightly from its previous manifestation to suggest that Hamdi and other enemy combatants *needed* to be held incommunicado (while being interrogated) to protect the country *and* to protect the attorneys in question. Moreover, this argument presented Hamdi as a racialized threat—in the words of the U.S. attorney, an "unconventional and unprincipled *savage* enemy"[56]—whose savagery was demonstrated by his willingness to "pass concealed messages through unwitting intermediaries such as attorneys."[57]

Elaborating on the need to protect the country and the public defender in question from such "savages," the U.S. attorney asserted:

> Although the government does not doubt the integrity or profession-alism of the Public Defender, there remains a substantial danger that even the most honorable of individuals might become the inadvertent, unknowing, and unwitting conduit for the transmission of nefarious messages, even when there is a good faith belief that such communi-cations are being made in pursuit of a client's representation.[58]

This argument appeared initially in the challenge from U.S. authorities to public-defender access for Hamdi, but it was developed in subsequent filings and even extended to suggest that the practice of confinement for Hamdi reflected a "humane" form of detention consistent with the U.S. position as a benevolent worldwide leader. Thus, in testimony from the acting commander of Joint Task 170 serving Guantanamo Bay, Cuba, Donald D. Woolfolk asserted:

> The United States does not employ any corporal means of coer-cion to gain information from persons being interrogated. Rather, the United States has adopted a *humane* approach to interrogation that relies upon creating an atmosphere of dependency and trust between detainees and the intelligence gathering staff assigned to that detainee.... A prime example of the effectiveness of this method of interrogation through dependency and trust can be found in the announcement this week of the U.S. Government's disruption and detention of a U.S. citizen working in coordination with al Qaida to detonate a "dirty bomb" in the United States. Knowledge and disrup-tion of this plot may not have occurred absent effective intelligence gathering through interrogation.
>
> Unlike any previous conflict, we face a foe that knows no borders and perceives all Americans as targets of opportunity. Under such circumstances the need to maintain the tightly controlled environ-ment, which has been established to create dependency and trust by the detainee with his interrogator, is of paramount importance. Disruption of the interrogation environment, such as through access to a detainee by counsel, undermines this interrogation dynamic. Should this occur, a critical resource may be lost, resulting in a *direct threat to national security*. (Emphasis added)[59]

Here, an image of the savage enemy intent on causing harm to Ameri-cans was proffered as a reasonable explanation for interrogating this prisoner.

In addition, mirroring the depiction of military inventions in Afghanistan as "humanitarian gestures," the interrogations of Hamdi were described as humane and ultimately efficient. The success of such techniques was further justified by pointing to Padilla's case, asserting that the tactics in question were delicate and required an intimate form of dependency that could be managed only by the U.S. military. Emphasizing the need for this centralized, unfettered, and unquestioned authority, the state further admonished that any deviation in this plan would ultimately threaten the entire country.[60]

In other words, the United States invoked the logic of masculine protectionism in presumably a magnanimous gesture of devotion to shield the country (and its deserving dependents) and even its own adversary (the public defender) from harm at the hands of a racialized savage, and it did so by stripping this savage of his access to representation. Again, these words mirrored the same benevolence invoked by Bush and the State Department in justifying the bombing of Afghanistan to protect an American "way of life" and even to shield helpless and hapless women from harm at the hands of the savage Taliban government.

Finally, the state's position as a masculine protector whose authority should be accepted uncritically and with deference was demonstrated in the government's reply to accusations of torture, and specifically to violations of the Geneva Convention. In response to a brief filed by Hamdi's attorneys alleging that the United States had defied the convention's requirement that a detainee's status as a prisoner of war be determined by a "competent tribunal," U.S. Attorney Ted Olson maintained that President Bush was the highest "competent authority" on the subject and had "conclusively determined that al Qaeda and Taliban detainees, including Hamdi, do not qualify for POW privileges." Moreover, when pressed on this question in oral arguments for Padilla's case, the U.S. attorney concluded the public needed simply to *trust* the government to do the right thing on their behalf:[61] "You have to recognize that in situations where there is a war—where the government is on a war footing, that you have to trust the executive to make the kind of quintessential military judgments that are involved in things like [constraints on torture]."[62]

In other words, the United States sought to confine and constrain Hamdi through multiple layers of restriction, even going so far as to invalidate the process of judicial review, the foundations of due process, the authority of the judiciary, and the political agency of citizens and asking that such expansions of authority be accepted readily with the argument "trust us."

Hamdi's case ended in September 2004 with a settlement agreement, subsequent to a Supreme Court decision that the Defense Department had to either charge him with a crime or release him. In this case, the Supreme Court reaffirmed the due process of citizens, requiring that even those held as enemy combatants be notified of the charges against them and be given the opportunity to rebut those charges in court, thereby rejecting the assertion of unfettered executive authority.[63] However, under the terms of the settlement reached, Hamdi agreed to forgo his U.S. citizenship and submit to voluntary deportation and confinement to Saudi Arabia for five years. He further agreed never to travel to Afghanistan, Iraq, Israel, Pakistan, Syria, the West Bank, or the Gaza Strip and to not travel to the United States for ten years (and then only with permission from the secretaries of Defense and Homeland Security) and to report to the U.S. embassy any intent to travel outside Saudi Arabia for fifteen years.[64] Thus, Hamdi's case came to a close when he was politically, legally, and geographically de-Americanized—that is, when he no longer possessed the political agency to resist his incarceration and could seek relief only by voluntarily relinquishing his citizenship. At this conclusion, Hamdi's status was not merely commensurate with immigrants; he literally became a noncitizen, and the slippage from natural-born citizen to racialized foreigner became complete.

José Padilla

While Hamdi's case demonstrated a significant escalation in the state's authority after 9/11, in many ways, the case of José Padilla represented the most extreme erosion of constitutional safeguards associated with citizenship in the context of securitization. As noted in the introduction, Padilla was not apprehended on a battlefield or in an instance of war, but on U.S. soil via civilian law enforcement. More importantly, Padilla's citizenship was never in question—that is, Padilla had lived most of his life in the United States and was surveilled even prior to his detention in 2002 despite the knowledge of his status as a natural-born citizen. In addition, his extensive detention and interrogation never yielded an actual finding of affiliation with the Taliban or Al Qaeda, despite unsubstantiated assertions by attorneys representing the Defense Department. Finally, while President Bush strongly denounced him as a "grave danger to national security" in his initial order designating him as an enemy combatant, this assertion proved baseless when in the briefest of memos—three years after Padilla's initial apprehension and without any new evidence—the president unilaterally waived his military detention and ordered him transferred to a civilian correctional facility to face criminal proceedings.

After Padilla's initial detention in Chicago, a limited effort was made to maintain due process. In particular, on May 15, 2002, he was transferred to a civilian correctional facility in New York with the intention of testifying before a grand jury as a material witness. Prior to his grand-jury testimony, Padilla appeared before Judge Michael B. Mukasey of the Second District

Court in southern New York, who assigned him counsel. However, before a case was brought against him, before he could meet with counsel, and even before he could testify before the grand jury, Padilla was declared an "enemy combatant" by order of the president and taken into military custody. From June 9, 2002, until November 2005, Padilla was held incommunicado. Specifically, he was not allowed to meet with or communicate with his lawyers or any family; he was confined to twenty-three-hour lockdown; he could not send or receive mail; and, like Hamdi, he lacked the means to file a petition to the courts on his own behalf.[65] Despite these restrictions, Padilla was subject to continual interrogations and possible abuse if not torture,[66] much of which formed the basis of the U.S. attorney's filings against him in federal court.[67]

Padilla's case followed the language and logic of Hamdi's. In fact, the two cases were tried almost simultaneously, with information and opinions traded between petitioners and respondents. Like Hamdi, Padilla was represented in absentia and presented through briefings submitted by the U.S. attorney as a threat to the country, as an Al Qaeda supporter, as a savage enemy, and ultimately as a potential terrorist. Unlike Lindh, both Hamdi and Padilla became enemy combatants without any due process, while Lindh was granted a trial, at which point he was prosecuted but not politically erased. In addition, as in Hamdi's case, the federal government asked for deference in its unilateral designation of Padilla as an enemy combatant, in his indefinite detention, and in the restrictions it imposed on due process.

However, Padilla's case differed slightly from Hamdi's in that it ultimately entailed multiple habeas petitions filed in different district courts, which reached two different circuit courts and produced two contradictory rulings. Without reviewing the details of the initial district court order, the Second Circuit Court and the Fourth Circuit Court came to opposing conclusions about the permissibility of Padilla's detention and the exercise of executive authority. On December 18, 2003, in a 2–1 decision, the Second Circuit ruled that Padilla's detention was a violation of the federal Non-Detention Act, which prohibited the detention of U.S. citizens by military authority under the designation of enemy combatant. Moreover, the Second Circuit Court rejected the broad reading of the AUMF, arguing that there was "no statutory or constitutional authority for the President to detain a U.S. citizen as an enemy combatant on U.S. soil."[68] Additionally, this court rejected the deference afforded to the executive office and the military in the Hamdi case and in its decision ordered that Padilla's case be remanded to the district court, that it issue a writ of habeas corpus, and that he be released from military control in thirty days.

Subsequent to this order, on July 2, 2004, Padilla filed a new habeas petition in the District Court of South Carolina. Similar to the Second Circuit Court, the district court held that the president lacked the authority to detain Padilla, that his detention was in violation of the U.S. Constitution and laws, and that he had to be criminally charged or released. Specifically, the court asserted that his detention and interrogation violated the U.S. Constitution, including the Fourth, Fifth, Sixth, and Eighth Amendments; the treason clause of Article III; the habeas suspension clause of Article I; and the Non-Detention Act.

However, the decision was overturned on September 9, 2005, by the Fourth Circuit Court of Appeals. In this case, the court affirmed President Bush's authority to detain a U.S. citizen as an "enemy combatant" and permitted Padilla's continual detention in the South Carolina brig without a criminal trial. Maintaining the same deference expressed in the Hamdi case, the Fourth Circuit Court argued that "the President is authorized by the Authorization for Use of Military Force to detain Padilla as a fundamental incident of the conduct of war."[69]

As mentioned earlier, in both Hamdi's and Padilla's cases, the courts battled over the question of deference, and specifically over the proper level of executive authority that could be exercised, particularly in relationship to the rights of U.S. citizens. In both cases, the district courts sided with the detainees and attempted to curtail the power of the military and the executive, and in both cases these efforts were rejected by the Fourth Circuit Court (albeit the dissension within the federal courts was apparent in the Second Circuit Court's concurrence with the lower courts detailed previously as well as the Supreme Court's rebuke of executive expansion). Particularly important in both cases were the repeated efforts of U.S. attorneys representing the executive and the Defense Departments to quash any judicial review of their actions, and specifically any gesture by the courts to intervene on their exercise of power, asserting security and protection concerns. However, when some adjudication of these cases appeared obvious, the state produced only scant and unsubstantiated evidence to support its fundamental argument that the men were enemy combatants—namely, the two declarations by Mobbs.

The paucity of information, let alone evidence, reported in the Mobbs Declarations cannot be underscored. As the attorneys representing Hamdi noted:

> This case raises the issue of whether the Executive branch may indefinitely detain an American citizen in solitary confinement in the United States by labeling that citizen an "enemy combatant," and supporting that allegation with nothing more than a two-page declaration containing hearsay allegations authored by a person who has done nothing more than review documents related to the case, while

at the same time depriving that citizen of all means, opportunity and ability to challenge the label and the allegations.[70]

When pushed for evidence, U.S. attorneys repeatedly asserted that the brief memos submitted by Mobbs were sufficient grounds to justify Hamdi's and Padilla's political erasure. However, both declarations failed to address the nature and authority of Mobbs relative to the executive office, what authority he had regarding classifications of enemy combatants, or even whether he was an officer of the United States, a member of the military, a CIA agent, a civil servant, or a paid government employee.[71] Moreover, in both declarations Mobbs claimed to have arrived at his conclusion about the threats posed by Hamdi and Padilla solely on the basis of his review of "government records and reports" (and no actual interviews), without any clarity as to how this review was conducted, which standards he used to arrive at the designation of enemy combatant, or what authority he had to engage in such a review.

In the end, the submission of these declarations as the central basis for the political erasure of Hamdi and Padilla reflected the pinnacle of the state's position as the ultimate authority capable of constraining judicial review and due process in service to an expansive security regime. While Hamdi's and Padilla's political agency was stripped throughout the course of their detention and they were held incommunicado, the United States depicted both men as dangerous, threatening, and foreign combatants through declarations that amounted to little more than the government's "say-so." In other words, the Mobbs Declarations became the closest thing to actual evidence the government presented to justify Hamdi's and Padilla's detentions. More importantly, in the course of these declarations, both men were reconstituted by the state as political subjects, but only for the purposes of establishing their alleged terrorist plots. Thus, we got a picture of Padilla after his release from prison and during his travels to the Middle East that confirmed previous government allegations of him as being a threat to homeland security:

> During his time in the Middle East and Southeast Asia, Padilla has been closely associated with known members and leaders of the Al Qaeda terrorist network. . . . While in Afghanistan in 2001, Padilla met with senior Usama Bin Laden lieutenant Abu Zubaydah. Padilla and an associate approached Zubaydah with their proposal to conduct terrorist operations within the United States.[72]

Several of the judges not only rejected these assertions made by the executive; they actively resisted these encroachments on citizenship and due process, limiting the restrictions on enemy combatants. In some instances, such as the dissenting opinions of Judges J. Michael Luttig and Diana Gribbon Motz in an appeal in Hamdi's case, the judges openly rejected efforts to unilaterally extend its executive authority and demand judicial deference, stating that courts "have no higher duty than the protection of the individual freedom guaranteed by our Constitution . . . in time of war."[73]

In the end, despite another round of conflicting opinions by a district court in South Carolina and the Fourth Circuit Court regarding the constitutionality of Padilla's capture and detention, the case was ultimately appealed to the Supreme Court. However, before a determination could be made regarding the constitutionality of Padilla's detention, and particularly his designation as an enemy combatant, the president signed a subsequent memorandum releasing Padilla from detention by the Defense Department and allowing his transfer to the DOJ for detention and criminal proceedings in a civilian court in Florida.[74] Five years after his initial apprehension, Padilla was convicted by a federal jury in Florida on conspiracy charges—namely, conspiring to "murder, kidnap and maim people abroad and support terrorists."[75]

Conclusion

Despite the seeming similarities in the cases of John Walker Lindh and Yaser Hamdi, including their American citizenship and the conditions of their apprehension, their treatments at the hands of U.S. officials deviated sharply, as did their constructions as threats to the state in the course of the legal proceedings. This shift from the state's performance of constitutionality that constructed Lindh as a dependent subject worthy of public protection (in the form of due process) to the construction of Hamdi as a foreign and threatening subject was subsequently extended to José Padilla.

In many ways, this abrupt shift is perplexing and leaves us looking for answers. Did something in Hamdi's and Padilla's cases justify their designation as "enemy combatants"—the distinction upon which much of their subsequent treatment was justified? In particular, were Hamdi and Padilla more threatening to the country and thus required the kinds of extrajudicial treatment they received? Unfortunately, the evidence in each of the cases merely confounds such elegant explanations. In particular, of the three cases involving American detainees suspected of terrorist activity, Lindh was the only individual who admitted to working on behalf of the Taliban, who admitted to fighting against the United States, and even admitted to having met with Osama bin Laden. In short, any effort to explain the erosion of citizenship represented in the three cases cannot be supported by claims related to their alleged threats to the country or their alliances and affiliations with terrorist organizations.

Similarly, throughout the legal proceedings, the U.S. attorneys representing the military and executive authorities engaged in sleight of hand by repeatedly justifying the use of the "enemy-combatant" label in the cases of Hamdi and Padilla without explaining how their cases differed from Lindh's, without actually showing any evidence to justify this designation (except the Mobbs Declarations), and without explaining their distinction from every other American citizen detained during wartime.[76]

A better understanding can be reached by looking outside the cases to the way the shifts in language were facilitated by the mounting fear generated through racialization and securitization—a fear accelerated by the federal government, particularly in 2002 and 2003. This manufactured fear, affirmed by the periodic apprehension of "enemy aliens" as some concrete manifestation of this threat, was used to justify a rapid expansion of executive authority and the national security regime from the creation of the first cabinet-level department in more than fifty years through the 2002 Homeland Security Act to the president's signing statements to reconfigure domestic policy. The federal government traded on this fear to extend its military presence abroad, launching military operations in Iraq and extending its presence in Afghanistan. Finally, this manufactured fear was used to justify a reconfiguration of U.S. citizenship, such as the National Security Agency's (NSA's) practice of monitoring everyday communications to revisions of the PATRIOT Act as well as the use of legal standards previously applied to immigrants with regard to American citizens. In short, the rapid and decisive extension of state authority would have been impossible without the compromises to citizenship facilitated through the cases of Hamdi and Padilla, and especially unlikely without their construction as foreign enemies in need of detention and isolation by a benevolent, masculine, and paternal state willing to protect the interests of its dependents.

Moreover, the erosion of citizenship in Hamdi's and Padilla's cases was facilitated by their racialization, which itself borrowed from and mirrored the discourses, technologies, and practices used against immigrants. To be succinct, Lindh's position as a middle-class white male whose childhood experiences closely resembled the ideals of American youth belied an easy erasure or "de-Americanization." To be sure, Lindh was subject to severe constraints on his status as a protected citizen; however, he was allowed rights that prevented his erasure and retained some degree of political agency, including transfer to a civilian prison, visitation with family, visitation from nongovernmental actors, formal criminal charges, the ability to marshal a defense, negotiation of a plea agreement, and permission to speak to the court. In the end, he maintained political agency and a semblance of due process not afforded to Hamdi and Padilla.

Ultimately, this chapter examines the reconfiguration of citizenship as racialized discourse on security and terrorism and the restrictions on due process, representation, and political agency applied to immigrants were transferred to natural-born American citizens. Just as the structure and administration of immigration politics shifted within the war on terror, generating harm to thousands of immigrants far removed from any actual terrorist activity, so too were the boundaries of citizenship fundamentally reconfigured, erasing select citizens and rendering others without rights, protections, and the possibility of redress. The question that loomed by the end of 2008 was whether these foundational shifts in immigration politics and citizenship were permanent features of the "new normal" or whether the coming Obama administration and efforts to rein in the security state would bring forth an end to the terrorization. These questions are taken up in the next chapter.

7

The End of Terror?

*A New Administration and a New Chapter
in Immigration Politics*

> *It is difficult to put into perspective the euphoria that is being
> caused, in the United States and the rest of the world, by the
> inauguration of Barack Obama's presidency. Two things explain
> it: a terrible global economic crisis and the personality of a man,
> very young, that assures us that the future will be better. . . . The
> promise of Barack is almost religious.*
>
> —JORGE RAMOS ÁVALOS, Univision anchorman, on the eve of
> the Obama inauguration[1]

> *We are extremely disappointed with President Obama and
> Congress for their lack of action. The reality is that current
> enforcement-only policies are terrorizing our communities across
> the nation and no one is taking responsibility.*
>
> —FELIPE MATOS, who along with three other students met with
> White House advisors in a push for immigration reform and
> passage of the DREAM Act[2]

From Arizona to Virginia, on November 4, 2008, Latina/o communities across the country pulsated with excitement as they watched Barack Obama win the presidential election and witnessed the end of the George W. Bush administration. Among the electorate, the registration and mobilization of unprecedented numbers of Latina/o voters and political elites were critical to Obama's win. Obama beat John McCain by a margin of two-to-one among Latina/o voters, garnering 67 percent and 31 percent of the vote, respectively. Moreover, Latinas/os constituted a larger percentage of the electorate (9 percent) than in any previous presidential election, with especially large increases in swing states, including Colorado, Florida, New Mexico, and Nevada. Obama not only bested his Republican opponent in these states; he outpaced previous Democratic presidential candidates among Latina/o voters and dramatically increased his own popularity between the primaries and the general election. According to the Pew Hispanic Center,

"No other major demographic voting group in the country swung so heavily to Obama as Latinos did between the primaries and the general election." In the end, while black voters were decisive in Obama's victory, Latinas/os played a critical role, particularly in Colorado, Florida, New Mexico, and Nevada.[3]

Elation over Obama's election was noted in the myriad cultural celebrations leading up to the inauguration, including an expanded list of official and unofficial balls, an impressive array of public musical celebrations in Washington, D.C., and a series of "community balls"—local versions of the official inaugural balls set in neighborhoods across the country and simulcast with the premiere "Unity" ball. The prominent inclusion of Latina/o artists, politicians, cultural performers, and elites in each of these venues, along with the first Latina/o-themed ball organized by the National Council of La Raza, marked the happiness, relief, and hope felt by many.

The opening quotation from Univision anchorman Jorge Ramos Ávalos captures the euphoria and relief that many Latinas/os and non-Latinas/os voiced during the course of the campaign while constructing a familiar narrative of candidate Obama as a "savior." The spiritual themes of deliverance and enlightenment at work in Ávalos's statement suggest that the Obama administration would not just bring "hope" and "change" but an end to the war on terror, and particularly the terrorizing effects exacted against Latinas/os.

Key to the mobilization of Latina/o voters and to the sense of deliverance captured by Ávalos was the widespread fear and frustration over the troubled immigration system. As research in previous chapters demonstrates, for many Latinas/os, the systematic restrictions coupled with the consistent racialization of Latinas/os as threatening foreigners enabled by an expansive national security regime produced an uneven burden and left entire communities, regardless of their actual status, feeling terrorized. The intensive post-9/11 campaign against immigrants resulted in the production of a masculinist security state that traded on racialized fears of nonwhite terrorists to justify increases in raids, detentions, deportations, and compromises to due process, which were felt prominently among Latina/o communities.

The 2008 National Survey of Latinos conducted by the Pew Hispanic Center noted that for the first time in the survey's history, half of the respondents said their situations had worsened in the previous year. Responses were even more dire among Latina/o immigrants, with 63 percent reporting that the situation for Latinas/os had worsened. Concerns over immigration were especially prominent among Latinas/os, with 57 percent expressing fear that they themselves, family members, or close friends may be deported.[4] Spurred in part by these restrictions as well as a coordinated national campaign to encourage citizenship and voting among Latinas/os,[5] the U.S. Citizenship and Immigration Services (CIS) Bureau reported a record number of immigrants applying for citizenship in 2007 and 2008.[6] For many, citizenship was a stepping-stone to voting and reforming the political land-scape, even as the fundamental protections for citizenship were eroding and the possibilities for a meaningful multiethnic and multiracial democracy became more tenuous.

The repeated promises of candidate Obama to introduce comprehensive immigration legislation, especially during his first year in office, and the inclusion of high-profile Latina/o political elites in his campaign, transition team, and staff signaled to many a cause for celebration.[7] However, despite some notable changes in both personnel and policy introduced by the new administration, by the end of Obama's first term, comprehensive immigration reform had been displaced by contentious battles over economic recovery, health care, energy, and a devastating oil spill in the Gulf of Mexico. Meanwhile the numbers of detainees and deportations surged, raids continued to take place, and immigrant backlash resurfaced, particularly in state legislative bodies openly hostile to immigration reform. Midway through Obama's first term, even support for the less contentious DREAM Act had collapsed, as neither congressional leaders nor the executive office could mobilize sufficient votes to pass the act as stand-alone legislation or as an amendment. Immigrant advocates, such as the students who pressed Congress to move on the bill, signaled their disapproval with language that compared the Obama administration with the Bush administration. In other words, the second opening quotation from student Felipe Matos registers their disappointment and denotes a sharp change from the elation described by Ávalos, instead charging the Obama administration with the same terrorizing tendencies that characterized immigration politics during the previous administration.

Not surprisingly, plans for immigration reform were revived in early 2012, and by June 2012, the Obama campaign was once again mobilizing Latina/o support for his reelection. While early tracking and field reports warned of a lackluster response from Latinas/os to the 2012 Obama campaign (as compared with 2008), the enthusiasm gap was eventually overcome, particularly following a string of executive actions aimed at relieving tensions for undocumented immigrants, including a new option for undocumented minors that mirrored the DREAM Act.

In the end, Latina/o electoral support for Obama proved pivotal to his reelection victory in 2012, as he garnered 71 percent of the Latina/o vote (compared with 27 percent for Republican challenger Mitt Romney). In fact, among key demographic groups composing the core of Obama's electoral success—African Americans, Latinas/os, women, younger voters, and independents—Latinas/os were the only group whose level of turnout *and* support for Obama substantially surpassed their levels in the 2008 presidential election. Ultimately, while President Obama's favorability ratings going into the 2012 campaign were affected by a bruising first term, resulting in decreased support among key constituents and whites generally, Latina/o turnout and support for Obama, particularly in Florida, Colorado, New Mexico, and Nevada, helped overcome setbacks elsewhere.[8] Acknowledging the significance of Latina/o voters, Obama issued a renewed call for immigration reform in his election night victory speech:

> You elected us to focus on your jobs, not ours. And in the coming weeks and months, I am looking forward to reaching out and working with leaders of both parties to meet the challenges we can only solve together. Reducing our deficit. Reforming our tax code. Fixing our immigration system. . . . We've got more work to do.[9]

With renewed momentum, Obama repeatedly called upon Congress to pass comprehensive immigration legislation in his second inauguration address in January 2013, and in his 2013 and 2014 State of the Union addresses. President Obama also convened multiple working groups on various aspects of immigration reform in the months after the election and delivered a rousing speech on immigration in late January 2013. By February 2013, the president and a bipartisan group of senators had outlined plans for comprehensive immigration reform legislation that was later passed in the Senate but ultimately failed in the House of Representatives, as Republicans mobilized against the bill. By the end of 2014, following a midterm election in which Republicans captured a number of key Senate and gubernatorial races and ultimately assumed majority control over both houses of Congress, the possibilities for comprehensive immigration reform legislation had once again vanished. In light of these changes, on November 21, 2014, the president signed an executive order authorizing widespread immigration reforms through administrative and policy changes. The changes were met with elation among many Latinas/os, even as Republicans once again promised political payback and the tenuousness of the change coming through executive action loomed large.

Given this context, how do we assess the Obama administration on immigration? Has the racialized terrorization of Latinas/os abated? Was the happiness expressed by so many during the election and inauguration warranted? Which of the opening quotations more closely approximates the character of immigration politics during the Obama administration? If the eight years after 9/11 were defined by masculinist securitization and racialized "terror" and the new administration promised change with respect to U.S. immigration policies, have we reached an end to the terror? And finally, what does the future hold for immigrants generally and for Latina/o immigrants in particular?

In this chapter, I examine the prospects for the future of immigration politics, starting with an analysis of reform within the Obama administration. A central feature of this analysis entails comparing the politics of immigration under the Obama administration against promises he made during the 2008 presidential campaign and against the politics of the previous Bush administration. I examine whether the fundamental shifts in immigration politics and securitization—particularly the construction of Latinas/os as terrorist threats, the proliferation of legislative and policy restrictions, and the escalation of large-scale raids—continued after Obama's inauguration in 2009. In addition, I examine the proliferation of state-level activity and the shifting racialization of Latina/o immigrants, as debates about "anchor babies" and efforts to curtail "birthright citizenship" resurfaced. Finally, I review recent administrative, legal, and political challenges to the nativist resurgence in the states and the prospects for reform in this context. Ultimately, this chapter is intended to examine the changes in immigration politics under the Obama administration and to compare them to the restructuring of immigration politics reviewed throughout the course of this book.

Immigration Reform: Campaign Promises and Governing Reality

On July 12, 2008, in a bid to augment his Latina/o support in the general election against McCain, Obama delivered his most pointed comments of the campaign on immigration to the annual meeting of the National Council of La Raza. In the address, he promised comprehensive immigration reform and signaled solidarity with those who had been subjected to the worst of the immigration-enforcement measures under the Bush administration:

> The system isn't working when twelve million people living in hiding and hundreds of thousands are crossing our border illegally each year. When companies hire undocumented immigrants instead of legal citizens because they want to avoid paying overtime or avoid unionization or are exploiting those workers. When communities are terrorized by ICE immigration raids, when nursing mothers are torn from their babies, when children come home from school to find their parents missing, when people are detained without access to legal counsel—when all that is happening, the system just isn't working, and we need to change it. . . . That's the commitment I'm making to you . . . and I will *make it a top priority in my first year as president of the United States of America.* (Emphasis added)[10]

This speech set the initial tone for Obama's immigration agenda, marked by a critique of terrorizing practices of Immigration and Customs Enforcement (ICE) under the previous administration (including the disruption of families and the challenges to due process)—a critique that resonated strongly with the preponderance of Latina/o voters across the country. In subsequent speeches and policy statements, candidate Obama spelled out the foundations of his immigration agenda, highlighting the apprehension of "criminal aliens" and additional restrictions against employers hiring unauthorized workers. Obama also pledged to increase working visas, remove backlogs, and develop a process to make legal status possible for the eleven to twelve million undocumented immigrants already present in the country.[11] In short, candidate Obama promised to "target enforcement efforts at criminals and bad-actor employees" and move away from large-scale raids apprehending unauthorized immigrants and individual immigrants who posed no threat to the country. Furthermore, candidate Obama emphasized repeatedly that these changes would be a priority his first year in office.[12]

Shortly after his inauguration, President Obama nominated former Democratic Governor of Arizona Janet Napolitano as secretary of the Department of Homeland Security (DHS). On January 30, 2009, soon after her confirmation, Secretary Napolitano ordered a review of all fugitive operation teams and established a new policy requiring ICE investigators to give priority to prosecuting employers. The new policy prevented ICE agents from arresting workers unless officials secured indictments, warrants, or a commitment by prosecutors to target managers first.[13] Napolitano also ordered reviews of the employment raids conducted under her predecessor.[14]

The nomination and confirmation of Eric Holder as the attorney general followed Napolitano's appointment and by June 2009, Attorney General Holder was leading the Department of Justice (DOJ) into investigations of particularly aggressive immigration-enforcement practices carried out by states and localities. For example, the DOJ launched a formal investigation into allegations of discrimination, unconstitutional searches and seizures, and racial profiling of Latina/o immigrants in the Maricopa County Sheriff's Office (MCSO) in Arizona, subsequently suing the MCSO in 2010 and ultimately finding a practice of "unconstitutional policing."[15] The DOJ's investigative work supported efforts by Napolitano at the DHS to curtail the overly aggressive and racialized practices of the MCSO, leading to a termination of the 287(g) agreement with Maricopa County, restrictions on its use of the Secure Communities Program, and a cessation of other agreements allowing deputies to enforce immigration laws.[16] In effect, the placement of Napolitano and Holder in high-profile administrative positions, and the tone they set by launching early investigations into aggressive enforcement measures, suggested that at the outset, the Obama administration was following through on his critiques of the previous administration and addressing some of the terrorizing enforcement practices.[17]

The Obama administration also set out to clear the backlog of applicants for citizenship and residency that had languished for years and led to cases of immigrants who were carefully following the law taking sixteen to eighteen months to complete their applications. Some successes were noted on this front, as CIS processed the backlog of more than a year's worth of identity checks on people seeking to work or live in the United States or become U.S. citizens within the administration's first year in office. In this same period, CIS also established a $1.2 million grant program for community-based organizations in the United States that aid immigrant populations to help further facilitate the application process.[18]

Efforts to uphold due process and to prevent the "disappearing" of immigrants into the vast detention system also met with some success under the Obama administration. For example, ICE launched a public online service in 2010 to track detainees through the penal system and make it easier for relatives and attorneys to find persons being held, particularly those who were transferred between facilities. ICE also announced it would conduct a review of its medical program (particularly the health care provided to detainees) and launch a new intake system aimed at reducing transfers and improving access to counsel.[19]

Noteworthy within the Obama administration were the lengths taken to aggressively pursue "criminal aliens," particularly by expanding the use of three key programs and operations begun under the Bush administration: the Secure Communities Program, designed to check the immigration status of virtually all those detained in local jails; Operation Community Shield, targeting immigrant gang members; and the National Fugitive Operations Program (NFOP), targeting immigrants with outstanding warrants or deportation orders. All of these programs required the cooperation and participation of state, local, and tribal enforcement officers, further entangling local jurisdictions with federal immigration.[20] As a result of these programs, the proportion of immigrants with criminal convictions being held in detention rose precipitously, from 27 percent in 2009 to 55 percent in 2010,[21] and the number of deportees with criminal convictions rose from 33 percent in 2008 to 59 percent in 2013.[22] By 2013, ICE had deported nearly 1.5 million people, including a record-breaking 409,847 in fiscal year 2012.[23] Underscoring the significance of these deportations to Latinas/os, the top-ten countries of removal were all in Latin America. In other words, of the 368,644 removals recorded by ICE in 2013, 97 percent were to Mexico, Central, South America, and the Caribbean.[24]

However, the rising deportation numbers were not exclusive to immigrants with criminal convictions for serious offenses, as most of those apprehended with criminal records were actually noncitizens guilty of minor offenses, such as traffic violations, disorderly conduct, or simply unlawful entry. In fact, the administration's focus on deporting criminals as a benchmark of successful immigration reform belied a more careful targeting of those with serious offenses, continued to construct undocumented immigrants as threatening, and further entangled local law enforcement in immigration enforcement. Thus, while the Obama administration was successful in fulfilling the campaign pledge to target and remove "criminal aliens," the enforcement of this promise, utilizing broad definitions of criminality, unjustly affected Latina/o communities across the country, leaving many with the deep-seated fear and vulnerability they experienced at the hands of the previous administration.

While the Obama administration failed to accurately parcel out actual threats, it also capitulated to the same masculinized discourse of border enforcement invoked during the Bush administration. In particular, Obama's position on immigration has frequently been described as "security first," prioritizing enforcement *before* comprehensive reform. Playing to the discourse of securitization and enhanced border enforcement at a news conference in April 2009, Obama stated, "If the American people don't feel like you can secure the borders, then it's hard to strike a deal that would get people out of the shadows and on a pathway to citizenship who are already here."[25]

In addition to making border enforcement central to its reform position, the White House consistently borrowed from conservative discourse in speeches emphasizing the need for "immigrant responsibility" and "accountability." Thus, in a speech intended to prod Republicans and assuage residents in border states, the president asserted, "Our nation has the right to control its borders and set laws for residency and citizenship. And no matter how decent they are or their reasons for being here, *they broke the laws and should be held accountable.*"[26] Even during the president's announcement of broad administrative reforms in November 2014, the focus was on the need for undocumented immigrants to take "responsibility" and "accountability" for their actions:

Even as we are a nation of immigrants, we're also a nation of laws. *Undocumented workers broke our immigration laws, and I believe that they must be held accountable,* especially those who may be dangerous. . . . What I'm describing is accountability. A commonsense middle-ground approach. If you meet the criteria, you can come out of the shadows and get right with the law. If you're a criminal, you'll be deported. If you plan to enter the U.S. illegally, your chances of getting caught and sent back just went up. (Emphasis added)[27]

Moreover, in a bid to outdo Republican opponents on the question of enforcement, the White House also authorized the deployment of an additional 1,200 Border Patrol agents, submitted a request to Congress for $500 million in supplemental funds for border protection, and continued to enforce the "zero-tolerance" policy, charging and incarcerating any immigrant caught crossing parts of the U.S.-Mexico border outside the official ports of entry and without proper authorization.[28] Finally, in response to Arizona's passage of a stringent anti-immigrant state law in May 2009, Secretary Napolitano announced a new set of measures that reframed the existing work of the administration as centrally focused on border enforcement and channeled actual resources to that end:

> Over the past 18 months, this administration has devoted more resources—including manpower, technology and infrastructure—to the Southwest border than at any point in America's history. We are committed to further bolstering our cooperation with our state, local and tribal law enforcement partners as we continue to implement strong, smart and effective enforcement strategies along our borders and throughout the nation.[29]

These enhancements to the existing security regime dominated the Obama administration's immigration agenda, relegating efforts to create humane reform or to abate the terrorizing practices of enforcement to suggestions at best. By the beginning of his second term, Obama had been far more successful in expanding securitization efforts than in ending the restrictive practices aimed at Latina/o communities, promoting immigration reform, or ameliorating the sense of fear among immigrants. The degree to which expanded enforcement became a cornerstone of Obama's immigration agenda was underscored in his February 2013 address to Congress announcing new parameters for congressional debate on immigration reform:

> The time has come to pass comprehensive immigration reform. *Real reform means strong border security, and we can build on the progress my administration has already made—putting more boots on the southern border than at any time in our history, and reducing illegal crossings to their lowest levels in 40 years.* Real reform means establishing a responsible pathway to earned citizenship—a path that includes passing a background check, paying taxes and a meaningful penalty, learning English, and going to the back of the line behind the folks trying to come here legally. And real reform means fixing the legal immigration system to cut waiting periods, reduce bureaucracy, and attract the highly-skilled entrepreneurs and engineers that will help create jobs and grow our economy. (Emphasis added)[30]

The "enforcement first" approach was reiterated in his immigration speech in January 2013 in Las Vegas, Nevada:

> First, we strengthened security at the borders so that we could final-ly stem the tide of illegal immigrants. We put more boots on the ground on the southern border than at any time in our history. And today, illegal crossings are down nearly 80 percent from their peak in 2000. Second, we focused our enforcement efforts on criminals who are here illegally and who endanger our communities. And today, deportations of criminals are at its highest level ever.[31]

Thus, while President Obama reaffirmed a desire for immigration reform that included amnesty and a path to citizenship for the millions of undocumented immigrants in the country, by the beginning of his second term, his administration was far more successful in expanding the reach of immigration-enforcement agents, increasing the rate of deportations, and enhancing border security with additional technology, personnel, and finan-cial resources.

Comparing Legislative and Policy Changes under the Obama Administration

In the analysis of immigration-related legislation conducted in Chapter 4, five areas of restrictions appeared prominently among the bills passed by Congress after 9/11: increased scrutiny of immigrants (particularly policing of immigrants' work authorizations, more federal agents and teams of offi-cers, higher budgets and more resources); increased possibilities for deten-tions, arrests, and/or deportations (including more arrests for violations that would not have resulted in detentions prior to 9/11); increased militariza-tion of the border; decreased access to publicly funded services (including a denial of state services); and expanded immigration enforcement through empowerment (or extension of capacity) of local- and state-level law enforce-ment to execute greater levels of investigation, review, apprehension, and/or cooperation with federal immigration authorities. Among these restrictions, the expansion of immigration enforcement to include greater involvement of local law enforcement was the most prevalent feature of new immigration legislation.

Despite the calls for a new tone on immigration and promises to reform policies and practices, by 2013, the entanglements not only continued but had been enhanced. In response to Arizona's new anti-immigrant state law in April 2010, Secretary Napolitano announced a new set of measures to enhance border security, including the "creation of new partnerships with state and local law enforcement" and upgraded "information sharing capabilities among all law enforcement partners."[32]

While much has been made of the problems with the 287(g) programs initiated under Bush, the Obama administration not only continued to add cities and states to these agreements but also announced the Southwest Border Law Enforcement Compacts—a new type of partnership to augment law enforcement at the border with local officers. In addition, while inaccuracies and abuses of information were commonly reported with the expansion of the National Crime Information Center (NCIC) database and its use with local law enforcement, the Obama administration created another integrated system designed to "fully link the information systems of all state, local and tribal law enforcement entities operating along the Southwest border" with those of the Departments of Homeland Security and Justice. The DHS expanded its targeting of "criminal aliens" with the use of local law enforcement via the addition of new "Joint Criminal Alien Removal Task Forces" and by "deploying 40 federal officers to state and local jails that are within 100 miles of the Southwest border to ensure the identification of all removable convicted criminal aliens detained in those jails."[33]

Finally Secretary Napolitano announced in 2010 that despite budget cutbacks elsewhere, funds for local law enforcement to develop border security measures had increased. Under the auspice of Operation Stonegarden," the DHS developed a grant program aimed at funding cooperative enforcement work between Border Patrol agents and state, local, and tribal law-enforcement agencies, with most of the funding concentrated on law-enforcement efforts in the Southwest border states.[34]

However, the comparisons with previous administrative initiatives, and specifically the laws and policies enacted as a function of the war on terror, are not limited to the expansion of immigration enforcement to local jurisdictions. Additional commonalities exist, such as increased scrutiny of immigrants (particularly policing of immigrants' work authorizations, more federal agents and teams of officers, and higher budgets) and the militarization of the border.

Under the Obama administration, the web-based work-authorization program "E-Verify" was extended and expanded as all business were encouraged to verify the authorization of all new hires, and (as of September 8, 2009) all federal contractors and subcontractors were required to use the program.[35] In addition, the DHS expanded the use of such administration tools as audits of workplace I-9 forms, leading to the detention, arrest, and deportation of immigrants found with falsified documents.[36] The DHS also swelled the number of Border Patrol agents in excess of twenty thousand;

"doubled the number of personnel assigned to Southwest Border Enforcement Security Task Forces; tripled the number of ICE intelligence analysts working along the U.S.-Mexico border; quadrupled deployments of Border Liaison Officers; and began screening 100 percent of southbound rail shipments."[37] Finally, in the expansion of law-enforcement duties, Secretary Napolitano announced that the DHS would also establish a "suspicious activities reporting program for the Southwest border," extending the prospects for immigrant scrutiny even beyond local law enforcement.[38]

Increasing militarization of the border was also evident in the physical fortification of the area, with new fences, sensors, and air surveillance. Construction of seven hundred miles of additional fencing along the border, authorized and appropriated under Bush, continued unabated under the Obama administration. In addition, the White House and Congress authorized the resumption of an $8 billion virtual fence comprising new technology, particularly an array of sensors and cameras.[39] In June 2010, the DHS announced it would expand the number of "air assets" along the Arizona border and deploy unmanned aircraft system flights along the Texas border and throughout the Gulf Coast region.[40] Finally in 2010, the DHS authorized the increased use of inspection technology to scrutinize passenger vehicles crossing at the border.[41]

From Noisy Raids to "Silent Audits"

Chapter 5 examined the return of large-scale immigrant raids with the rise of homeland-security fears and their particular impacts on Latina/o immigrants. Despite being described in racially neutral language and targeting "terrorist threats" (as opposed to specific ethnic/racial populations), the raids—which were concentrated in federally secured facilities, employment sites, and residential areas—disproportionately affected Latinas/os and spread fear throughout neighborhoods. The election of President Obama and the early changes in the administration (including the appointment of Secretary Napolitano and directives aimed at curtailing previous ICE strategies) suggested that the terrorizing effects of these large-scale roundups had come to an end. However, evidence from ICE as well as independent reporting indicates that the noisy raids of the Bush administration were replaced by "silent audits."[42] That is, under the Obama administration, immigration agents shifted their attention from conducting public raids targeting groups of individual immigrants to reviewing companies' hiring records and conducting audits where they suspected high concentrations of unauthorized laborers. This process enabled federal authorities to review hundreds of companies at a time, and while the burden of compliance shifted to employers, immigrants caught up in the audits still suffered a loss of unemployment, accompanied in some cases by detention and deportation, along with widespread fear of apprehension.[43]

According to the *New York Times*, between 2009 and 2011, ICE agents conducted audits on more than 2,900 companies in 2010 alone and levied $3 million in civil fines. Companies found in violation of immigration laws were forced to fire all suspected unauthorized laborers on their payrolls.[44] Investigations of Chipotle Mexican Grill exemplified this shift, as the company fired hundreds of workers at its restaurants across the country following a federal investigation in 2011.[45] Similarly, following a federal audit in 2009, ABM Industries, Inc., a large office-cleaning contractor, fired 1,200 janitors in Minneapolis, Minnesota.[46]

In contrast, under the Bush administration, raids were carried out as public spectacles, with hundreds of agents descending at once, generating fear and intimidation across entire towns. In some cases, such as the raids executed with local law enforcement in Arizona, deputies detained everyone present within the vicinity of the location being raided, with mass detentions of innocent individuals lasting for extended periods of time.[47] Moreover, hundreds of workers were apprehended in these raids, including citizens lacking proper identification and immigrants legally authorized to work. Raids conducted between 2001 and 2009 typically resulted in laborers without proper documentation facing a combination of incarceration, deportation, and fines, while very few employers faced any civil or criminal charges.[48] In this way, the audits conducted under the Obama administration removed the public spectacle of large-scale raids and roundups and properly held employers accountable; however, the proliferation of these audits meant more employment sites were targeted, resulting in greater scrutiny of these immigrants, more immigrants losing their jobs, and, ultimately, continuing fear of detection and apprehension.

Crafting Immigration Reform through Administrative Action

At the federal level, while legislative momentum for comprehensive immigration gained little traction, the Obama administration shifted energy and efforts to providing relief to immigrants in the form of revised policy guidelines and administrative directives. Specifically, in 2010, CIS debated internal reforms intended to provide "administrative relief options to reduce the threat of removal for certain individuals present in the United States without authorization," while the deportation of unauthorized immigrant students virtually ceased altogether.[49]

In 2011, through a series of memos, ICE Director John Morton clarified the administration's enforcement priorities: "namely the promotion of national security, border security, public safety, and the integrity of the immigration system."[50] More importantly, Morton authorized all field office directors, field agents, and counsel to use "prosecutorial discretion" in the management of immigrant enforcement cases and to focus on individuals who posed a national security risk, serious felons, known gang members, and "individuals with an egregious record of immigration violations." In short, the memo advised agents and officers to show leniency to some individual immigrants who posed no public risk.[51] Responding to mounting deportations and criticisms of the record number of immigrant apprehensions, the Obama administration also issued a memo in November 2011 announcing a review of new immigration cases, a prioritization of cases involving immigrants with dangerous criminal records (as well as egregious immigration law violators), and the closing of "low-priority" cases involving immigrants with no criminal histories. In December 2011, it began applying the same focus to approximately three hundred thousand deportation cases that were pending in federal criminal courts.[52] In May 2012, ICE announced a policy shift on the contentious Secure Communities Program, whereby immigrants arrested for minor traffic violations would not get flagged for deportation until they had been convicted. In its easing of the program, ICE wrote, "ICE agrees that enforcement action based solely on a charge for a minor traffic offense is generally not an efficient use of government resources."[53] Aiming to ease the pressure generated by legislative inaction and to evade a deadlocked debate with Republicans, these policy alternatives mitigated the terrorizing effects and immediate threat of deportation or detention on certain segments of the immigrant community, but they were not long-term solutions.

However, President Obama created more substantial relief for more than six hundred thousand undocumented immigrants with the signing of an executive order in June 2012 creating Deferred Action for Childhood Arrivals (DACA)—a policy cousin to the DREAM Act. The new policy permitted undocumented immigrants ages thirty or younger, with clean criminal records, who had lived in the United States for at least five years and were in school (or were high school graduates or military veterans in good standing) to remain in the United States without fear of deportation. For immigrants who came forward and qualified, the DHS would grant deferred action—preventing their deportation through a two-year reprieve. Moreover, the policy cleared the way for these young immigrants to work legally, specifically permitting them to apply for work permits and possibly obtain other significant documents, such as driver's licenses.[54]

In August 2013, once again acting through ICE, the Obama administration issued a new policy entitled the Parental Interests Directive, urging immigration authorities to consider alternatives to detention for undocumented immigrants when minor children were involved.[55] The new policy called for "making sure that detained parents have as much involvement with their children—and any child welfare requirements and proceed-ings—as possible," especially "keeping detained parents close to where their children live, as opposed to holding them in another state, and bringing back deported parents who are in danger of losing their children so they can participate in hearings and regain custody."[56] The directive came on the heels of research by the Applied Research Center noting that in 2011, roughly 5,100 citizen children of unauthorized immigrants apprehended by ICE were living in foster care and that in some cases, immigrants deported or held for lengthy periods without consultation and communication with child welfare had their parental rights severed and their children placed in adoption proceedings.

The most significant executive action came on November 20, 2014, when the president outlined broad reforms providing relief from deporta-tion for segments of the immigrant population and reiterating the focus on border security and apprehending criminals. Of the many reforms outlined, Deferred Action for Parental Accountability provoked the strongest reaction from opponents while affecting the largest number of immigrants. The pro-vision allowed "parents of U.S. citizens and lawful permanent residents who have been present in the country since January 1, 2010, to request deferred action and employment authorization for three years."[57] The 2014 execu-tive action also extended eligibility and work authorization for DACA, loos-ened eligibility requirements for a waiver program for individuals seeking green cards, and created opportunities for authorized immigrants seeking to change their statuses to "parole-in-place."

While these executive actions were regarded as the Obama administra-tion's boldest reforms, in many ways they were consistent with the immigra-tion agenda at work throughout his term in office. In particular, the action announced on November 20, 2014, also dedicated additional resources for border control and enforcement, prioritized "criminal aliens" for removal, and provided only temporary relief for specified groups of undocumented immigrants, with no prospects for legal status or long-term reform.[58] More-over, the dominant narrative surrounding the order remained focused on the alleged responsibility of undocumented immigrants and the need for greater immigrant "accountability."

What changed with DACA and the 2014 reforms was the clear specifi-cation of relief for particular categories of immigrants. Rather than merely prioritizing the removal of dangerous criminal immigrants, the orders spelled out protections from deportation for certain immigrants—namely, childhood arrivals and parents of lawfully present children. In this way, the executive orders represented the strongest and most wide-reaching measure of reform under the Obama administration. The defense of these popula-tions was a welcome and necessary step in the process of reform, but the fact that the relief arrived so late in the administration's term and neglected more than half of the undocumented immigrant population minimized its impact and did little to change the structure of immigrant politics within the new security regime.

In the end, the reforms had the potential of providing temporary relief for select segments of the immigrant population in relationship to federal enforcement; however, at the time of publication, the orders were halted by an injunction issued in connection with a federal lawsuit led by Republicans looking to block implementation. In addition, the executive actions left untouched renewed immigrant restrictions within individual states, highlighted by the passage of SB 1070 in Arizona.

Arizona and the Resurgence of Nativism among States and Localities

Tensions surrounding immigration restrictions at the state and local levels were reignited in April 2010, when the Arizona state legislature passed a highly restrictive state law and reinserted immigration into the national debate during a critical midterm election.[59] The Support Our Law Enforcement and Safe Neighborhoods Act, commonly referred to as SB 1070, created state penalties related to immigration law enforcement for trespassing, harboring and transporting undocumented immigrants, failing to carry immigrant registration documents, and human smuggling, among several other provisions. The most contentious section of the bill, and the first of its kind among states, created a state trespassing violation for unlawful presence—meaning that an undocumented immigrant could be jailed for a state violation by Arizona law enforcement. In addition, SB 1070, along with subsequent revisions in HB 2162, further emboldened state and local law enforcement to act as immigration agents by permitting them to detain and arrest individuals they encountered (while enforcing any other law or ordinance) whom they "reasonably suspect[ed]" were in the country illegally. Finally, the new laws enabled legal residents to sue state and local entities for failure to comply with the acts and failure to enforce federal immigration law.[60]

The new law quickly reignited tensions surrounding immigration and once again gave license to nativist concerns regarding immigrant invasions. However, unlike the language of previous legislation, such as the USA PATRIOT Act, the Homeland Security Act, or the Enhanced Border Security Act, much of the debate surrounding SB 1070 centered on critiques of the federal government (particularly for its failure to halt the entry of unauthorized immigrants) and the danger of increasingly violent drug cartels. In this context, the security discourse shifted from protecting the homeland and its dependents to safeguarding the needs of individual property owners and the state's desire to withhold public services to protect its budget. These themes were clear in the defense of the bill offered by its principal architect, State Senator Russell Pearce:

> Why did I propose SB 1070? I saw the enormous fiscal and social costs that illegal immigration was imposing on my state. I saw Americans out of work, hospitals and schools overflowing, and budgets strained. Most disturbingly, I saw my fellow citizens victimized by illegal-alien criminals. . . . When do we stand up for Americans and the rule of law?[61]

While the bill's immediate catalyst was the death of local rancher Robert Krentz, as Pearce suggests, the issue was animated by the frustrations over the increased costs to tax payers due to the flow of undocumented immigrants into the state, the weakened economy, and the rise of drug-related violence. Partisan politics also shaped the discourse, with much of the blame centering on the federal government and members of the Obama administration in a year of critical midterm elections and conservative efforts to recapture control of Congress.[62] Thus, in Arizona, Republican state legislators regularly invoked failures of the federal government as the rationale for SB 1070 and presented immigration as the most significant problem facing the state:

> The federal government has dropped the ball on this issue for over 20 years and elected officials of both parties have been pointing their fingers east to Washington, saying, "It's a federal issue." Well, we have an obligation in this state to also do what we can to protect life, liberty, and property in this state, and that's what we're about here today. . . . The illegal alien situation in this state is costing us collectively over $2 billion a year in related costs to education, incarceration, and medication . . . and that is what's causing a lot of the budget problems that we've been wrestling with. . . . *This bill goes a long way to bringing law and order to this state. That's our number one obligation as government. It's not the education, or the health, or other aspects of our daily lives, but it's the protection of life, liberty, and property.* (Emphasis added)[63]

Testimony in the Arizona House and Senate followed a similar pattern, with a call for urgent action to deal with perceived criminal threats to property and persons.[64] In many ways, this shift mirrored more closely the nativism expressed in border-states in the 1990s around the passage of Proposition 187 than the heightened concerns over national security that characterized immigration debates after 9/11.[65] Ironically, despite the common refrain among state legislators that they were "doing the job that the federal government refused to do," in reality the state itself was replicating legally and politically the kind of racialized terrorization of Latina/o immigrants that had taken place at the federal level since 9/11. That is, the effect of the legislative campaign was to intimidate and terrify entire communities in the state (and outside) and enhance the vulnerability of a population already deeply encumbered by restrictions enacted over the previous decade.

Ultimately, the shift in discourse did not remove the racialization of immigrants as terrorist threats; it simply altered the type of threat and the need for their containment and/or removal. As Governor Jan Brewer noted shortly after signing the bill into law:

> Well, we all know that the majority of the people that are coming to Arizona and trespassing are now becoming drug mules. . . . The drug cartels have taken control of the immigration. So they are criminals. They're breaking the law when they are trespassing and they're criminals when they pack the marijuana and the drugs on their backs. . . . [T]he human rights violations that have taken place (by the cartels) victimizing immigrants and their families are abhorrent.[66]

In short, the bill still had the effect of targeting Latina/o immigrants and constructing them as threatening, thereby legitimating their scrutiny, detention, and removal. In addition, the law still produced a terrorizing effect, even without the discourse of securitization and terrorism.[67] In the days leading up to the law's implementation, there were numerous reports of Latina/o immigrants leaving the state, often selling possessions, businesses, and even land quickly to avoid the scrutiny and harassment the law portended.[68]

While the image of Latina/o immigrants as terrorist threats waned, nativists looking to capitalize on racialized and gendered fears of immigrant fertility reintroduced the "anchor baby" as a cause for concern. Focusing on immigrant women, proponents of this discourse maintained that undocumented pregnant women were manipulating their way into the United States for the sole purpose of delivering a U.S.-born citizen who would serve as an "anchor" to support family members via social welfare and state-supported services and ultimately sponsor additional relatives for admission to the United States. While this narrative circulated for decades among anti-immigrant groups,[69] it gained mainstream popularity with the publication of Samuel Huntington's 2004 article "The Hispanic Challenge" (and attendant book), in which Latina/o immigration and fertility are described as "the single most immediate and most serious challenge to America's traditional identity."[70]

By late 2010 and early 2011, fears about hordes of Latinas entering the United States to give birth and manipulate American resources became part of broadcast television and cable news reporting when conservatives in Arizona (buoyed by the political success of SB 1070) announced their plans to introduce a "birthright citizenship" bill to restrict citizenship from children born to undocumented immigrants. The movement quickly gained support among dozens of legislators across the country, including congressional Representative Steve King (R-IA), who formally introduced HR 140, the Birthright Citizenship Act, on January 3, 2013.[71]

In their efforts to galvanize additional support for restrictive measures, such as SB 1070, conservatives relied on a racialized and sexualized construction of Latina immigrants as breeders intent on "having children on U.S. soil for the sheer purpose of gaming the system."[72] Here, Latina immigrants rather than Latino workers were the perceived threat and catalyst for destruction, as their presence promised to overwhelm the country's fragile social-welfare system and presumably gain an unfair advantage for themselves and their children. In this narrative, the protections of citizenship (that have been tethered to whiteness and masculinity since its inception in the United States) were purportedly coming under threat from the hypersexuality of nonwhite and nonnative women. Moreover, the only way to control the threat was to control and regulate the admission of Latina women and to mark their children as permanent foreigners. Thus, pregnant Latinas were racialized and sexualized as imminent threats to the country's financial welfare and to the value of citizenship in much the same way that Latina/o immigrants were depicted as public security threats during the war on terror. However, in this iteration of threat, the actions required to control and regulate entailed the curtailment of citizenship for women and children. By the end of the 113th congressional session, the Birthright Citizenship bill had died in committee, but the codification of the "anchorbaby" discourse into legislation confirmed the strength of this racialized and gendered demonization of Latina/o immigrants, even as discussions of terrorist threats waned.

Court Challenges and Resistance

In December 2011, the Supreme Court announced it would take up the case challenging Arizona's SB 1070, and in June 2012—in a surprise to many— it delivered a split decision striking down three of the four provisions on immigration but upholding the most restrictive component. Specifically, the

Court sustained section 2 (B) of the law, which required state law-enforcement officers conducting a stop, detention, or arrest to verify the person's immigration status if they had reason to suspect the person was in the country illegally. The Court struck down three other measures, including those that created state misdemeanors for unauthorized immigrants who failed to comply with federal immigrant-registration requirements and those who sought or engaged in work.[73]

While the legal challenges to Arizona's laws created a temporary respite from the state's aggressive crackdown on undocumented immigrants,[74] the battle over immigration reform had already expanded to other states seeking to emulate Arizona's restrictive legislation. By July 2010, South Carolina, Pennsylvania, Minnesota, Rhode Island, and Michigan had all introduced legislation mimicking SB 1070. Both Tennessee and Michigan introduced resolutions supporting Arizona's action against immigrants. These actions followed additional efforts from individual states to pass restrictive immigration legislation, including the denial of publicly funded services to immigrants and the empowerment of local law-enforcement agents to act on immigration matters. Despite the fact that immigrants were already barred from voting, many states eager to capitalize on anti-immigrant campaigns strengthened restrictions against immigrants voting and denied financial aid and tuition waivers to undocumented immigrants.

The movement that led to the passage of Arizona's law was linked to a larger national campaign created and supported by conservative anti-immigrant groups, including the Federation for American Immigration Reform (FAIR), the Center for Immigration Studies, the Immigration Reform Law Institute (IRLI), and NumbersUSA. Professional and financial backing from these groups (including working with state legislators to draft legislation, providing financial support to candidates who supported immigration restrictions, and defending such laws in court challenges), coupled with public anxiety and rising nativism directed at Latina/o immigrants, produced hundreds of additional state bills aimed at curtailing immigration and immigrant rights.[75] While thousands of restrictive immigration bills were introduced in state legislatures during the height of the war on terror, Arizona's actions reflected an even more aggressive posture in this long trajectory of state activity.[76]

Following Arizona's lead, Alabama, Georgia, Indiana, South Carolina, and Utah extended the reach of immigration authority by "requiring state and local law enforcement agencies [to] check the immigration status of anyone encountered during a lawful stop or arrest for whom they possess 'reasonable suspicion' of lacking valid immigration status; requiring local law enforcement officials [to] check the immigration status of anyone booked into custody, held in custody, or convicted of a crime; [and] authorizing law enforcement officials to make warrantless arrests for civil immigration violations."[77] Mirroring federal legislation, these state efforts also added new levels of burden and scrutiny to the daily activities and work of immigrants by "making it a state crime to fail to carry immigration registration documents; making it a state crime for unauthorized immigrants to solicit or to perform work; making it a state crime to hire unauthorized day laborers or for day laborers to solicit work in a roadway or get into a vehicle . . . and requiring primary and secondary schools to check the immigration status of all students enrolling in the school, and denying unauthorized students access to postsecondary educational institutions."[78] Finally, the most restrictive state laws added new challenges to potential employers, business partners, and the courts by "making the E-Verify system mandatory for all businesses in the state; making it illegal to enter into business transactions with unauthorized immigrants; and preventing the courts from enforcing any contracts entered into by an unauthorized immigrant."[79]

As was the case with SB 1070, each of these laws was challenged in court, with the most restrictive provisions tied to law enforcement and requirements for identification blocked and eventually either struck down or scrapped by the states themselves. For example, federal courts struck down or severely limited "stop-and-verify" provisions and provisions enabling local law enforcement to arrest without a warrant persons who had removal orders pending. In addition, the courts blocked provisions requiring schools to report the number of unauthorized students and parents in their schools, those making it illegal for unauthorized residents to engage in business transactions and contracts or to look for work, and those barring the use of Matricula Consular identification cards. The courts upheld local law enforcement's ability to review legal status in cases of routine stops where "reasonable suspicion" of a person's legal status existed; however, they also held that detaining individuals solely to verify their immigration status would raise constitutional concerns, particularly without federal discretion and supervision.[80]

Ultimately, the decade of restrictive federal action, the resurgence of state-level nativism, and the particularly aggressive anti-immigrant discourse galvanized activists and advocates at the state level to push for a halt to the most restrictive practices, especially a cessation to the mounting number of deportations. In the face of costly legal challenges, the push to pass blanket enforcement laws, such as SB 1070, lost energy by 2013, with more states adopting a nuanced approach to immigration law and a number of states even expanding rights for immigrants in the wake of more restrictive laws. For instance in December 2013, New Jersey joined Oregon, Colorado, and Minnesota in passing tuition-equity laws allowing undocumented immigrants who fulfilled residency and high school graduation requirements to become eligible for in-state tuition rates. By 2014, fifteen states had enacted such statutes, while university boards in Hawaii, Michigan, and Rhode Island had also granted undocumented students meeting certain eligibility standards access to in-state tuition rates.[81]

In addition, in 2013, Nevada joined Vermont, Maryland, California, and Washington, D.C., in enacting new state legislation enabling undocumented immigrants to receive driver authorization cards. Finally, California joined Connecticut in 2013 in passing legislation lessening the severity of the Secure Communities Program and the level of cooperation with federal enforcement.[82] The California law, also known as the Trust Act, directed local law enforcement to hold immigrants for federal immigration enforcement and possible deportation only in instances where they had committed serious crimes, including offenses involving child abuse, drug trafficking, and gang activity.[83]

Opposition to Arizona's law also galvanized organizations and individuals supporting immigrant rights, a number of professional organizations, and even foreign countries. Thus, the California Senate, the Illinois House, and the New York Senate introduced resolutions opposing the Arizona law.[84] In addition, the Major League Baseball Players Association issued a statement critiquing the law, and individual players openly expressed their opposition, including Rod Barajas (Mets), Albert Pujols (Cardinals), Yorvit Torrealba (Padres), and Jerry Hairston (Padres).[85] Mexico, Uruguay, Panama, Ecuador, Bolivia, Guatemala, Cuba, Turkey, Senegal, Micronesia, and Ghana issued letters condemning the law.[86] Finally, several professional organizations, such as the US Human Rights Network and the American Educational Research Association, refused to hold their conventions in states where the most restrictive legislation was passed, costing those states millions in lost lodging revenue, in-town transportation, retail sales, and food sales.

Thus, while clashes between state legislatures and the federal government were frequent, especially in the Southwest, passage of SB 1070 was significant for a number of reasons. First, at the time of its passage, it was the most restrictive and far-reaching state-level immigration law. Moreover, the passage of SB 1070 emboldened other state legislatures and anti-immigrant groups to go further than they had in the past in restricting immigrants and immigration activity through state law and local enforcement. The movement in Arizona also revived nativist debates about citizenship and belonging for all Latina/o immigrants, leading to the racialized demonization of immigrant women's bodies in the discourse surrounding birthright citizenship and "anchor babies." Finally passage of SB 1070 also galvanized advocates of immigration reform, prompting political and legal challenges at the federal level and organized resistance at the local level.

Conclusion

This book began from an effort to understand the escalation of state authority that I witnessed in my own life in the form of police spying that disrupted my ability to conduct research and produced unwarranted scrutiny. As it turns out, the intensification of spying and scrutinizing to everyday activities was just the tip of the iceberg. More pressing was the emergence of a national security regime that was deeply racialized and consistently constructed immigrants as foreigners and potential terrorist threats. This new security discourse enabled additional restrictions of immigrants as well as the fundamental restructuring of immigration politics and policy that served as a platform to erode the rights and protections of natural-born citizens. This restructuring manifested in multiple forms, from the creation of the Department of Homeland Security and the concentration of virtually all immigration administration within the department to new layers of enforcement that made use of local law-enforcement agents to multiply and extend the reach of immigration authority. Immigration legislation passed since 2001 has also reflected an increasingly restrictive agenda intent on curtailing the resources, rights, and mobility of immigrants, the majority of whom are Latina/o.[87] Moreover, the new legislation coupled with the return of large-scale domestic raids and roundups traded on racialized depictions of Latinas/os as foreign and threatening while simultaneously subjecting the same population to terrifying forms of ethnic intimidation, harassment, abuse, and discrimination.

While the new security regime and the racialization of immigrants as public-security threats gained traction and escalated after 9/11, they were rooted in a history of immigrant racialization manifest throughout twentieth-century immigration politics. In other words, a central feature of the research presented here is its linking of the history of Latina/o immigration racialization, political exclusion, and the escalation of state capacity and authority within immigration policy with the terrorization of immigrants prevalent in the contemporary security regime. Contextualizing the modern security state within this longer trajectory offers a fuller understanding of how immigration restructuring has evolved as well as the challenges and obstacles to creating long-standing reform. The process by which this long-standing trajectory of racialization has intersected with gendered modes of subordination, creating new layers of restriction and rearticulating the meaning of immigrants in the United States, is also a central feature of the analysis.

Examining how race and gender intersect in the war on terror demonstrates the complexity of these topics as sites of analysis especially relevant for studies of immigration politics while reflecting on nuances in the patterns of restriction and the discourses legitimating them in the new security regime.

Overall, the national security regime relied heavily on the production of security discourse founded upon racialized fears and a gendered logic of protection to legitimate aggressive military mobilization abroad and restrictions at home that were aimed at immigrants but had the effect of reconfiguring citizenship. Changes in immigration politics filtered into case law, as the imprint of "enemy combatant" cases involving foreign-born persons extended to cases involving natural-born citizens, transferring the vulnerability of immigrants to particular classes of citizens and undermining traditional guarantees of due process. Altogether, the security regime produced multiple configurations of subordination in which race was salient and central. Documenting these multiple and intersecting forms of subordination required the use of conceptual and heuristic tools that point to a different application of race and provide a fuller accounting of the multiple sources of constraint, manipulation, and subjugation at work in their execution.

What remains to be seen is the degree to which the restructuring of immigration politics that took place during the war on terror can be reversed or reformed in the foreseeable future. Certainly, the redirection of federal institutions, such as the Departments of Homeland Security and Justice, away from large-scale raids aimed at publicly terrorizing entire communities; the legal and political challenges from the Obama administration to particularly aggressive states and actors; and the efforts to find administrative and policy solutions, such as DACA, are changing the terms of the debate. That is, on one level, these changes have deviated from the racialization of immigrants as foreign and threatening and lessened the degree to which immigration law and practices are grounded in the construction of immigrants as potential terrorists. Moreover, the abatement of rhetoric at the federal level capitalizing on fear of foreign and domestic enemies and of disciplinary mechanisms that chastise, encumber, and regularly incarcerate political opponents of the state have lessened the effect of masculine protectionism. However, these changes in the terms of debate have not sufficiently realigned the necessary political institutions and processes, nor have they succeeded in opening up enough political space for comprehensive immigration reform that is not driven by further restrictions on immigrant labor, services, or admissions.

Thus, while many initial Obama supporters, such as the student quoted in the opening of this chapter, have lamented the lack of progress on substantive immigration reform, the review of campaign promises conducted here and the comparison of Obama and Bush on immigration politics suggest that changes have occurred at the federal level. These changes have been concentrated in administrative and policy decisions that facilitate applications, remove backlogs, and delay or deflect scrutiny and possible deporta-tions. They also extend to the review and subsequent abatement of aggressive enforcement strategies employed by specific agencies (including ICE Fugitive Operation Teams), specific states (including the DOJ's investigation of the MCSO and the executive office's suit against the state of Arizona subsequent to its passage of SB 1070), and even specific individuals (including the nonre-newal of a 287(g) agreement with Maricopa County Sheriff Arpaio). Finally, there has been a notable shift away from discourse, legislation, and policies that present immigrants generally, and Latina/o immigrants specifically, as terrorist threats.

However, to the degree that substantive changes have occurred at the federal level, the disproportionate attention to enforcement and restriction and the persistent construction of immigration as a security concern still work to displace other interests from the immigration agenda. Most notably, finding a means for undocumented persons to adjust their statuses (specifi-cally by offering a pathway to citizenship or legal permanent residency) as well as efforts to increase available visas and to achieve a modicum of stabil-ity for Latina/o immigrants have effectively been erased from the national debate. Instead, programs that emerged from the era of terror—including the Secure Borders Initiatives, the Secure Communities Program, and the Fugitive Operations Program gained new life, and record numbers of immi-grants have been deported.[88]

In the end, while President Obama continues to call for "genuine, com-prehensive immigration reform," there is a persistent lack of institutional momentum for such legislative change. Moreover, while language highlight-ing the racialization of immigrants as terrorist threats has abated, an active discourse focused on the criminality of immigrants has resurfaced, coupled with a criminalization of immigrant women's bodies in efforts to further constrict opportunities for citizenship. Trading the racialized language of terrorism for criminality does little to alleviate the continued scrutiny and targeting of immigrants, suggesting that while we have reached an end to the war on terror, the terrorization of Latina/o immigrants persists.

Notes

PREFACE

1. Cherrie Moraga, *Loving in the War Years: Lo Que Nunca Paso por Sus Labios* (Boston: South End Press, 1983).

2. Anna Sampaio, "Transforming Chicana/o and Latina/o Politics: Globalization and the Formation of Transnational Resistance in the U.S. and Chiapas," in *Transnational Latino/a Communities: Politics, Process, and Culture,* ed. Carlos Vélez-Ibáñez and Anna Sampaio (Boulder, CO: Rowman and Littlefield, 2002), 47–71.

3. Anna Sampaio, "Transnational Feminisms in a New Global Matrix: *Hermanas en La Lucha,*" *International Feminist Journal of Politics* 6, no. 2 (2004): 181–206.

CHAPTER 1

1. The defendants were eventually exonerated of the misdemeanor trespassing charges in a jury trial because the defense demonstrated that members of the group could not have been trespassing, as they had been allowed—actually, *invited*—into the luncheon. Ana Davico, "Protesters Disrupt Owens Luncheon[;] Three Supporters of Mexican Civil Rights Placed under Arrest," *Rocky Mountain News,* September 17, 1999.

2. Often the names of people appeared in the files even if they made only quick trips to Denver as part of a lecture series or as invited keynote speakers at a local campus. In several of these cases, their sponsorship by a group targeted by the DPD was enough to land them in the criminal intelligence database.

3. John Ingold, "Webb Orders Spy-File Review[;] Police Misinterpreted Policy, Mayor Says," *Denver Post,* March 14, 2002.

4. John Ingold, "Police Locate More 'Spy Files' in Search Connected with Suit[;] Chief Unhappy They Weren't Found Earlier," *Denver Post,* September 17, 2002.

5. American Friends Service Committee et al. v. City and County of Denver, Civil

Action No. 02-N—0740 (D. Colo.). A copy of the complaint filed by the litigants in the case is available at www.aclu-co.org/news/complaints/complaint_spyfiles.htm.

6. Ibid.

7. Ingold, "Police Locate More 'Spy Files.'"

8. Several of the communities I visited as part of my research in Chiapas were communities in the midst of "low-intensity" warfare with the Mexican state. This relationship was characterized by constant monitoring of the residents of these communities by local immigration and military officials. Particularly menacing were the military camps established in the post-1994 escalations, with visible state and military lookout posts that served as a perpetual reminder of the communities' surveillance. These military camps were responsible for an increase in violence against these "communities in resistance," including gender-based violence from harassment to rape. As such, anyone traveling into and out of these communities would be subject to monitoring, and the presence of suspicious persons often provoked additional scrutiny and harassment. For an understanding of the conflict and the ensuing low-intensity war, see Neil Harvey, *The Chiapas Rebellion: The Struggle for Land and Democracy* (Durham, NC: Duke University Press, 1998); Guillermo Rovira, *Mujeres de Maiz: La Voz de las Indígenas de Chiapas y la Rebelion Zapatista* (Mexico City, Mexico: Virus, 1996); and John Womack Jr., *Rebellion in Chiapas: An Historical Reader* (New York: New Press, 1999). As a consequence, few visitors were able to enter or exit these communities without the Mexican government's knowledge, and the existence of problematic visitors—particularly those who carried the charge of "criminal extremist"—could easily be used as justification for the surveillance or, worse, as an excuse for incursion into these areas.

9. This was not the first instance in which local or federal law enforcement had illegally targeted individuals and organizations working in an international and transnational context in Latin America. According to Nancy Chang, "The FBI's overblown foreign intelligence investigation of a law-abiding domestic organization that opposed United States military aid to El Salvador in the 1980s—the Committee in Solidarity with the People of El Salvador (CISPES)—reveals how insensitive the FBI can be to the exercise of First Amendment rights. During the course of the FBI's surveillance of CISPES, agents 'took thousands of photographs at peaceful demonstrations . . . , surveilled churches and church groups, sent an informant to numerous meetings, rummaged through trash, collected mailing lists, took license plate numbers of vehicles parked outside public meetings, and obtained long distance telephone billing records from telephone companies.' Through the use of informants, the FBI gathered information on the political activities of approximately 2,375 individuals and 1,330 organizations, and initiated 178 related investigations that appear to have been based on political ideology rather than on suspicion of criminal activity. Yet this massive government intrusion into the lives of thousands of lawful political activists failed to yield a single criminal charge, let alone a criminal conviction." Nancy Chang, *Silencing Political Dissent: How Post–September 11 Anti-terrorism Measures Threaten Our Civil Liberties* (Washington, DC: Center for Constitutional Rights, 2002), 36.

10. Jack Cloherty and Jason Ryan, "FBI Spied on PETA, Greenpeace, Anti-war Activists," ABC News, September 20, 2010, available at http://abcnews.go.com/News/Blotter/fbi-spied-peta-greenpeace-anti-war-activists/story?id=11682844.

11. Multiple secretive spying operations were authorized and executed by the federal government. In some cases, these operations targeted U.S. citizens, such as the order granted to the FBI to indiscriminately collect communications "metadata" from millions of Americans' cell phones. Other programs, such as Prism, authorized fed-

eral agents to collect data on foreigners via specific websites, such as Google, Facebook, and Apple. The programs allowed for the e-mails and Internet activities of Americans, regardless of whether they were the surveilled targets, to be captured in the database without an individualized court order when they communicated with people overseas. Glenn Greenwald, "NSA Collecting Phone Records of Millions of Verizon Customers Daily," *The Guardian,* June 5, 2013, available at www.theguardian.com/world/2013/jun/06/nsa-phone-records-verizon-court-order; and Charlie Savage, Edward Wyatt, and Peter Baker, "U.S. Confirms That It Gathers Online Data Overseas," *New York Times,* June 6, 2013, available at http://www.nytimes.com/2013/06/07/us/nsa-verizon-calls.html?emc=eta1.

12. Thomas Peele and Daniel J. Willis, "Surveillance: Civil Rights Groups Seek End to Collection of Government Reports on 'Suspicious Activity' by Americans," SanJose-MercuryNews.com, September 20, 2013.

13. John K. Webb, "Use of the Social Security Fraud Statute in the Battle against Terrorism 42 U.S.C. Sec. 408 (a)(7)(A)(C)," *United States Attorney's Bulletin* 50, no. 3 (2002).

14. Ibid.

15. Kristen Lombardo, "American Nightmare," *Boston Globe,* May 5, 2002; National Hispanic Leadership Agenda ,"How the Latino Community's Agenda on Immigration Enforcement and Reform Has Suffered since 9/11," Washington, DC, June 2004; Amy Smith, "Operation Tarmac: Overkill?" *Austin Chronicle,* March 14, 2003; Matthew Wald, "Officials Arrest 104 Airport Workers in Washington Area," *New York Times,* April 24, 2002; Webb, "Use of the Social Security Fraud Statute."

16. Department of Homeland Security, "Remarks by Secretary of Homeland Security Michael Chertoff, Immigration and Customs Enforcement Assistant Secretary Julie Myers, and Federal Trade Commission Chairman Deborah Platt Majoras at a Press Conference on Operation Wagon Train," December 13, 2006, available at www.dhs.gov/xnews/releases/pr_1166047951514.shtm.

17. Jennifer Talhelm, "Raids in Six States May Be Largest Ever," Associated Press, December 13, 2006.

18. Seth Motel and Eileen Patten, "Statistical Portrait of the Foreign-Born Population in the United States, 2011: Table 5," Pew Research Hispanic Trends Project, January 29, 2013. Available at www.pewhispanic.org/2013/01/29/statistical-portrait-of-the-foreign-born-population-in-the-united-states-2011/.

19. A compelling indicator of this shift in immigration politics and policy and its impact on Latinas/os was evident in a 2007 nationwide survey of Latina/o adults performed by the Pew Hispanic Center. The center found that more than half of Latina/o adults in the United States were worried that they, family members, or close friends could be deported, and the concern was even more widespread among foreign-born Latinas/os, where two-thirds of the population registered fear of deportation. Moreover, approximately half of the Latinas/os surveyed reported that the increased public attention on immigration issues negatively affected them personally in a number of ways, including decreased access to employment and housing, more frequent demands to produce documents to prove their immigrant status, less access to government services, and a diminished capacity to travel abroad. Finally, Pew surveyors found that 41 percent of Latina/o adults reported that they, family members, or close friends had faced discrimination in the previous five years—a 3 percent increase over the number reporting discrimination in 2006 and a 10 percent increase over reports of discrimination since 2002. Pew Hispanic Center, "National Survey of Latinos: As Illegal Immigration Issue Heats Up, Hispanics Feel a Chill," Washington, DC, 2007. Available at www.pew

hispanic.org/2007/12/13/2007-national-survey-of-latinos-as-illegal-immigration-issue-heats-up-hispanics-feel-a-chill/.

20. Raymond Rocco, *Transforming Citizenship: Democracy, Membership, and Belonging in Latino Communities* (East Lansing: Michigan State University Press, 2014), 114–115.

21. Ibid.

22. See Leo Chavez, *The Latino Threat: Constructing Immigrants, Citizens, and the Nation* (Stanford, CA: Stanford University Press, 2008); Alfonso Gonzales, *Reform without Justice: Latino Migrant Politics and the Homeland Security State* (New York: Oxford University Press, 2013); Joseph Nevins, *Operation Gatekeeper and Beyond: The War on "Illegals" and the Remaking of the U.S.-Mexico Boundary,* 2nd ed. (New York: Routledge, 2010); and Rocco, *Transforming Citizenship.*

23. Aarti Kohi, Peter Markowitz, and Lisa Chavez, "Secure Communities by the Numbers: An Analysis of Demographics and Due Process," a report from the Chief Earl Warren Institute on Law and Social Policy, October 2011, available at www.law.berkeley.edu/files/Secure_Communities_by_the_Numbers.pdf.

24. Operation Return to Sender, which began on May 26, 2006, is a nationwide interior enforcement initiative that brings together the National Fugitive Operations Program (NFOP) operating through the Immigration and Customs Enforcement (ICE) bureau with federal, state, and local law-enforcement entities to identify and apprehend immigrants classified as "fugitives." The Secure Communities Program, launched in March 2008, followed the trend of mobilizing local law-enforcement agencies' resources to enforce federal immigration policies by requiring local jurisdictions to share electronic data on immigrants arrested. The program "transformed the landscape of immigration enforcement by allowing ICE to effectively run federal immigration checks on every individual booked into a local county jail, usually while still in pre-trial custody" (ibid., 2). See also Julie Myers, Assistant Secretary, U.S. Department of Homeland Security, Letter to Ms. Christina DeConcini, Director of Policy, National Immigration Forum, July 6, 2007, qtd. in Kohli, Markowitz, and Chavez, "Secure Communities by the Numbers."

In 2014, the Obama administration replaced the Secure Communities Program with a new initiative entitled Priority Enforcement, designed to target for removal immigrants who are convicted of specific serious crimes or who pose a clear threat to national security. The new program also replaces ICE requests for detention issued to local law-enforcement agencies with requests for notification, shifting the responsibility of local agents from prolonged detention of immigrants to notification of pending release.

25. See American Civil Liberties Union, "Documents Obtained by ACLU Show Sexual Abuse of Immigration Detainees Is Widespread National Problem," ACLU.org, October 19, 2011, available at www.aclu.org/immigrants-rights-prisoners-rights-prisoners-rights/documents-obtained-aclu-show-sexual-abuse; and American Civil Liberties Union, "Sexual Abuse in Immigration Detention—Raquel's Story," ACLU.org, October 16, 2011, available at www.aclu.org/immigrants-rights/sexual-abuse-immigration-detention-raquels-story.

CHAPTER 2

1. See Laura Bush, "The Taliban's War against Women," Radio Address to the Nation, Crawford, Texas, November 17, 2001, available at www.state.gov/g/drl/rls/rm/2001/6206.htm.

2. David Cole, *Enemy Aliens: Double Standards and Constitutional Freedoms in the War on Terrorism* (New York: New Press, 2003).

3. Ibid., 49.

4. Margaret Graham Tebo, "The Closing Door: U.S. Policies Leave Immigrants Separate and Unequal," *American Bar Association Journal* 8, no. 9 (2002): 43–47.

5. Jef Huysmans, *The Politics of Insecurity: Fear, Migration, and Asylum in the EU* (London: Routledge, 2006), xi–xii.

6. Ibid., 7.

7. Nira Yuval-Davis, *The Politics of Belonging: Intersectional Contestations* (London: Sage, 2011), 40.

8. See especially Antje Ellermann, *States against Immigrants: Deportation in Germany and the United States* (New York: Cambridge University Press, 2009); Terri E. Givens, Gary P. Freeman, and David L. Leal, ed., *Immigration Policy and Security: U.S., European, and Commonwealth Perspectives* (New York: Routledge, 2009); Jonathan Xavier Inda, *Targeting Immigrants: Government, Technology and Ethics* (Oxford, UK: Blackwell, 2006); David C. Brotherton and Philip Kretsedemas, ed., *Keeping Out the Other: A Critical Introduction to Immigration Enforcement Today* (New York: Columbia University Press, 2008); and Joseph Nevins, *Operation Gatekeeper and Beyond: The War on "Illegals" and the Remaking of the U.S.-Mexico Boundary,* 2nd ed. (New York: Routledge, 2010); and Leo Chavez, *The Latino Threat: Constructing Immigrants, Citizens, and the Nation* (Stanford, CA: Stanford University Press, 2008).

9. Natsu Saito, "Symbolism under Siege: Japanese American Redress and the 'Racing' of Arab Americans as 'Terrorists,'" *Asian Law Journal* 8 (2001): 12.

10. Raymond Rocco, *Transforming Citizenship: Democracy, Membership and Belonging in Latino Communities* (East Lansing: Michigan State University Press, 2014), 114–115.

11. See specifically Sandra Harding, *The Science Question in Feminism* (New York: Cornell University Press, 1986); Sandra Harding, *Whose Science? Whose Knowledge: Thinking from Women's Lives* (New York: Cornell University Press, 1991); Joan Scott, "Gender: A Useful Category for Historical Analysis," *American Historical Review* 91 (1986): 1053–1075; Kimberlé Crenshaw et al., ed., *Critical Race Theory: The Key Writings That Formed the Movement* (New York: New Press, 1995); and Richard Delgado and Jean Stefanic, *Critical Race Theory: An Introduction,* 2nd ed. (New York: New York University Press, 2011).

12. While multiple intellectual trajectories evolved into the current discourse of "intersectionality," when using this term, I am invoking "third-world" feminism, womanism, and variations of *mestizaje,* hybridity, as well as studies of double and triple oppression that emerged from women of color caught between the gendered movements for women's liberation that marginalized concerns of racial and ethnic discrimination and the masculinized agency of the civil rights movements that erased gendered divisions. In short, the first wave of intersectionality points to an alternative form of social and political organization and identity simultaneously attentive to multiple manifestations of race, ethnicity, class, gender, sexual orientation, and difference. See specifically Gloria Anzaldúa, *Borderlands/La Frontera: The New Mestiza* (San Francisco: Spinsters/Aunt Lute Press, 1987); Irene Blea, *La Chicana and the Intersection of Race, Class, and Gender* (New York: Praeger, 1992); Teresa Córdova et al., ed., *Chicana Voices: Intersections of Class, Race, and Gender* (Austin: University of Texas, Austin, Center for Mexican American Studies Publications, 1986); Kimberlé Crenshaw, "Mapping the Margins:

Intersectionality, Identity Politics, and Violence against Women of Color," *Stanford Law Review* 43, no. 6 (1991): 1241–1299; Patricia Hill Collins, *Black Feminist Thought: Knowledge, Empowerment, and Consciousness* (New York: Routledge, 2000); Cherrie Moraga and Gloria Anzaldúa, ed., *This Bridge Called My Back: A Collection of Writings by Radical Women of Color* (Watertown, MA: Persephone Press, 1981); Chela Sandoval, "U.S. Third World Feminism: The Theory and Method of Oppositional Consciousness in the Postmodern World," *Genders* 10 (1991): 1–24; and Alice Walker, *In Search of Our Mothers' Gardens: Womanist Prose* (Orlando, FL: Harcourt Brace Jovanovich, 1983). While these authors all speak to "the multidimensionality of marginalized subjects' lived experiences" (Crenshaw 1991, 8), as cultivated in relationship to dominant sources of power and privilege in the U.S., Floya Anthias and Nira Yuval-Davis remind us of the simultaneous interventions in intersectional analysis among postcolonial critics writing in relationship to Europe. See especially Floya Anthias and Nira Yuval-Davis, "Contextualising Feminism: Gender, Ethnic and Class Divisions," *Feminist Review* 15 (November 1983): 62–75; and Floya Anthias and Nira Yuval-Davis, *Racialized Boundaries: Race, Nation, Gender, Colour and Class and the Anti-racist Struggle* (London: Routledge, 1992).

13. Mary Hawkesworth, "Congressional Enactments of Race-Gender: Toward a Theory of Raced-Gendered Institutions," *American Political Science Review* 97, no. 4 (2003): 529–550; Mary Hawkesworth, *Feminist Inquiry: From Political Conviction to Methodological Innovation* (New Brunswick, NJ: Rutgers University Press, 2006); Scott, "Gender"; and Iris Marion Young, "The Logic of Masculinist Protection: Reflections on the Current Security State," *Signs: Journal of Women in Culture and Society* 29 (2003): 1–25.

14. Rita Dhamoon, *Identity/Difference Politics: How Difference Is Produced, and Why It Matters* (Vancouver, BC: University of British Columbia Press, 2009), 11–12.

15. See specifically Ange-Marie Hancock, "When Multiplication Doesn't Equal Quick Addition: Examining Intersectionality as a Research Paradigm," *Perspectives on Politics* 5, no. 1 (2007): 63–79; Hawkesworth, "Congressional Enactments of Race-Gender"; Hawkesworth, *Feminist Inquiry*; and Anne L. Schneider and Helen M. Ingram, *Policy Design for Democracy* (Lawrence: University Press of Kansas, 1997).

16. Hawkesworth, *Feminist Inquiry*.

17. Anne L. Schneider and Helen M. Ingram, "Social Construction of Target Population: Implications for Politics and Policy," *American Political Science Review* 87, no. 2 (1993): 334–347.

18. Judith Butler, *Gender Trouble: Feminism and the Subversion of Identity* (New York: Routledge, 1990), 1.

19. Hawkesworth, "Congressional Enactments of Race-Gender," 531.

20. Young, "The Logic of Masculinist Protection." Young's work parallels political theory work examining the discourse of war through feminization by V. Spike Peterson, Krista Hunt, and Kim Rygiel. See specifically V. Spike Peterson, "Thinking through Intersectionality and War," *Race, Gender and Class* 14, nos. 3–4 (2007): 10–27; and Krista Hunt and Kim Rygiel, ed., "(En)gendered War Stories and Camouflaged Politics," in *(En)gendering the War on Terror: War Stories and Camouflaged Politics* (Burlington, VT: Ashgate, 2006), 1–24.

21. See Judith Stiehm, "The Protected, the Protector, the Defender," *Women's Studies International Forum* 5, no. 3 (1982): 367–376; and Jean Bethke Elshtain, *Women and War* (Chicago: University of Chicago Press, 1987).

22. Iris Marion Young, "The Logic of Masculinist Protection: Reflections on the Current Security State." *Signs: Journal of Women in Culture and Society* 29 (2003): 4.

23. Young, "The Logic of Masculinist Protection," 5.

24. Susan Rae Peterson, "Coercion and Rape: The State as a Male Protection Racket," in *Feminism and Philosophy,* ed. Mary Vetterling-Braggin, Frederick A. Elliston, and Jane English (Totowa, NJ: Littlefield Adams, 1977), 360–371.

25. To be clear, identifying the current security regime as gendered is not the same as saying it is at the exclusive control of men or that men as a class are somehow deliberately engaging in acts of overtly dominative aggression with the intent of suppressing women for their own privilege or pleasure. As Young notes, this framing speaks to more traditional and yet less conceptually nuanced understandings of gender and sexism as a political force. By distinction, the gendering happening in the context of the current security regime is far more subtle, enticing even—operating within the confines of logic emanating from patterns of paternal hierarchy. This kind of gendering lacks the typical cues of blatant aggression or hypersexualization and instead enables paternal domination through seemingly benevolent claims to protection and assurance for "our way of life." In short, this is a question about framing, logic, and the conceptual tools used by the state to justify the security regime and the subtle, coded, and yet insidious ways they play on pervasive ideas about gender and race. As such, this framing of gender is irrespective of the individual actors or their intentions. I deal with additional manifestations and intersections of gender in the form of specific subjects and identities in other areas of the book (particularly in the discussion of raids), as it is an important take on the problematic effects of shifts in immigration politics in the context of the war on terror, but this is not the guiding focus of this chapter or book.

26. Richard Cheney, "Interview of the Vice President by CBS's *60 Minutes II*," White House, November 14, 2001, available at www.whitehouse.gov/vicepresident/news-speeches/speeches/vp20011114.html.

27. U.S. Department of State, "Report on the Taliban's War against Women: Executive Summary," Washington, DC, November 17, 2001, available at www.state.gov/g/drl/rls/6183.htm.

28. Ibid.

29. Laura Flanders, "Beyond the Burqa: The Rights Women Need in Afghanistan are Basic Human Rights," Common Dreams, December 13, 2001, available at www.commondreams.org/cgi-bin/print.cgi?file=/views01/1214-03.htm.

30. George W. Bush, "President Delivers State of the Union Address," January 29, 2002, available at http://georgewbush-whitehouse.archives.gov/news/releases/2002/01/20020129-11.html.

31. Nancy Chang, *Silencing Political Dissent: How Post–September 11 Anti-terrorism Measures Threaten Our Civil Liberties* (Washington, DC: Center for Constitutional Rights, 2002).

32. Peterson, "Coercion and Rape."

33. U.S. General Accounting Office, "Report to Congressional Committees-Aviation Security: Computer-Assisted Passenger Prescreening System Faces Significant Implementation Challenges," GAO-04-385, February 2004.

34. Nancy Cordes, "New Airport Screening Bares All," *CBS Evening News,* May 23, 2009, available at www.cbsnews.com/stories/2009/05/23/eveningnews/main5036146.shtml.

35. Saito, "Symbolism under Siege."

36. Bill Ong Hing, *Defining America through Immigration Policy* (Philadelphia: Temple University Press, 2004); and Kevin Johnson, *The "Huddled Masses" Myth: Immigration and Civil Rights* (Philadelphia: Temple University Press, 2003).

37. Ian Haney Lopez, *White by Law: The Legal Construction of Race in America* (New York: New York University Press, 2006).

38. Mae M. Ngai, *Impossible Subjects: Illegal Aliens and the Making of Modern America* (Princeton, NJ: Princeton University Press, 2004).

39. Lina Newton, "'It is Not a Question of Being Anti-immigration': Categories of Deservedness in Immigration Policymaking," in *Deserving and Entitled: Social Constructions and Public Policy,* edited by Anne Schneider and Helen Ingram (New York: State University of New York Press, 2005), 139–171.

40. Hing, *Defining America through Immigration Policy,* 260.

41. Roger Daniels, *Prisoners without Trial: Japanese Americans in World War II* (New York: Hill and Wang, 1993); and Ronald Takaki, *Strangers from a Different Shore: A History of Asian Americans* (New York: Little, Brown, 1989).

42. Rodolfo Acuña, *Occupied America: A History of Chicanos,* 3rd ed. (New York: HarperCollins, 1987).

43. Cole, *Enemy Aliens.*

44. Jonathan Peterson, "Response to Terror: INS Fugitives to Be Listed on FBI Database," *Los Angeles Times,* December 6, 2001.

45. Ted Bridis, "US Lifts FBI Criminal Database Checks," Associated Press, March 25, 2002.

46. Arnoldo Garcia, *When Collaboration Is a Dirty Word* (Oakland, CA: National Network for Immigrant and Refugee Rights, 2003); and National Hispanic Leadership Agenda, *How the Latino Community's Agenda on Immigration Enforcement and Reform Has Suffered Since 9/11,* Washington, DC, 2004.

47. Chris Adams, "INS to Put in Federal Criminal Databases the Names of People Ordered Deported," *Wall Street Journal,* December 6, 2001; Peterson, "Response to Terror"; and Mary Beth Sheridan, "INS Seeks Law Enforcement Aid in Crackdown Move: Targets 300,000 Foreign Nationals in U.S. Despite Deportation Orders," *Washington Post,* December 6, 2001.

48. U.S. Department of Justice, Office of the Inspector General, "The September 11 Detainees: A Review of the Treatment of Aliens Held on Immigration Charges in Connection with the Investigation of the September 11 Attacks," Washington, DC, April 2003.

49. Chang, *Silencing Political Dissent.*

50. Bonnie Honig, *Democracy and the Foreigner* (Princeton, NJ: Princeton University Press, 2003).

51. Ibid., 11.

CHAPTER 3

1. The constitution of the Republic of Texas was developed in 1836 when Texas gained its independence from Mexico and prior to its annexation by the United States. Its constitution granted citizenship to the Republic to Mexicans living in Texas on independence day, an action extended via congressional resolution in 1845 after Texas was annexed. Similarly, Articles VIII and IX of the Treaty of Guadalupe Hidalgo conferred U.S. citizenship and protections for property upon Mexicans living in the territory of the Southwest ceded to the United States at the end of the Mexican-American War.

2. Arnoldo De León, *In Re Ricardo Rodríguez: An Attempt at Chicano Disenfranchisement in San Antonio, 1896–1897* (San Antonio, TX: Caravel Press, 1979).

3. Ian Haney Lopez, *White by Law: The Legal Construction of Race in America* (New York: New York University Press, 2006).

4. Ibid.

5. See *The Handbook of Texas Online*, available at www.tsha.utexas.edu/handbook/online/articles/II/pqitw_print.html.

6. Ibid.

7. As noted, the history of immigration politics in the United States is rife with contradictions and complications, leading to wide disparities in opportunities and obstacles among various classes of Latinas/os. Recognizing that a full accounting of this complicated history is beyond the scope of both this chapter and this book, the examination here focuses on Mexican immigrants, because they are the largest population of immigrants and because their experiences often serve as the imprimatur for other Latina/o ethnic groups. At key junctures, I consider important distinctions as they relate to Puerto Ricans, Cubans, and Central Americans, but I do not intend to fully account for the differences within each of these populations. Although the focus is on the relationship between Mexican immigrants and immigration politics, this relationship is contextualized within a larger process of racialization that draws upon and affects European, Asian, and other immigrants within each period.

8. See specifically George Borjas, ed., *Mexican Immigration to the U.S.* (Chicago: University of Chicago Press, 2007); George Borjas, *Heaven's Door: Immigration Policy and the American Economy* (Princeton, NJ: Princeton University Press, 2001); Alma Garcia, *The Mexican Americans* (Westport, CT: Greenwood Press, 2002); Camile Guerin-Gonzales, *Mexican Workers and American Dreams: Immigration, Repatriation, and California Farm Labor, 1900–1939* (New Brunswick, NJ: Rutgers University Press, 1994); David Gregory Gutiérrez, ed., *Between Two Worlds: Mexican Immigrants in the United States* (Wilmington, DE: Scholarly Resources, 1996); David Gregory Gutiérrez, *Walls and Mirrors: Mexican Americans, Mexican Immigrants, and the Politics of Ethnicity* (Berkeley: University of California Press, 1995); Douglas S. Massey, Jorge Durand, and Nolan J. Malone, *Beyond Smoke and Mirrors: Mexican Immigration in an Era of Economic Integration* (New York: Russell Sage Foundation, 2003); Marcelo Suárez-Orozco, "Latin American Immigration to the United States," in *The United States and Latin America: The New Agenda*, ed. V. Bulmer-Thomas and J. Dunkerly (Cambridge, MA: Harvard University Press, 1999), 227–244; Alejandro Portes and Robert L. Bach, *Latin Journey: Cuban and Mexican Immigrants in the United States* (Berkeley: University of California Press, 1985); and Alejandro Portes and Ruben Rumbaut, *Immigrant America* (Berkeley: University of California Press, 1990).

9. See specifically John Bodnar, *The Transplanted: A History of Immigrants in Urban America* (Bloomington: Indiana University Press, 1985); Roger Daniels, *Guarding the Golden Door: American Immigration Policy and Immigrants since 1882* (New York: Hill and Wang, 2004); Roger Daniels, *Coming to America: A History of Immigration and Ethnicity in American Life,* 2nd ed. (New York: Harper Perennial, 2002); Oscar Handlin, *The Uprooted: The Epic Story of the Great Migrations That Made the American People,* 2nd ed. (Boston: Little, Brown, 1973); and John Higham, *Strangers in the Land, Patterns of American Nativism (1860–1925)* (New Brunswick, NJ: Rutgers University Press, 1963).

10. Specifically, the treaty stipulated:

Article VIII—Mexicans now established in territories previously belonging to Mexico, and which remain for the future within the limits of the United States, as defined by the present treaty, shall be free to continue where they now reside, or to remove at any time to the Mexican Republic, retaining the property which they possess in the said territories, or disposing thereof, and removing the proceeds wherever they please, without their being subjected, on this account, to any contribution, tax, or charge whatsoever.

Those who shall prefer to remain in the said territories may either retain the title and rights of Mexican citizens, or acquire those of citizens of the United States. But they shall be under the obligation to make their election within one year from the date of the exchange of ratification of this treaty; and those who shall remain in the said territories after the expiration of that year, without having declared their intention to retain the character of Mexicans, shall be considered to have elected to become citizens of the United States.

Article IX—The Mexicans who, in the territories aforesaid, shall not preserve the character of citizens of the Mexican Republic, conformably with what is stipulated in the preceding Article, shall be incorporated into the Union of the United States, and admitted as soon as possible, according to the principles of the Federal Constitution, to the enjoyment of all the rights of citizens of the United States. In the meantime, they shall be maintained and protected in the enjoyment of their liberty, their property, and the civil rights now vested in them according to the Mexican laws. With respect to political rights, their condition shall be on an equality with that of the inhabitants of the other territories of the United States.

11. Raymond Rocco, *Transforming Citizenship: Democracy, Membership and Belonging in Latino Communities* (East Lansing: Michigan State University Press, 2014).

12. Sister Mary Collete Standart, "The Sonoran Migration to California, 1848–1856: A Study in Prejudice," *Southern California Quarterly* 57 (Fall 1976): 333–357.

13. According to State Department records, between 1869 and 1879 the Chinese population virtually doubled, increasing from 63,000 Chinese immigrants to the United States to 120,000, and by 1882 approximately 300,000 Chinese had entered the country. Bill Ong Hing, *Defining America through Immigration Policy* (Philadelphia: Temple University Press, 2004), 29.

14. This included the 1850 Foreign Miner's License Tax in California, requiring all foreign-born persons who had not become citizens under the 1848 Treaty of Guadalupe Hidalgo to acquire a license to mine at the cost of $20 a month, as well as the adoption of anti-Chinese provisions in the California state constitution of 1877. Similarly, in 1880 the San Francisco Board of Supervisors passed an ordinance prohibiting laundry facilities from operating in buildings made of wood without the consent of the board. The ordinance was clearly directed at the population of Chinese immigrants, who owned 75 percent of the laundry facilities in San Francisco, virtually all of which were housed in wooden buildings. The challenge to the San Francisco ordinance on laundry facilities, which ultimately reached the Supreme Court in the case of *Yick Wo v. Hopkins (1886)*, marked a unique departure from the federal government's position relative to Chinese immigrants in this period. In its decision, the Supreme Court affirmed the right of Chinese immigrant Yick Wo to be free from discrimination resulting from the San Francisco ordinance and affirmed the extension of those same protections to other immigrants, regardless of status.

15. An important gendered exception to this exclusion existed. As a condition of the agreements, those laborers already in the United States could leave and return with

"close family members," spawning an industry of "picture brides"—Japanese women who entered into arranged marriages with Japanese laborers in Hawaii and the mainland to gain entrance into the United States. Sucheng Chan, *Asian Americans: An Interpretive History* (Boston: Twayne, 1991).

16. Clara Rodriguez, "A Summary of Puerto Rican Migration to the United States," in *Challenging Fronteras: Structuring Latina and Latino Lives in the U.S.*, ed. Mary Romero, Pierrette Hondagneu-Sotelo, and Vilma Ortiz (New York: Routledge, 1997), 101–113; Pedro A. Caban, *Constructing a Colonial People: Puerto Rico and the United States: 1898–1932* (Boulder, CO: Westview Press, 2009); and Mario Murillo, *Islands of Resistance: Puerto Rico, Vieques, and U.S. Policy* (New York: Seven Stories Press, 2011).

17. Higham, *Strangers in the Land*, 202.

18. In particular, the law excluded from admission any immigrant from a newly constructed "Asiatic Barred Zone," a region that included Afghanistan, Arabia, Asiatic Russia, Burma, the East Indies, India, Indochina, the Malay States, the Polynesian Islands, and Thailand. Hing, *Defining America through Immigration Policy*, 60.

19. Lisa Garcia Bedolla, *Latino Politics* (Cambridge, UK: Polity Press, 2009); and Jose Cabranes, *Citizenship and the American Empire* (New Haven, CT: Yale University Press, 1979), 14–17. To this day, Puerto Rican island residents may participate in presidential primaries but may not vote in the general election.

20. As Fred H. Bixby of the American Cattle Raiser's Association observed, "We have no Chinamen; we have not the Japs. The Hindu is worthless; the Filipino is nothing, and the white man will not do the work." As quoted in Mark Reisler, "Always the Laborer, Never the Citizen: Anglo Perceptions of the Mexican Immigrant during the 1920s," *Pacific Historical Review* 45, no. 2 (1976): 231–254.

21. Ibid., 236.

22. Francisco Balderrama and Raymond Rodriguez, *Decade of Betrayal: Mexican Repatriation in the 1930s* (Albuquerque: University of New Mexico Press, 1995).

23. The 1921 Quota Law also extended the practice of distinguishing between admissible and inadmissible immigrants based on class and wealth. As such, the law introduced a new class of "nonquota immigrants"—those whose entrance would not count against the total quota allocated by Congress—that included immigrants returning from visits abroad, professional actors, artists, lecturers, singers, nurses, ministers, and professors. In addition, after 1924, all wives and dependent children of U.S. citizens were allowed to enter as nonquota immigrants, as were immigrants belonging to any recognized learned profession.

24. As a condition of the act, a minimum number of one hundred visas were allotted to each eligible nation, but immigrants ineligible for citizenship were barred from access to these visas altogether. Hing, *Defining America through Immigration Policy*.

25. U.S. Department of Labor, Annual Report of the Commissioner-General of Immigration, Washington, DC, 1924, 9; and Roger Daniels and Otis L. Graham, *Debating American Immigration, 1882–Present* (Lanham, MD: Rowman and Littlefield, 2001), 24.

26. Daniels and Graham, *Debating American Immigration*, 22.

27. U.S. Department of Labor, Annual Report of the Commissioner-General of Immigration, 9.

28. Manuel Garcia y Griego, "The Importation of Mexican Contract Laborers to the United States, 1942–1964," in *The Border That Joins: Mexican Migrants and U.S. Responsibility*, ed. Peter G. Brown and Henry Shue (Totowa, NJ: Rowman and Littlefield, 1983), 49–98.

29. Rodolfo Acuña, *Occupied America: A History of Chicanos,* 3rd ed. (New York: HarperCollins, 1987).

30. During the first phase of the program, outlined under the 1942 bilateral agreement, Mexico had a distinct advantage in negotiating the terms of the agreement, a factor it used to stipulate a series of conditions for Mexican workers that would be largely erased or ignored in subsequent legislation governing the program. For example, as a condition of agreeing to send Mexican laborers to the United States, the United States had to demonstrate that recruitment would be based on a written labor contract, that recruitment would be based on need (so that Mexican laborers would not displace domestic labor or lower its wage), that employers or the U.S. government would pay transportation and subsistence costs between the recruitment center in Mexico and the worksite, that contract workers would be permitted to remain permanently in the United States, and that racial discrimination would be unacceptable. Garcia y Griego, "The Importation of Mexican Contract Laborers to the United States."

31. Ernesto Galarza, *Strangers in Our Fields* (Washington, DC: Report of the Fund for the Republic, 1956), 13. In addition to the international executive agreements, workers were protected by standard work contracts signed prior to migrating to the United States, by specific state laws, by occupational risk insurance required of bracero employers, by nonoccupational insurance paid for by each bracero worker, and by the basic civil rights accorded to all U.S. residents. Collectively, these protections further promised braceros "hygienic lodgings adequate to the climatic conditions of the area . . . free of charge, including blankets, cots and mattresses"; work compensation in the case of injury; proper tools, supplies, and equipment free of charge; adequate transportation to work; and the option of purchasing regular meals that would not exceed more than $1.75 a day. Ibid., 15–17.

32. Ibid.

33. Julian Samora, *Los Mojados: The Wetback Story* (Notre Dame, IN: University of Notre Dame Press, 1971).

34. Garcia y Griego, "The Importation of Mexican Contract Laborers to the United States."

35. Ibid., 49–98; Reisler, "Always the Laborer, Never the Citizen," 231–254; and Samora, *Los Mojados.*

36. Garcia y Griego, "The Importation of Mexican Contract Laborers to the United States," 49–98; and Samora, *Los Mojados.*

37. Daniels and Graham, *Debating American Immigration, 1882–Present,* 22.

38. The Alien Registration Act was further bolstered in 1950 by passage of the Internal Security Act, which required the exclusion or deportation of all immigrants who had been communist party members or had belonged to "front" organizations. In short, while the Alien Registration Act criminalized association with radical organizations, the Internal Security Act went a step further and facilitated the deportation of immigrants engaged in such associations.

39. Natsu Saito, "Symbolism under Siege: Japanese American Redress and the 'Racing' of Arab Americans as 'Terrorists,'" *Asian Law Journal* 8 (2001): 11–26.

40. Ironically, this shift in racial formations was arguably most notable in the congressional repeal of the Chinese Exclusion Act, while persons of Japanese descent were detained and incarcerated. Specifically, beginning in December 1943, Congress repealed fifteen separate statutes affecting Chinese exclusion and made foreign-born Chinese eligible for naturalization. Symbolically, this shift reflected changes in the global political

climate, whereby China had become a U.S. ally; however, politically, the repeal was insignificant, since China continued to receive only a token quota of 105 visas for immigrants seeking admission to the United States and remained the one exception to an immigration policy that continued to exclude all other Asians until 1952. For a fuller account of this history, see Chan, *Asian Americans*; Peter Irons, *Justice at War: The Story of the Japanese-American Internment Cases* (Berkeley: University of California Press, 1993); Ronald Takaki, *Strangers from a Different Shore: A History of Asian Americans* (New York: Little, Brown, 1989); and Gary Okihiro, *Whispered Silences: Japanese Americans and World War II* (Seattle: University of Washington Press, 1996).

41. Daniels and Graham, *Debating American Immigration, 1882–Present.*

42. Hing, *Defining America through Immigration Policy*, 76.

43. Building on reforms in the 1952 immigration legislation, the Hart-Cellar Act also abandoned the "Asian-Pacific Triangle," resulting in the restoration of normalized quotas for Asian countries and a substantial increase in the population of Asian immigrants post-1965. Ibid.

44. Ibid.

45. Daniels, *Coming to America.*

46. Susan Tiano, *Patriarchy on the Line: Labor, Gender, and Ideology in the Mexican* Maquila *Industry* (Philadelphia: Temple University Press, 1994); see also Leslie Sklair, *Assembling for Development: The* Maquila *Industry in Mexico and the United States* (San Diego: Center for U.S.-Mexican Studies, 1993).

47. Anna Sampaio, "Transforming Chicana/o and Latina/o Politics: Globalization, and the Formation of Transnational Resistance in the U.S. and Chiapas," in *Transnational Latino/a Communities: Politics, Process, and Cultures,* edited by Carlos Vélez-Ibáñez and Anna Sampaio (Boulder, CO: Rowman and Littlefield, 2002), 47–71.

48. Immigration Reform and Control Act of 1986, 8 USC 1101 note, Sec. 314. A less controversial diversity program added to the law made visas available to "non-preference immigrants," resulting in the allocation of five thousand visas between 1987 and 1998 to qualified immigrants who were natives of foreign states adversely affected by the Immigration Act of 1965.

49. Ibid., Sec. 274A.

50. Ibid., Sec. 111.

51. Hing, *Defining America through Immigration Policy.*

52. Congress supported this concentrated enforcement strategy by doubling the INS budget for enforcement between 1993 and 1997, from $400 million to $800 million. See Joseph Nevins, *Operation Gatekeeper and Beyond: The War on "Illegals" and the Remaking of the U.S.-Mexico Boundary* (New York: Routledge, 2010).

53. Ibid.

54. Ibid.

55. Ibid., 191. In response to the rising death toll, the INS initiated a new public awareness program in 1997 entitled "Stay Out, Stay Alive," and a Border Safety Initiative in 1998. Collectively, these efforts were designed to warn potential crossers of the increased risks, increase search and rescue in particularly dangerous routes, and identify bodies. Despite these efforts, migrant deaths along the border continue, and efforts to abate these cruelties have consistently met with resistance.

56. Hing, *Defining America through Immigration Policy.*

57. Personal Responsibility and Work Opportunity Reconciliation Act of 1996. H.R. 3734. ENR, Title IV, Sec. 400.

58. Ibid., Sec. 401(C)(A)(B).

59. As Ange-Marie Hancock notes, the debates surrounding welfare reform and the masculinized rhetoric of shaping up economic dependents to promote self-sufficiency was largely aimed at African American women. However, the specific language on eligibility with regard to noncitizens served to reignite the image of Latinas/os as economic threats. This renewed debate opened the door for a wave of anti-immigrant legislation at the state level intended to deny state services to immigrants. Despite the fact that long-standing requirements already existed for government aid to immigrants (regardless of their status) in emergency medical situations, for disaster relief, for public health programs (such as the treatment of communicable diseases), in public housing, and generally for the protection of life and safety, the new legislation assumed an aggressive posture cloaked in the language of self-sufficiency to deny benefits to immigrants. Ange-Marie Hancock, *The Politics of Disgust: The Public Identity of the Welfare Queen* (New York: New York University Press, 2004).

60. Illegal Immigration Reform and Immigrant Responsibility Act of 1996, Pub.L. 104-208, Div. C, 110 Stat. 3009-546, Title I.

61. Ibid., Title II.

62. In 2001, the Supreme Court limited the scope of the law's retroactive application by preventing an immigrant who had pleaded guilty of a deportable offense prior to the 1996 legislation from being deported if that crime did not constitute grounds for deportation prior to IIRIRA.

63. Office of Public Affairs, U.S. Department of Homeland Security, "Fact Sheet: Section 287(g) Immigration and Nationality Act, U.S. Immigration and Customs Enforcement," August 16, 2006.

64. See Immigration and Human Rights Policy Clinic, *The Policies and Politics of Local Immigration Enforcement Laws: 287(g) Program in North Carolina*, University of North Carolina, Chapel Hill, February 2009, 6. See also U.S. Government Accountability Office, *Immigration Enforcement: Better Controls Needed over Program Authorizing State and Local Enforcement of Federal Immigration Laws*, GAO-09-109, Washington, DC, January 2009.

CHAPTER 4

1. The research presented here builds specifically from the arguments of prominent national immigrants' rights groups who have critiqued federal action. In particular, the National Hispanic Leadership Agenda, the National Council of La Raza, the American Friends Service Committee, the American Civil Liberties Union, the National Network for Immigrant and Refugee Rights, the American Immigration Lawyers Association, the National Immigration Forum, and the National Immigration Law Center have issued memos, reports, and calls for action with respect to specific practices emanating from shifts in immigration politics at the federal level, which they argue are negatively affecting Latina/o immigrants. This chapter builds upon these critiques by reviewing all the legislation dealing with immigration introduced to Congress during the height of the war on terror, giving particular consideration to those bills that were ultimately signed into law.

2. In this analysis, I examined bills that were introduced and passed into public law that amended an existing immigration statute, created a new one, or substantially contributed in discourse to a congressional agenda on immigration. I did not analyze

private bills or those in which the term "immigration" was flagged but did not deal centrally with the subject.

3. One area of legislation not tracked in this review is allocations for immigration enforcement or immigration-related programs, services, agencies, and so on. Because immigration-related programs can be found in a wide-reaching array of federal departments, agencies, and units, it is beyond the scope of this chapter to track such changes in funding. While funding is not tracked in a systematic manner, some notable instances of large federal allocations are discussed in the review of legislation presented here. See, for instance, Intelligence Authorization Act for Fiscal Year 2003. Public Law No. 107-306, 116 STAT. 2383, November 27, 2002; Consolidated Appropriations Resolution, 2003. Public Law No. 108-7. 117 STAT. 11, February 20, 2003; National Defense Authorization Act for Fiscal Year 2004. Public Law No. 108-136, 117 STAT. 1392, Title XVII, Sec. 1701–1704, November 24, 2003; Department of Homeland Security Appropriations Act, 2004. Public Law No. 108-90. 117 STAT. 1137, October 1, 2003; and Department of Homeland Security Appropriations Act, 2005. Public Law No. 108-334. 118 STAT. 1298, October 18, 2004.

4. Enhanced Border Security and Visa Entry Reform Act of 2002. Public Law No. 107-173. 116 STAT. 543. Title III, Sec. 103, 301–303, May 14, 2002.

5. Ibid., Title I, Sec. 101–102.

6. Enhanced Border Security and Visa Entry Reform Act of 2002. Public Law No. 107-173. 116 STAT. 543, Title I, Sec. 201–204, May 14, 2002; Department of Homeland Security Appropriations Act, 2004. Public Law No. 108-90. 117 STAT. 1137. Title IV, October 1, 2003; Department of Homeland Security Appropriations Act, 2005. Public Law No. 108-334. 118 STAT. 1298. Title II, October 18, 2004; and Department of Defense and Emergency Supplemental Appropriations for Recovery from and Response to Terrorist Attacks on the United States Act, 2002. Public Law No. 107-117. 115 STAT. 2230, January 10, 2002.

7. Consolidated Appropriations Act, 2005. Public Law No. 108-447. 118 STAT. 2810. Sec. 426, December 8, 2004.

8. Enhanced Border Security and Visa Entry Reform Act of 2002. Public Law No. 107-173. 116 STAT. 543. Title III, Sec. 303–304, May 14, 2002.

9. Ibid., Title IV, Sec. 401–404.

10. Intelligence Authorization Act for Fiscal Year 2003. Public Law No. 107-306, 116 STAT. 2383. Sec. 341–342, November 27, 2002.

11. Consolidated Appropriations Resolution, 2003. Public Law No. 108-7. 117 STAT. 11. Sec. 112, February 20, 2003; and National Defense Authorization Act for Fiscal Year 2004. Public Law No. 108-136, 117 STAT. 1392. Sec. 803, November 24, 2003.

12. Enhanced Border Security and Visa Entry Reform Act of 2002. Public Law No. 107-173. 116 STAT. 543. Title V, Sec. 501–502, May 14, 2002; Departments of Commerce, Justice, and State, the Judiciary, and Related Agencies Appropriations Act, 2002, Public Law No. 107-77. 115 STAT. 748. Title I, Sec. 115, 621, November 28, 2001; and Cyber Security Research and Development Act of 2002. Public Law No. 107-305, 116 Stat. 2367, Sec. 16–17, November 27, 2008. A related feature of this legislation was the practice of extending restrictions to persons or entities who failed to comply with the restrictions placed upon immigrants, particularly their review and scrutiny. In the case of the 2002 Cyber Security Research and Development Act, universities that were deemed out of compliance with monitoring and reporting of foreign students faced their own penalties.

13. Basic Pilot Extension Act of 2001, Public Law No. 107-128. 115 STAT. 2407, January 16, 2002; and Basic Pilot Extension and Expansion Act of 2003, Public Law No. 108-156. 117 STAT. 1944. Sec. 2–4, December 3, 2003.

14. Enhanced Border Security and Visa Entry Reform Act of 2002. Public Law No. 107-173. 116 STAT. 543. Title II, Sec. 4. May 14, 2002.

15. Department of Homeland Security Appropriations Act, 2004. Public Law No. 108-90. 117 STAT. 1137, October 1, 2003; and Department of Homeland Security Appropriations Act, 2005. Public Law No. 108-334. 118 STAT. 1298, October 18, 2004.

16. Implementing Recommendations of the 9/11 Commission Act of 2007. Public Law No. 110-53. 121 STAT. 266. Title V, Subtitle B, Sec. 512, August 3, 2007.

17. Enhanced Border Security and Visa Entry Reform Act of 2002. Public Law No. 107-173. 116 STAT. 543. Title IV, Sec. 306, May 14, 2002.

18. Consolidated Appropriations Act, 2005. Public Law No. 108-447. 118 STAT. 2809, December 8, 2004.

19. Identity Theft Penalty Enhancement Act, 2005. Public Law No. 108-275. 118 STAT. 831, Sec. 2–3, July 15, 2004.

20. National Defense Authorization Act for Fiscal Year 2004. Public Law No. 108-136, 117 STAT. 1392, Title XVII, Sec. 1701–1704, November 24, 2003.

21. Terrorist Bombings Convention Implementation Act of 2002. Public Law No. 197-197, 116 STAT. 721, June 25, 2002.

22. For example, the Intelligence Authorization Act for Fiscal Year 2003 not only excluded immigrants from serving on the influential 9/11 Commission; it reinforced provisions stipulating that only citizens and permanent residents could request information about themselves from the National Reconnaissance Office. Intelligence Authorization Act of Fiscal Year 2003. Public Law No. 107-306, 116 STAT. 2383, November 27, 2002.

23. Enhanced Border Security and Visa Entry Reform Act of 2002. Public Law No. 107-173. 116 STAT. 543. Title I, Sec. 101, May 14, 2002.

24. Aviation and Transportation Security Act. Public Law No. 107-71. 115 STAT. 597, November 19, 2001.

25. See especially allocation in the following legislation: Enhanced Border Security and Visa Entry Reform Act of 2002. Public Law No. 107-173. 116 STAT. 543, May 14, 2002; Department of Homeland Security Appropriations Act, 2004. Public Law No. 108-90. 117 STAT. 1137, October 1, 2003; and Department of Homeland Security Appropriations Act, 2005. Public Law No. 108-334. 118 STAT. 1298, October 18, 2004.

26. Secure Fence Act of 2006. Public Law No. 109-367. 120 STAT. 2638, October 26, 2006.

27. By 2005, these efforts went beyond attempts to restrict immigrants from accessing government services, a practice often presented as a cost-saving measure to cash-strapped states, and took on more enforcement qualities as law enforcement and civil servants were increasingly compelled to report or apprehend persons suspected of being in the country without proper documentation.

28. Cyber Security Research and Development Act. Public Law No. 107-305. 116 STAT. 2387, November 27, 2002.

29. Social Security Protection Act of 2004. Public Law No. 108-203. 118 STAT. 493. Sec. 211, March 2, 2004. This was a response to reports from the *New York Times* that undocumented immigrant laborers were contributing millions of dollars each year to Social Security and Medicaid without compensation and the subsequent push to remunerate the population.

30. Aviation and Transportation Security Act. Public Law No. 107-71. 115 STAT. 597, November 19, 2001.

31. Intelligence Authorization Act for Fiscal Year 2003. Public Law No. 107-306, 116 STAT. 2383, November 27, 2002.

32. Maritime Transportation Security Act of 2002. Public Law No. 107-295. 116 STAT. 2064, November 25, 2002; emphasis added.

33. Cyber Security Research and Development Act. Public Law No. 107-305. 116 STAT. 2387, November 27, 2002.

34. Trafficking Victims Protection Reauthorization Act of 2003. Public Law No. 108-193. 117 STAT. 2875. Sec. 4, December 19, 2003.

35. National Defense Authorization Act for Fiscal Year 2004. Public Law No. 108-136, 117 STAT. 1392, Title XVII, Sec. 1701–1704, November 24, 2003.

36. Implementing Recommendations of the 9/11 Commission Act of 2007. Public Law No. 110-53. 121 STAT. 266. Subtitle B, Sec. 71, August 3, 2007.

37. Aviation and Transportation Security Act. Public Law No. 107-71. 115 STAT. 597, November 19, 2001; and Intelligence Authorization Act for Fiscal Year 2003. Public Law No. 107-306, 116 STAT. 2383, November 27, 2002.

38. Enhanced Border Security and Visa Entry Reform Act of 2002. Public Law No. 107-173. 116 STAT. 543, May 14, 2002; Maritime Transportation Security Act of 2002. Public Law No. 107-295. 116 STAT. 2064, November 25, 2002; and 2002 Supplemental Appropriations Act for Further Recovery from and Response to Terrorist Attacks on the United States. Public Law No. 107-206. 116 STAT. 820, August 2, 2002.

39. Bob Stump National Defense Authorization Act for Fiscal Year 2003. Public Law No. 107-314. 116 STAT. 2458, December 2, 2002; National Defense Authorization Act for Fiscal Year 2004. Public Law No. 108-136, 117 STAT. 1392, November 24, 2003; Consolidated Appropriations Act, 2004. Public Law No. 108-199. 118 STAT. 3, January 23, 2004; and William Wilberforce Trafficking Victims Protection Reauthorization Act of 2008. Public Law No. 110-457. 122 STAT. 5044, December 23, 2008.

40. Bob Stump National Defense Authorization Act for Fiscal Year 2003. Public Law No. 107-314. 116 STAT. 2458. December 2, 2002; National Defense Authorization Act for Fiscal Year 2004. Public Law No. 108-136, 117 STAT. 1392, November 24, 2003; and Consolidated Appropriations Act, 2004. Public Law No. 108-199. 118 STAT. 3, January 23, 2004.

41. See 2002 Supplemental Appropriations Act for Further Recovery from and Response to Terrorist Attacks on the United States. Public Law No. 107-206. 116 STAT. 820, August 2, 2002; Department of Homeland Security Appropriations Act, 2004. Public Law No. 108-90. 117 STAT. 1137, October 1, 2003; Department of Homeland Security Appropriations Act, 2005. Public Law No. 108-334. 118 STAT. 1298, October 18, 2004; Consolidated Appropriations Resolution, 2003. Public Law No. 108-7. 117 STAT. 11, February 20, 2003; and Consolidated Appropriations Act, 2005. Public Law No. 108-447. 118 STAT. 2810, December 8, 2004.

42. Department of Defense and Emergency Supplemental Appropriations for Recovery from and Response to Terrorist Attacks on the United States Act, 2002. Public Law No. 107-117. 115 STAT. 2230, January 10, 2002; and National Defense Authorization Act for Fiscal Year 2004. Public Law No. 108-136, 117 STAT. 1392, November 24, 2003.

43. 2002 Supplemental Appropriations Act for Further Recovery from and Response to Terrorist Attacks on the United States. Public Law No. 107-206. 116 STAT. 820, August 2, 2002. These particular provisions were significant to immigration investigations, because they provided specific direction to officers to coordinate instances of driver's

license fraud with social security fraud (a process that undoubtedly would lead to the apprehension of unauthorized immigrant laborers).

44. Aviation and Transportation Security Act. Public Law No. 107-71. 115 STAT. 597, November 19, 2001.

45. Violence Against Women and Department of Justice Reauthorization Act of 2005. H.R. 3402. Public Law No. 109-162. STAT. 2960.

46. William Kandel, "Immigration Provisions of the Violence Against Women Act (VAWA)," Congressional Research Services, May 15, 2012, available at www.fas.org/sgp/crs/misc/R42477.pdf.

47. Paul Gilroy, *Postcolonial Melancholia* (New York: Columbia University Press, 2006).

48. Sharmila Lodhia, "Constructing an Imperfect Citizen-Subject: Globalization, National 'Security,' and Violence against South Asian Women," *WSQ: Women's Studies Quarterly* 38, nos. 1–2 (2010): 168.

49. In their report on residential raids conducted by the NFOP, Margot Mendelson, Shayna Strom, and Michael Wishni note that in 2003, 32 percent of the immigrants apprehended and arrested by the teams had criminal convictions, a number that dropped to 17 percent in 2006 and 9 percent by 2007. In other words, by 2007, the preponderance of immigrants apprehended by the Fugitive Operations Teams as part of the war on terror had no connection to terrorism *and* no evidence of criminal convictions in their records. See Margot Mendelson, Shayna Strom, and Michael Wishni, *Collateral Damage: An Examination of ICE's Fugitive Operations Program,* a Report of the Migration Policy Institute, Washington, DC, 2009.

50. Violence Against Women and Department of Justice Reauthorization Act of 2005. H.R. 3402. Public Law No. 109-162. STAT. 2960. Sec. 1196.

51. Ibid., Sec. 1111.

52. Trafficking Victims Protection Reauthorization Act of 2003. Public Law No. 108-193. 117 STAT. 2875. Sec. 3., December 19, 2003.

53. Ibid.

54. Lodhia, "Constructing an Imperfect Citizen-Subject," 168.

55. Nancy Chang, *Silencing Political Dissent: How Post–September 11 Anti-terrorism Measures Threaten Our Civil Liberties* (Washington, DC: Center for Constitutional Rights, 2002).

56. Procedurally, the act was significant because it was debated and passed by Congress within six weeks after September 11 and in the wake of anthrax attacks that exiled several legislators from their offices. Moreover, despite the scale of the legislation, the act was passed with virtually no public hearing or debate and without a conference or a committee report. Ultimately, despite a lack of careful review or extended debate and amendments, the bill passed handily in both the House (356–66), and the Senate (98–1).

57. USA PATRIOT Act, Sec. 412(a), adding 8 U.S.C. Sec. 1226A(a)(3) and (5).

58. Robyn E. Blumner, "Ashcroft's Power to Detain without Charges Continues without Oversight," *St. Petersburg Times,* May 5, 2002.

59. USA PATRIOT Act, Sec. 312, adding new INA section 236A(a)(3) and (a)(6).

60. Ibid., Sec. 411(a), amending 8 U.S.C. Sec. 1182 (a)(3)(B)(iv)(IV)(bb) and (cc), (V)(bb) and (cc), and (VI)(cc) and (dd).

61. Ibid., Sec. 411(a), amending 8 U.S.C. Sec. 1181(a)(3)(B)(vi)(I) and (II).

62. Chang, *Silencing Political Dissent,* 63.

63. Blumner, "Ashcroft's Power to Detain without Charges Continues without Oversight."

64. In 2005, Congress reauthorized and expanded provisions of the USA PATRIOT Act. Surveillance-related provisions of the act that were set to expire were made permanent. (Two provisions of this surveillance regarding roving surveillance authority under FISA and applications for tangible documents by the FBI in foreign intelligence and international terrorism investigations were extended through December 2009.) Beyond this, the revision added to the existing structure of anti-terrorism work affecting immigrants by increasing penalties for terrorism financing and money laundering and adding forms of narco-terrorism to the list of acts that may constitute a form of terrorism in the United States. Finally, the revised law opened new doorways for scrutiny and review of Mexican immigrants by specifically seeking collaboration with Mexican law-enforcement authorities to combat the production and trafficking of methamphetamine through enhanced border security. H.R. 3199 USA PATRIOT Improvement and Reauthorization Act of 2005, Public Law 109-77.

65. Homeland Security Act of 2002. Public Law No. 107-296. 116 STAT. 2192. Subtitle D, Sec. 441–443, November 25, 2002.

66. Ibid., 116 STAT. 2177. Subtitle E, Sec. 451, November 25, 2002.

67. Ibid., Subtitle A, Sec. 401–403, November 25, 2002.

68. Ibid., 116 STAT. 2195. Subtitle E, Sec. 451, November 25, 2002.

69. Ibid., Sec. 452–459, November 25, 2002.

70. U.S. Customs and Border Protection, "Secure Borders, Safe Travel, Legal Trade: U.S. Customs and Border Protection Fiscal Year 2009–2014 Strategic Plan," July 2009; and U.S. Customs and Border Protection, "CBP Statistics as of Fiscal Year 2009," February 16, 2010.

71. U.S. Immigration and Customs Enforcement, "ICE Strategic Plan FY 2010–2014," 2010.

72. Ibid.

73. Emergency Supplemental Appropriations Act for Defense, the Global War on Terror, and Tsunami Relief, 2005. Public Law No. 109-13, 119 STAT. 306. Division B, Title 1, Sec. 103, May 11, 2005.

74. Ibid., 119 STAT. 308–311. Division B, Title I, Sec. 104–106, May 11, 2005.

75. Ibid., 119 STAT. 306. Division B, Title I, Sec. 103, May 11, 2005.

76. Ibid., 119 STAT. 316–317. Division B, Title III, Sec. 302, May 11, 2005.

77. Ibid., 119 STAT. 317–318. Division B, Title III, Sec. 303, May 11, 2005.

78. The legislation "authorized a trier of fact, considering the totality of the circumstances and all relevant factors, to base credibility determinations in asylum cases on the: (1) demeanor, candor, or responsiveness of the applicant or witness; (2) inherent plausibility of the applicant's or witness's account; (3) consistency between the applicant's or witness's written and oral statements; (4) internal consistency of each such statement; (5) consistency of such statements with other evidence of record [including the Department of State's report on country conditions]; and (6) any inaccuracies or falsehoods in such statements regardless of whether they go to the heart of the applicant's claim." Moreover under the terms of the legislation, there was no presumption of credibility for the applicant. Emergency Supplemental Appropriations Act for Defense, the Global War on Terror, and Tsunami Relief, 2005. Public Law No. 109-13, 119 STAT. 302–306. Division B, Title I, Sec. 101, May 11, 2005.

79. Ibid., 119 STAT. 312–315. Division B, Title II, Sec. 202, May 11, 2005.

CHAPTER 5

1. Kristen Lombardo, "American Nightmare," *Boston Globe,* May 5, 2002.

2. Amy Smith, "Operation Tarmac: Overkill," *Austin Chronicle,* March 14, 2003.

3. National Hispanic Leadership Agenda, *How the Latino Community's Agenda on Immigration Enforcement and Reform Has Suffered since 9/11,* Washington, DC, 2004; National Network of Immigrant and Refugee Rights, "Increased Security Scrutiny Keeps Refugee Families Apart," Fall/Winter 2003; and Matthew Wald, "Officials Arrest 104 Airport Workers in Washington Area," *New York Times,* April 24, 2002.

4. Bruce Finley, "Migrant Cases Burden System," Denver Post.com, October 2, 2006.

5. Pew Hispanic Center, *National Survey of Latinos: As Illegal Immigration Issue Heats Up, Hispanics Feel a Chill,* Washington, DC, 2007.

6. Department of Homeland Security, "Fact Sheet: Section 287(g) Immigration and Nationality Act," August 16, 2006.

7. Roberto Lima and Bassina Farbenblum, "Freedom of Information Act Request/ Expedited Processing Request," Seton Hall School of Law, Center for Social Justice, December 13, 2007.

8. Ibid., 9.

9. *Seton Hall School of Law, Center for Social Justice and Evicao El Brasilera v. United States Department of Homeland Security (DHS)*; United States Immigration and Customs Enforcement (ICE); and United States Citizenship and Immigration Services (USCIS), U.S. District Court of New Jersey, January 28, 2008. In their lawsuit, the plaintiffs again remind us of the lack of available information from the federal sources on the raids, stating, "The public remains critically uninformed about these activities, with no access to vital information—including records, statements, and policy guidelines—concerning the methods ICE agents are using to target, locate, and arrest immigrants in increasing numbers inside their homes" (2).

10. While the search of materials extends from 2001 to 2010, the focus in this chapter is on the period immediately following the attacks on 9/11 through 2008 for three reasons: First, this represents the height of securitization efforts conducted under the war on terrorism in the United States; second, a greater array of documentation and analysis regarding large-scale roundups and deportations exists after 2009 but not in the years prior; and third, this timeline is consistent with the examination of legislative and policy shifts outlined in the previous chapter.

11. Joanna Dreby, *How Today's Immigration Enforcement Policies Impact Children, Families, and Communities: A View from the Ground,* a Report from the Center for American Progress, August 2012, available at www.americanprogress.org.

12. According to Bill Ong Hing, the first deportation law in the United States was included in the 1798 Alien and Sedition Acts and was aimed at Irish and French immigrants as well as any immigrant "dangerous to the peace and safety of the United States." However, no one was ever deported under this provision, which expired in 1800. Bill Ong Hing, *Defining America through Immigration Policy* (Philadelphia: Temple University Press, 2004), 209.

13. Ibid., 213.

14. Ibid.

15. Ibid.

16. Natsu Saito, "Symbolism under Siege: Japanese American Redress and the 'Racing' of Arab Americans as 'Terrorists,'" *Asian Law Journal* 8 (2001): 11–26.

17. Ibid.

18. See Julie Charlip, "Sanger Sweep Stirs Questions on Civil Rights Violations," *Fresno Bee*, October 14, 1984; Hing, *Defining America through Immigration Policy*, 150–151.

19. Nina Bernstein, "Immigrant Workers Caught in Net Cast for Gangs," *New York Times*, November 25, 2007; Nick Norlen, "Immigration Raid Tactics Alarm Princeton Advocates," *Princeton Packet*, January 25, 2008.

20. Nicholas de Genova,"The Deportation Regime: Sovereignty, Space, and the Freedom of Movement," in *The Deportation Regime*, edited by Nicholas de Genova and Nathalie Peutz (Durham, NC: Duke University Press, 2010), 33–62; Tanya Maria Golash-Boza, *Immigration Nation: Raids, Detentions, and Deportations in Post-9/11 America* (Boulder, CO: Paradigm Press, 2011); and Dan Kanstroom, *Deportation Nation: Outsiders in American History* (Cambridge, MA: Harvard University Press, 2007). One indicator of how drastically conditions for Mexican migrants changed after 9/11 is evident in the congenial discourse around the passage of immigrants between the United States and Mexico that took place in and around the White House in 2000 and 2001. Shortly after assuming office in 1999, President Bush met with then President Vincente Fox to discuss immigration reform and announced subsequent to that meeting that "harmonizing" immigration policy would be a top priority for his administration. In light of this congenial rhetoric, President Fox called for a policy of open borders, and specifically a plan for population movements to match the mobility of goods and capital between the two countries.

By July 2001, Secretary of State Colin Powell and Attorney General John Ashcroft were in discussions to develop a temporary guest-worker program through which one to two million undocumented Mexicans in the United States could receive legal status. At the time, U.S. policymakers in both parties indicated interest in proposals to receive Mexican guest workers, with a formal draft agreement scheduled for production in early 2002. Even in the aftermath of the attacks on 9/11, momentum for easing the immigration flow from Mexico still existed, as congressional leaders of the Democratic Party visited the state of Puebla in November 2001, saying they hoped to provide access to U.S. citizenship for all Mexican migrants. Nevertheless, by 2002, all hopes of reform without restrictions were effectively quashed, as new legislation, such as the PATRIOT Act and the Homeland Security Act, was passed, and the first round of immigrant detentions began to take place.

21. Sensitive facilities included but were not limited to airports, nuclear power plants, chemical plants, military bases, defense facilities, and seaports. "Dozens Use Fake IDs to Work at Chicago Airport," Agence France Presse, November 8, 2007.

22. The estimates in Table 5.1 are based on newspaper reports of raids conducted in federally secured facilities and "sensitive areas" (including airports, military bases, nuclear-power plants, chemical plants, military bases, defense facilities, and seaports as well as locations that are typically adjacent to these facilities), private worksites, and residential neighborhoods. Estimates of apprehensions are based on the same newspaper accounts rather than from individual apprehensions, detentions, or arrests made by ICE, CPB, state patrols, sheriff's officers, or any other immigration authorities in the course of their daily work. Finally, the estimates of apprehensions refer to persons who were held or detained for any length of time, including persons who were held and later released; persons who were held and subsequently arrested, indicted, deported, or transferred; and persons who were taken into custody but not charged with a crime. Ultimately,

given the absence of public records on the raids conducted prior to 2009 and the indirect method of accounting for the raids and apprehensions, the estimates presented here differ from, for example, the total number of arrests made by Fugitive Operation Teams between 2003 and 2008 as reported by ICE and the total number of undocumented immigrants arrested in conjunction with worksite raids. See ICE, "ICE multifaceted strategy leads to Record Enforcement Results," News Release, October 23, 2008, 8; and U.S. Immigration and Customs Enforcement, "Fact Sheet: Worksite Enforcement Overview" (Washington, DC: U.S. Department of Homeland Security), April 30, 2009, available at www.ice.gov/news/library/factsheets/worksite.htm.

23. Operation Return to Sender, which began on May 26, 2006, was a nationwide interior enforcement initiative that brought together the National Fugitive Operations Program (NFOP), operating through the Immigration and Customs Enforcement (ICE) Bureau, with federal, state, and local law-enforcement entities to identify and apprehend immigrants classified as "fugitives." The Secure Communities Program, launched in March 2008, followed the trend of mobilizing local law-enforcement agencies resources to serve federal immigration enforcement by requiring local jurisdictions to share electronic data on immigrants arrested. The program "transformed the landscape of immigration enforcement by allowing ICE to effectively run federal immigration checks on every individual booked into a local county jail, usually while still in pre-trial custody." See Aarti Kohi, Peter Markowitz, and Lisa Chavez, *Secure Communities by the Numbers: An Analysis of Demographics and Due Process. A Report from the Chief Earl Warren Institute on Law and Social Policy*, October 2011, available at www.law.berkeley.edu/files/Secure_Communities_by_the_Numbers.pdf; and Julie Myers, Assistant Secretary, U.S. Department of Homeland Security, letter to Ms. Christina DeConcini, Director of Policy, National Immigration Forum, July 6, 2007.

24. The names often reflected the multitude of agencies involved in the raids. For example, Operation Tarmac referred to the portion of a joint agreement operated through the INS/DHS, whereas Operation Safe Harbor (sometimes referred to as Operation Safe Travel) referred to the portion of the program under the direction of the Social Security Administration, specifically the Office of the Inspector General. Together these were sometimes referred to as Operation Safe Sky, but more commonly they were referred to as simply Operation Tarmac. John K. Webb, "Use of the Social Security Fraud Statute in the Battle against Terrorism 42 U.S.C. Sec. 408 (a)(7)(A)(C)," *United States Attorney's Bulletin* 50, no. 3 (2002).

25. Rosanna Ruiz, "Airport Sweep Nets 143 Arrests: Workers Charged with False IDs," *Houston Chronicle,* September 10, 2002.

26. Webb, "Use of the Social Security Fraud Statute."

27. Paul Street, "Background Check: Operation Tarmac and the Many Faces of Terror," *Z Magazine,* January 11, 2003, available at www.zmag.org/sustainers/content/2003-01/11street.cfm;and Janet Rausa Fuller and Robert C. Herguth, "Feds Charge 25 in Airport Probe," *Chicago Sun-Times,* December 11, 2002. By June 2002, the INS testified that the U.S. government had expended resources auditing more than 190,000 Employment Eligibility Verification Forms at more than 1,900 airport businesses, arresting 500 immigrant workers and deporting 260. National Hispanic Leadership Agenda, *How the Latino Community's Agenda on Immigration Enforcement and Reform Has Suffered since 9/11*; see also Wald, "Officials Arrest 104 Airport Workers in Washington Area."

28. The most common charges included use of false documentation, including fake

work permits, which violated the felony fraud section of the Social Security Act. Under section 408(a)(7) of the act, a person is subject to criminal penalties if he or she

1. willfully, knowingly, and with an intent to deceive use[d] a social security number on the basis of false information furnished by the SSA (408 (a)(7)(A));
2. falsely represent[ed], with an intent to deceive, a number to be the social security number assigned to him or her or to another person (408 (a)(7)(B)); or
3. knowingly altered a social security card issued by the SSA, bought or sold a card that was, or was purported to be, a card so issued, counterfeited a social security card, or possessed a social security card with an intent to sell or alter it (408 (a)(7)(C)).

See Webb, "Use of the Social Security Fraud Statute," 1.

29. Ruiz, "Airport Sweep Nets 143 Arrests."

30. Daniel G. Bogden, "Joint Law Enforcement Investigation Promotes Airport Security: Workers at Reno-Tahoe Airport Face Federal Charges," U.S. Attorney, District of Nevada, U.S. Department of Justice, available at www.usdoj.gov/usao/nv/home/pressrelease/february2002/tarmac222.htm.

31. John Suthers, "Over 100 Workers at DIA Indicted for Falsifying Security Applications—All Had Access to Restricted Areas," Press Release, United States Attorney's Office, Colorado, September 17, 2002, available at www.usdoj.gov/usao/co/091702Frame1Source1.htm.

32. Michael Hedges, "Hundreds of Airport Workers Picked Up in Crackdown," *Houston Chronicle*, April 24, 2002.

33. Suthers, "Over 100 Workers at DIA Indicted for Falsifying Security Applications."

34. "Jones Reacts to Arrest of Illegal Aliens Working at Seymour Johnson Air Force Base," Congressional Press Releases, July 7, 2005.

35. Suthers, "Over 100 Workers at DIA Indicted for Falsifying Security Applications."

36. Hedges, "Hundreds of Airport Workers Picked Up in Crackdown."

37. Ruiz, "Airport Sweep Nets 143 Arrests."

38. Rosanna Ruiz, "Airport Sweep Outpaces Other Cities' Efforts: Houston Nets Most Indictments," *Houston Chronicle*, September 11, 2002.

39. "ICE Arrests 60 Illegals Working in Sensitive Areas," *Washington Times*, May 21, 2005.

40. "Illegal Immigrants Nabbed in California Raid," Associated Press, September 22, 2004.

41. In reality, by 2006, there was virtually no distinction between worksite raids and raids conducted at sensitive facilities, such as airports, nuclear-power plants, chemical plants, military bases, defense facilities, and seaports, as all became part of Operation Return to Sender. See "Dozens Use Fake IDs to Work at Chicago Airport."

42. U.S. Immigration and Customs Enforcement, "Fact Sheet: Worksite Enforcement Overview," April 30, 2009, available at www.ice.gov/news/library/factsheets/worksite.htm.

43. Donna Leinwand, "Immigration Raid Linked to ID Theft, Chertoff Says," *USA Today*, December 13, 2006, available at www.usatoday.com/news/nation/2006-12-13-immigration_x.htm.

44. Efforts to appease a Republican base and shore up support for a guest-worker program advanced by the Bush administration were evident in Secretary Chertoff's press conference in response to the Swift meat-packing raids. See Department of Homeland Security, "Remarks by Secretary of Homeland Security Michael Chertoff, Immigration and Customs Enforcement Assistant Secretary Julie Myers, and Federal Trade Commission Chairman Deborah Platt Majoras at a Press Conference on Operation Wagon Train," December 13, 2006, available at www.dhs.gov/xnews/releases/pr_1166047951514.shtm.

45. Leinwand, "Immigration Raid Linked to ID Theft."

46. Randy Capps et al., *Paying the Price: The Impact of Immigration Raids on America's Children* (Washington, DC: Urban Institute, 2007); and "ID Thieves Targeted in Immigration Raids: Feds Raid Swift Meat-Packing Plants at Six Locations across Country," Associated Press, December 12, 2006, available at www.msnbc.msn.com/id/16169899/.

47. Department of Homeland Security, "Remarks by Secretary of Homeland Security Michael Chertoff."

48. Ibid.

49. According to Secretary Chertoff, the number of apprehensions and arrests made in conjunction with Operation Wagon Train would have been greater had Swift not take steps to inform employees prior to the raid. In the press conference held by DHS subsequent to the raids, Chertoff maintained that Swift first attempted to stop the raids by filing an injunction in federal district court and then terminated approximately four hundred employees prior to the raid. Ibid.

50. Ibid.

51. Ibid.

52. Ibid.

53. Margot Mendelson, Shayna Strom, and Michael Wishni, *Collateral Damage: An Examination of ICE's Fugitive Operations Program* (Washington DC: Migration Policy Institute, 2009).

54. U.S. Department of Homeland Security, as quoted in ibid., 3.

55. Myers, "Letter to Ms. Christina DeConcini," 3.

56. See Mendelson, Strom, and Wishni, *Collateral Damage*, 2.

57. Descriptions of the raids conducted by the Fugitive Operations Teams highlighted these problems:

> In a typical raid, between three and ten ICE agents surround a home believed to house one or multiple immigrant families. This occurs in the pre-dawn hours of the morning. The agents pound furiously on the door, and in many cases shout "police." The occupants are awoken and a person rushes to the door, assuming an emergency. In some instances, the person opens the door. In other cases, the person asks who is there, to which the ICE agents respond "police" and in some cases demand that the door be opened. In other instances the ICE agents state that they are police, looking for a particular individual who is unknown to the occupants of the home, which then leads the occupant to open the door in order to assist with the inquiry. As the door is opened, the agents enter the home, typically without requesting consent. In some cases, if the agents do not have a clear path of entry, they forcibly push the door and the individual who opened it. It has been reported that agents have even broken down doors to gain entry.

Upon information and belief, the agents typically do not have a search warrant authorizing entry to the premises. Multiple armed agents then move through the home and order all of the individuals out of bed and to a central location in the home. Often these occupants include small children, many of whom are U.S. citizens. ICE agents have pointed guns directly at the occupants of a home, including in some instances, children. The ICE agents often state that they are looking for a particular individual. Regardless of whether that individual is known to the occupants (in many cases, the occupants have never heard of the person), or whether the individual is present in the home, the agents typically question all of the occupants about their identity and immigration status. There are several first-hand reports of ICE agents confiscating individuals' cell phones, checking telephone numbers stored on these phones, and forcing the owners of the phones to divulge details about relatives and friends whose numbers were stored in the phones.

It has been reported that ICE agents are sometimes verbally abusive, and if the occupants are uncooperative, physically abusive as well. In front of children and other family members, ICE agents typically handcuff individuals they suspect are unlawfully present in the United States and place them in a van outside the home. They often do not allow the person to change out of his or her bedclothes. Nor do they typically tell the family where they are taking the person. ICE agents then move on to other houses in the neighborhood and repeat this sequence filling the van with arrestees. (*Seton Hall School of Law, Center for Social Justice and Evicao El Brasilera v. United States Department of Homeland Security [DHS]*; United States Immigration and Customs Enforcement [ICE]; and United States Citizenship and Immigration Services [USCIS], U.S. District Court of New Jersey, January 28, 2008, 8–9)

58. David Cole, *Enemy Aliens: Double Standards and Constitutional Freedoms in the War on Terrorism* (New York: New Press, 2003).

59. Department of Homeland Security, "Fact Sheet: Secure Border Initiative," November 2, 2005, available at www.dhs.gov/xnews/releases/press_release_0794.shtm.

60. Fugitive operation teams operate in more than thirty states. In addition to Operation Return to Sender and Operation Community Shield, these teams have conducted residential raids across the country, but especially in locations with high concentrations of Latina/o immigrants, including Operation City Lights in Las Vegas, Operation Phoenix in Florida, Operation Deep Freeze in Chicago, and Operation FLASH in the Northeast. California had one of the largest concentrations of fugitive operations teams, with thirteen operating in the state from San Diego to San Francisco.

61. Mendelson, Strom, and Wishni, *Collateral Damage*.

62. Ibid.

63. Ibid.

64. Michelle Garcia, "N.Y. Using Terrorism Law to Prosecute Street Gang: Critics Say Post-9/11 Legislation Is Being Applied Too Broadly," *Washington Post*, February 1, 2005.

65. Kohi, Markowitz, and Chavez, *Secure Communities by the Numbers*.

66. Spencer S. Hsu, "Immigration Raid Jars a Small Town," *Washington Post*, May 18, 2008, available at www.washingtonpost.com/wp-dyn/content/article/2008/05/17/AR2008051702474.html; and Robin Shulman, "Immigration Raid Rips Families," *Wash-*

ington Post, March 18, 2007, available at www.washingtonpost.com/wp-dyn/content/article/2007/03/17/AR2007031701113.html.

67. American Civil Liberties Union, "Documents Obtained by ACLU Show Sexual Abuse of Immigration Detainees Is Widespread National Problem," ACLU.org, October 19, 2011, available at www.aclu.org/immigrants-rights-prisoners-rights-prisoners-rights/documents-obtained-aclu-show-sexual-abuse; and American Civil Liberties Union, "Sexual Abuse in Immigration Detention—Raquel's Story," ACLU.org, October 16, 2011, available at www.aclu.org/immigrants-rights/sexual-abuse-immigration-detention-raquels-story.

68. American Civil Liberties Union, "Sexual Abuse in Immigration Detention."

69. Ibid.

70. Dreby, *How Today's Immigration Enforcement Policies Impact Children, Families, and Communities.*

71. Ibid, 10.

72. Capps et al., *Paying the Price*, 2.

73. Dreby, *How Today's Immigration Enforcement Policies Impact Children, Families, and Communities.*

74. National Immigrant Justice Center, "Fact Sheet: Children Detained by the Department of Homeland Security in Adult Detention Facilities," May 2013.

75. A report from the Applied Research Center found that in 2010, 5,100 children of immigrant adults were placed in foster homes. See Seth Freed Wessler, *The Perilous Intersection of Immigration: Enforcement and the Child Welfare System* (Applied Research Center, 2011), available at http://arc.org/shatteredfamilies.

76. As with past "sting operations" in which undocumented immigrants were lured to an immigration processing center on a false premise (e.g., an offer to buy a car), a similar form of deception was used on July 7, 2008, in a raid at the Seymour Johnson Air Force Base in Goldsboro, North Carolina. In this operation, workers were tricked by ICE into thinking they were attending an OSHA-held meeting on workplace safety. In the end, forty-nine individuals were arrested. See "U.S. Ends Job 'Safety' Immigration Raids," Associated Press, March 29, 2006.

77. U.S. Attorney Michael Selby, as quoted in Ruiz, "Airport Sweep Nets 143 Arrests."

78. "Local Officials Adopt New, Harder Tactics on Illegal Immigrants," *New York Times,* June 9, 2008.

CHAPTER 6

1. *Padilla v. C.T. Hanft, U.S.N. Commander, Consolidated Naval Brig,* 2005.

2. "Declaration of Michael Mobbs," Special Advisor to the Undersecretary of Defense for Policy, Unclassified Memo, August 27, 2002, available at http://news.findlaw.com/hdocs/docs/padilla/padillabush82702mobbs.pdf.

3. Ibid.

4. Executive Order to the Secretary of Defense, June 9, 2002.

5. Ibid.

6. Aihwa Ong, *Buddha Is Hiding: Refugees, Citizenship, the New America* (Berkeley: University of California Press, 2003), xix.

7. While Foucault's reading of governmentality extends beyond the formal practices of the state to consider the micropractices of control and the way these become disci-

plining mechanisms shaping subjects as well as points of negotiation and resistance, my analysis remains largely tied to interventions of the new security state, the way these are racialized and gendered, and their effect in reconstituting citizenship. See specifically Michel Foucault, "On Governmentality," in *The Foucault Effect: Studies in Governmentality,* ed. Graham Burchell, Colin Gordon, and Peter Miller (Chicago: University of Chicago Press, 1991), 87–104; and Michel Foucault, *Discipline and Punish: The Birth of the Prison* (New York: Vintage, 1979).

8. Executive Order to the Secretary of Defense, June 9, 2002.

9. To clarify, I am invoking an understanding of agency here synonymous with individual will, self-definition, intentionality, purposefulness, choice, and the ability to resist subordination. In effect, I am focusing on the capacity for individuals to shape the world they live in and to effect change when they have been harmed. By focusing on the loss of political agency, I am highlighting the unwarranted restrictions on individual rights that leave subjects without choice or the capacity to express themselves, defend themselves, or act on their own, particularly in relationship to the judicial branch and defense against loss of liberties. The choice to frame agency in these terms is meant to underscore the loss of basic juridical protections for natural-born citizens, a key feature of modern citizenship claims in the United States; however, I recognize that such a limited definition comes with a concomitant naturalization of freedom and liberty as a social ideal that does not capture the range of possibilities that agency embodies. While others have done more work in reimagining the boundaries of agency to understand more complex forms of action, such a redefinition is beyond the scope of this particular chapter. See specifically Saba Mahmood, "Feminist Theory, Embodiment, and the Docile Agent: Some Reflections on the Egyptian Islamic Revival," *Cultural Anthropology* 16, no. 2 (2001): 202–236; and Mustafa Emirbayer and Anne Mische, "What Is Agency?" *American Journal of Sociology* 103, no. 4 (1998): 962–1023.

10. The specific doctrine invoked in these cases is "next-of-friend" standing established in *Whitmore v. Arkansas 195 U.S.* (1990). In this case, the Supreme Court noted that next-of-friend standing "has long been an accepted basis for jurisdiction in certain circumstances" and has been typically invoked "on behalf of detained prisoners who are unable, usually because of mental incompetence or inaccessibility, to seek relief themselves" (162). Moreover, a "'next friend' does not himself become a party to the habeas corpus action in which he participates, but simply pursues the cause on behalf of the detained person, who remains the real party in interest" (163). The doctrine has since been affirmed in statute as well.

11. Opinion, United States 4th Circuit Court of Appeals, *Yaser Hamdi et al. v. Donald Rumsfeld et al.*, June 26, 2002, 6; and Memorandum of Points and Authorities in Support of Respondent's Objection to Magistrate Judge's Order of May 20, 2002, Regarding Access, May 23, 2002, 9.

12. Opinion, United States 4th Circuit Court of Appeals, *Yaser Hamdi et al. v. Donald Rumsfeld et al.*, June 26, 2002, 7.

13. Emergency Motion for Stay Pending Appeal, May 21, 2002, 3.

14. While the courts acted in this context to limit executive authority in important ways that are detailed later in this chapter, Congress proved much less willing to exercise such checks on the administration. As David Cole notes, "[Congress] did nothing to challenge the president's assertion of enemy-combatant authority, to respond to the abuses of immigrants after 9/11, or even to call for an independent investigation of the

torture scandal." See David Cole, *Enemy Aliens: Double Standards and Constitutional Freedoms in the War on Terrorism* (New York: New Press, 2003), xxvii.

15. Ibid.

16. Military Order of November 13, 2001, 66 Federal Registry 57, 833 (November 16, 2001), Sec. 2 (a).

17. Ibid., Sec. 1(f).

18. Ibid., Sec. 2(a)(ii).

19. "Authorization for Use of Military Force" Pub.L. No. 107-40, Sec. 2(a) 115 STAT. 224 (September 18, 2001). The law stipulated: "The President is authorized to use all necessary and appropriate force against those nations, organizations or persons he determines planned, authorized, committed, or aided the terrorist attacks that occurred on September 11, 2001, or harbored such organizations or persons, in order to prevent any future acts of international terrorism against the United States by such nations, organizations or persons."

20. Dick Cheney, as quoted in Cole, *Enemy Aliens*, 2.

21. John Ashcroft, "John Walker Lindh Press Conference," Department of Justice Conference Center, January 15, 2002.

22. Ibid.

23. "At the Sheberghan prison [Afghanistan], Hamdi was *determined by the U.S. military* screening team to meet the criteria for enemy combatants over whom the U.S. was taking control. . . . [B]ased upon his interviews and in light of this association with the Taliban, Hamdi was considered *by military forces* to be an enemy combatant" (emphasis added). "Declaration of Michael Mobbs."

24. While the list of terrorism-related cases heard in federal courts extends long before 9/11, these cases are distinct from those highlighted here for a variety of reasons. First, the most recent cases, in particular those surrounding the first World Trade Center bombing, involved foreign nationals and not natural-born citizens. Second, cases involving natural-born citizens, such as the Oklahoma City bomber Timothy McVeigh, did not invoke terrorism charges (in part because of the lack of federal law to define their actions as domestic terrorism) and presented the defendants as criminal anomalies as opposed to symbols of a greater threat from an entire ethnic or religious population. In short, they were not actively racialized by the state as foreigners or terrorists—legally or politically.

25. Anne E. Asbury, Affidavit in Support of a Criminal Complaint and an Arrest Warrant, January 15, 2002.

26. Ibid.

27. Ibid.

28. George C. Harris and William B. Cummings, "Defendant's Memorandum of Points and Authorities in Support of Motion to Suppress Involuntary Statements," *USA v. John Phillip Walker Lindh*, US District Court, Eastern District of Virginia.

29. An additional distinction in Lindh's handling is the formal advisement of his rights. According to the Departments of Defense and Justice, once he was identified as a U.S. citizen, Lindh was advised of his Miranda Rights and subsequently "acknowledged that he understood his rights, that he was waiving these rights, and that he agreed to be questioned by the FBI outside the presence of a lawyer" (Asbury, Affidavit in Support of a Criminal Complaint and an Arrest Warrant, 2). However, Lindh's lawyer challenged this acknowledgment, alleging that U.S. interrogators did not inform him of his rights

for several days and subjected him to extremely debilitating conditions, including star-vation, sleep deprivation, public humiliation, withholding of medical treatment, and continued questioning that amounted to coercive conduct (Harris and Cummings, "Defendant's Memorandum of Points and Authorities in Support of Motion to Suppress Involuntary Statements").

30. Alissa J. Rubin, "Afghans Detail Detention in 'Black Jail' at U.S. Base," *New York Times,* November 28, 2009, available at www.nytimes.com/2009/11/29/world/asia/29bagram.html?_r=1&hpw.

31. Antonio M. Taguba, as quoted in Seymour M. Hersh, "Annals of National Secu-rity: Torture at Abu Ghraib," *New Yorker,* May 10, 2004, 2.

32. Ibid., 4.

33. Both Hazel Carby and Jaspir K. Puar note that the spectacle of racialized, gen-dered, and sexualized torture captured in the treatment of prisoners at Abu Ghraib was not exceptional but rather inimical to the foundation of the United States. As Carby notes, "It is these enslaved and disposed—who were brutally slaughtered and driven from their lands or dragged in chains across the Atlantic to build the foundation of wealth upon which the modern United States of America rests—who have lived the consequences of this Janus face of American freedom and non-freedom" (2). While I agree with both that the use of gendered and racialized violence has been foundational in U.S. development, I would refine this argument by adding that in its performance of constitutionality, the state also has a long history of publicly permitting such violence to foreign subjects while repeatedly asserting that the constitution protects *citizens* from similar abuses. In the case of Abu Ghraib, the state, as represented by the U.S. military, employed such abusive imprisonment and again justified its practices as reasonable and necessary means for interrogating foreign prisoners while simultaneously upholding due process for Lindh. In doing so, the state differentiated the status of foreign sub-jects captured in war from U.S. citizens (even those hostile to the state) apprehended in the same time period. See Hazel Carby, "A Stranger and Bitter Crop: The Spectacle of Torture," *openDemocracy,* October 10, 2004, available at www.opendemocracy.net/media-abu_ghraib/article_2149.jsp; and Jaspir K. Puar, "Abu Ghraib: Arguing against Exceptionalism," *Feminist Studies* 30, no. 2 (2004): 522–534.

34. Defendant's Sentencing Memorandum, 1, September 26, 2002.

35. "Plea Agreement," *U.S. v. John Lindh,* U.S. District Court, July 15, 2002, 7.

36. Ibid., 8.

37. Marilyn Walker and Frank Lindh, "Interview with Amy Goodman," *Democ-racy Now,* July 31, 2009, available at www.democracynow.org/2009/7/31/exclusive_john_walker_lindhs_parents_discuss.

38. Prepared Statement of John Walker Lindh to the Court, October 4, 2002, 1–2.

39. Defendant's Sentencing Memorandum, September 26, 2002, 8, 10.

40. Harris and Cummings, "Defendant's Memorandum of Points and Authorities," 1.

41. Ibid., 2.

42. Ibid., 23.

43. "Plea Agreement," *U.S. v. John Lindh,* U.S. District Court, July 15, 2002, 3.

44. Birth Certificate, Yaser Esam Hamdi, September 26, 1980.

45. Petition for Writ of Habeas Corpus, June 11, 2002, Petition filed in the U.S. District Court for the Eastern District of Virginia, Norfolk Division in the case of *Yaser Hamdi, Esam Hamdi v. Donald Rumsfeld,* Commander Paulette.

46. Ibid., 4.

47. Emergency Motion for Stay Pending Appeal, May 21, 2002, 3, 14; and Memorandum of Points and Authorities in Support of Respondent's Objection to Magistrate Judge's Order of May 20, 2002, Regarding Access, May 23, 2002.

48. Brief for Respondents-Appellants, Paul J. McNulty et al. in the case of *Yaser Esam Hamdi et al. v. Donald Rumsfeld et al.*, filed with the 4th Circuit Court of Appeals, June 19, 2002, 14–15.

49. Emergency Motion for Stay Pending Appeal, May 21, 2002, 7. In its opinion, the district court also ordered that the meeting with Hamdi was to be "private between Hamdi, the attorney, and the interpreter, without military personnel present, and without any listening or recording devices of any kind being employed in any way." Opinion, United States 4th Circuit Court of Appeals, *Yaser Hamdi et al. v. Donald Rumsfeld et al.*, June 26, 2002, 3–4.

50. Emergency Motion for Stay Pending Appeal, May 21, 2002, 14–15.

51. "Brief for Respondents-Appellants," 31.

52. Published opinion, United States 4th Circuit Court of Appeals, *Yaser Hamdi et al. v. Donald Rumsfeld et al.*, July 12, 2002, 7, 9, 11–12.

53. Order Directing Government to Provide More Information, *Yaser Hamdi and Esam Hamdi v. Donald Rumsfeld and Commander Paulette*, in the U.S. District Court for the Eastern District of Virginia Norfolk Division, 7, 14.

54. Majority Opinion, *Jose Padilla v. Donald Rumsfeld* (U.S. Court of Appeals—2nd Circuit—Case Nos. 03-2235, 03-2438), December 18, 2003.

55. *Jose Padilla v. Commander C.T. Hanft, USN* (U.S. Court of Appeals—4th Circuit—Case No. 05-6396).

56. Emergency Motion for Stay Pending Appeal, May 21, 2002, 3 (emphasis added).

57. Ibid.

58. Ibid., 15.

59. "Declaration of Colonel Donald D. Woolfolk," Attachment C, Executed on June 13, 2002, 1–2. See also "Brief for Respondents-Appellants," 37–38.

60. In other filings, the U.S. attorneys representing the military built on their presentation of the Defense Department and its tactics as "humane" by arguing that all enemy combatants were "protected from harm or other reprisals, given medical care and treated humanely and may be visited by the International Committee of the Red Cross" ("Brief for Respondents-Appellants," 21). These claims appear vacuous if not completely fabricated, as reports of torture and coercive conduct at the hands of U.S. military officials were uncovered shortly thereafter. In addition, there was no evidence of Hamdi himself being visited by international observers or receiving any other protections, such as medical care.

61. Theodore B. Olson, "Excerpts from Government's Brief in Hamdi," as quoted in H. L. Pohlman, *Terrorism and the Constitution: The Post-9/11 Cases* (Boulder, CO: Rowman and Littlefield, 2008), 100.

62. Paul Clement in "Excerpts from Oral Argument in Padilla," as quoted in ibid., 116. As if to underscore the absurdity of this position, fewer than twenty-four hours after the U.S. attorney delivered these remarks in front of the Supreme Court, the graphic torture of prisoners in Abu Ghraib at the hands of American soldiers in the 372nd Military Police Company was revealed to the public.

63. In its ruling, the Supreme Court asserted that the president did have authority to

detain citizens captured on a foreign battlefield during the war on terror by virtue of the AUMF. However, it rejected the arguments of the U.S. attorney justifying their incommunicado detention and continued interrogation, stating that the detainees had the right to due process and specifically to challenge their designation as enemy combatants before a neutral decision maker. Moreover, most of the justices resisted the expansion of executive power in their opinions, with a particularly pointed rebuke signed by Justices O'Conner, Rehnquist, Kennedy, and Breyer:

> The position that the courts must forgo any examination of the individual case and focus exclusively on the legality of the broader detention scheme cannot be mandated by any reasonable view of separation of powers, as this approach serves only to condense power into a single branch of government. We have long since made clear that a state of war is not a blank check for the President when it comes to the rights of the Nation's citizens. . . . Any process in which the Executive's factual assertions go wholly unchallenged or are simply presumed correct without any opportunity for the alleged combatant to demonstrate otherwise falls constitutionally short. (*Hamdi v. Rumsfeld*, 542 U.S. 507 [2004])

64. "Settlement Agreement," *Yaser Esam Hamdi v. Donald Rumsfeld*, September 17, 2004.

65. *Padilla v. C. T. Hanft*, District Court of South Carolina, 3; and Amended Petition for Writ of Habeas Corpus, *Padilla v. Bush et al.*, June 19, 2002, 2–3.

66. Pohlman, *Terrorism and the Constitution*, 133.

67. Amended Petition for Writ of Habeas Corpus, *Padilla v. Bush et al.*, June 19, 2002.

68. *Padilla v. Rumsfeld*, August 2003, 4, available at www.fas.org/sgp/jud/padilla1203.pdf.

69. *Padilla v. C. T. Hanft, U.S.N. Commander, Consolidated Naval Brig*, 2005, 12.

70. "Reply Brief for Respondents-Appellants," *Yaser Hamdi et al. v. Donald Rumsfeld et al.*, in the U.S. Court of Appeals for the 4th Circuit, 5.

71. In the "Mobbs Declaration" filed against Padilla, Michael Mobbs asserted, "The Under Secretary of Defense for Policy has directed me to head his Detainee Policy Group. Since mid-February 2002, I have been substantially involved with matters related to the detention of enemy combatants in the current war against the Al Qaeda terrorists and those who support and harbor them" (1). However, no additional details about this "Special Advisor" are ever provided. In short, Mobbs was empowered with a tremendous amount of authority relative to the restrictions on citizenship, but for all intents and purposes, he was a virtual unknown.

72. "Declaration of Michael Mobbs."

73. *Hamdi v. Rumsfeld*, 337 F.3d 335, 357–68 (4th Cir. 2003). The resistance within the federal courts is also demonstrated in the contradictory rulings described earlier and several of the amicus briefs filed in support of Hamdi and Padilla, such as one filed by a group of retired federal judges, including appointments from Republican presidents. Moreover, in subsequent cases not taken up here, the courts resisted the expansion of executive authority by requiring that Guantanamo detainees be given access to counsel and limiting federal power in two sections of the USA PATRIOT Act and in the procedures established for military tribunal. See *Hamdi v. Rumsfeld*, 124 S. Ct. 2633 (2004);

Doe v. Ashcroft, 334 F. Supp. 2d 1 (D.D.C. 2004); *Humanitarian Law Project v. Ashcroft*, 309 F. Supp. 2d 1185 (C.D. Cal. 2004); *Al Odah v. Bush*, 346 F. Supp 2d 1 (D.D.C. 2004).

74. White House, "Memorandum for the Secretary of Defense," November 20, 2005.

75. Jury Verdict Form in Terrorism Support Trial, *U.S. v. Jose Padilla, Adham Amin Hassoun, and Kifah Wael Jayyousi*, August 16, 2007.

76. "Brief for Respondents-Appellants," 20.

CHAPTER 7

1. "*Es difícil poner en perspectiva la euforia que está causando, en Estados Unidos y en el resto del mundo, el inicio de la presidencia de Barack Obama. Dos cosas la explican: una terrible crisis económica mundial y la personalidad de un hombre, muy joven, que nos asegura que el futuro será mejor. . . . La promesa de Barack es casi religiosa*" (translation mine). Jorge Ramos Ávalos, "Mensaje a Obama: No Nos Falles," January 19, 2009, available at www.univision.com.

2. Devin Dwyer, "Immigrant Students Seeking Executive Order Disappointed after White House Meeting," ABC News, June 15, 2010.

3. See Mark Hugo Lopez, *The Hispanic Vote in 2008* (Washington, DC: Pew Hispanic Center, 2008); and Susan Minushkin and Mark Hugo Lopez, *The Hispanic Vote in the 2008 Democratic Presidential Primaries* (Washington, DC: Pew Hispanic Center, 2008). Also see CNN Election 2008, specifically the individual state and national exit polls, available at www.cnn.com/ELECTION/2008/.

4. See Mark Hugo Lopez and Susan Minushkin, *2008 National Survey of Latinos: Hispanics See Their Situation in the U.S. Deteriorating; Oppose Key Immigration Enforcement Measures* (Washington, DC: Pew Hispanic Center, September 2008).

5. For details on the national campaigns spearheaded and funded by several national organizations, principally the National Association of Latino/a Elected Officials (NALEO), the National Council of La Raza (NCLR), the Service Employees International Union (SEIU), and the We Are America Alliance, along with major Latina/o media outlets, including Univision, Entravision, and Impremedia, see Ya Es Hora ¡Ciudadania! "Sobre Ya Es Hora/About Ya Es Hora," 2007, available at www.yaeshora.info/sobre_ya_es_hora.

6. Bruce Finley, "Road to U.S. Citizenship Slow, Crowded, under Construction," Denver Post.com, January 13, 2008.

7. The Obama administration nominated more Latinas/os to senior government positions than any previous White House. Notable among these nominations is the first Latina Supreme Court Justice, Sonia Sotomayor, as well as the first Latinas/os as heads of the Departments of Labor (Hilda Solis) and the Interior (Ken Salazar), and Cecelia Munoz (former president of the National Council of La Raza) as director of the White House Domestic Policy Council. See Barack Obama, "Remarks by the President at Cinco de Mayo Reception," White House, Office of the Press Secretary, May 5, 2010, available at www.whitehouse.gov/the-press-office/remarks-president-cinco-de-mayo-reception.

8. Latinas proved to be a key factor driving President Obama's increased support among Latinas/os. In the years leading up to the election, Latinas outpaced Latinos in rates of naturalization, and in both 2008 and 2012, larger proportions of Latinas voted in the election and supported Obama. Moreover, tracking data from Impremedia/ Latino Decisions polls showed that while Latinas and Latinos strongly favored Obama throughout the campaign, by September 2012, Obama held a 53-point lead over Romney

among Latinas, compared to a 29-point lead with Hispanic men. Owing in part to their preferences for Obama's position on immigration reform, a 13-point gender gap existed between Latinas and Latinos, as compared to a 9-point gender gap among all voters. See Anna Sampaio, "Latinas and Electoral Politics: Expanding Participation and Power in State and National Elections," in *Gender and Elections: Shaping the Future of American Politics*, 3rd ed., ed. Susan J. Carroll and Richard Fox (New York: Cambridge University Press, 2014), 146–167.

9. Barack Obama, "Transcript: Obama's Victory Speech," November 7, 2012, *Political Ticker . . .*, available at http://politicalticker.blogs.cnn.com/2012/11/07/transcript-obamas-victory-speech/.

10. Barack Obama, "Address to the National Council of La Raza," NCLR Annual Conference, San Diego, CA, July 12, 2008.

11. Ken Dilanian, "Tough Enforcement against Illegal Immigrants Is Decried," *Los Angeles Times*, July 12, 2010.

12. Julia Preston, "Obama to Push Immigration Bill as One Priority," *New York Times*, April 9, 2009.

13. In spite of these changes, large-scale detentions and arrests as well as individual prosecutions of nonthreatening Latina/o students, nannies, and caregivers have continued, albeit with fewer deportations of noncriminal immigrants. See "Secretary Seeks Review of Immigration Raid," *New York Times*, February 26, 2009.

14. Spencer S. Hsu, "Little New in Obama's Immigration Policy," *Washington Post*, May 20, 2009.

15. Thomas E. Perez, Assistant Attorney General, U.S. Department of Justice, Civil Rights Division, Letter to Mr. Bill Montgomery, County Attorney, Maricopa County, Re: United States' Investigation of the Maricopa County Sheriff's Office, December 15, 2011.

16. "Homeland Security Cuts Ties with Arizona Sheriff," Associated Press, December 15, 2011.

17. Jacques Billeaud and Amanda Lee Myers, "Arizona Files Appeal as Sheriff Launches New Sweep," *Denver Post*, July 29, 2010.

18. See Department of Homeland Security, "Department Responsibilities: Enforcing Our Immigration Laws," July 14, 2010, available at www.dhs.gov/xabout/gc_1240610592951.shtm.

19. Anna Gorman, "Detained Immigrants Can Now Be Located Online," *Los Angeles Times*, July 24, 2010.

20. The Secure Communities Program uses biometric data to identify "criminal aliens" in local jails, and in May 2009 the administration announced the expansion of the program to enable the sharing of this biometric data across jurisdictions. According to DHS records, since the inception of the Secure Communities Program in 2008, more than 34,900 "criminal aliens" have been identified and 46,929 undocumented immigrants have been deported. Moreover, the department reports that under Operation Community Shield, more than 1,800 gang members have been arrested nationwide, and through the Fugitive Operations Programs, more than 11,000 "alien absconders" have been located. See Department of Homeland Security, "Department Responsibilities"; see also Tim Hoover, "Ritter Weighs Civil Rights v. Enforcement System That Flags Jailed Illegal Immigrants," *Denver Post*, August 1, 2010.

21. See Department of Homeland Security, "Fact Sheet: Southwest Border Next Steps," June 23, 2010, available at www.dhs.gov/ynews/releases/pr_1277310093825.shtm;

and Jim Barnett, "U.S. Deportations Reach Historic Levels," CNN, October 18, 2011, available at www.CNN.com.

22. U.S. Immigration and Customs Enforcement, "FY 2013 ICE Immigration Removals, ERO Annual Report," available at www.ice.gov/doclib/about/offices/ero/pdf/2013-ice-immigration-removals.pdf.

23. U.S. Immigration and Customs Enforcement, "FY 2012 Immigration Removals," available at www.ice.gov/removal-statistics/2012statistics.htm; and Brian Bennett, "Deportations from U.S. Drop for First Time in Obama's Tenure," *Los Angeles Times,* December 19, 2013.

24. U.S. Immigration and Customs Enforcement, "FY 2013 ICE Immigration Removals."

25. Hsu, "Little New in Obama's Immigration Policy."

26. President Obama, as quoted in Devin Dwyer, "President Obama Prods Republicans in Speech on Comprehensive Immigration Reform," ABC News, July 1, 2010, available at http://abcnews.go.com/Politics/obama-renews-push-comprehensive-immigration-reform/story?id=11062758; emphasis added.

27. Barack Obama, "Transcript: Obama's Immigration Speech," *Washington Post,* November 20, 2014, available at www.washingtonpost.com/politics/transcript-obamas-immigration-speech/2014/11/20/14ba8042-7117-11e4-893f-86bd390a3340_story.html.

28. Hsu, "Little New in Obama's Immigration Policy."

29. Department of Homeland Security, "Readout of Secretary Napolitano's Remarks on Border Security and Law Enforcement at the Center for Strategic and International Studies," June 23, 2010, available at www.dhs.gov/ynews/releases/pr_1277311620062.shtm.

30. Barack Obama, "Remarks of President Barack Obama—As Prepared for Delivery, State of the Union Address," White House, Office of the Press Secretary, February 12, 2013.

31. Barack Obama, "Remarks by the President on Comprehensive Immigration Reform, Del Sol High School, Las Vegas, Nevada," White House, Office of the Press Secretary, January 29, 2013.

32. See Department of Homeland Security, "Fact Sheet: Southwest Border Next Steps."

33. Ibid.

34. Ibid.

35. Due to persistent problems with accuracy and verification, it was not mandated by all employers. According to the Social Security Administration, 4.1 percent, or 17.8 million, records submitted to E-Verify contained discrepancies. A 2007 independent study of the program found that "the database used for verification was still not up sufficiently up to date to meet the Illegal Immigration Reform and Immigrant Responsibilities Act requirement of accuracy verification." See Ann Morse, "E-Verify: Frequently Asked Questions," Immigrant Policy Project, National Conference of State Legislatures, February 4, 2010, available at www.ncsl.org/default.aspx?tabid=13127.

36. According to its own records, ICE conducted more than 1,400 I-9 audits of employers suspected of hiring unauthorized workers, more than three times the number of audits conducted the previous year.

37. See Department of Homeland Security, "Fact Sheet: Southwest Border Next Steps."

38. See Department of Homeland Security, "Fact Sheet: Southwest Border Next

Steps"; and Department of Homeland Security, "Readout of Secretary Napolitano's Remarks on Border Security."

39. Hsu, "Little New in Obama's Immigration Policy."

40. See Department of Homeland Security, "Fact Sheet: Southwest Border Next Steps."

41. Ibid.

42. "U.S. Replaces Noisy Immigration Raids at Place of Employment with 'Silent Audits,'" *Business of Homeland Security,* July 12, 2010.

43. While most raids taking place after 2009 were far less public, incidences of large-scale raids still existed, albeit with far less consensus across enforcement arms. Thus, for example, in February 2009, ICE agents conducted a raid at Yamato Engine Specialists, a car-refurbishing plant in Washington State. Twenty-eight immigrants were arrested as a result of the raid. Shortly after the action, Secretary Napolitano ordered an investigation into the raid and other ICE plans. In Arizona, despite having been stripped of the power to conduct immigration sweeps and make federal arrests, as of 2012, Sheriff Joe Arpaio had continued to target Latina/o immigrants in sweeps— utilizing the authority of state law as opposed to federal statutes. See "Secretary Seeks Review of Immigration Raid"; and Billeaud and Myers, "Arizona Files Appeal as Sheriff Launches New Sweep."

44. "U.S. Replaces Noisy Immigration Raids at Place of Employment with 'Silent Audits.'"

45. In Minnesota, unofficial estimates indicate that as many as 700 of its 1,200-member workforce were fired for lack of proper work authorization. Lisa Baertlein, Mary Milliken, and Ed Stoddard, "U.S. Fast Food Caught in Immigration Crosshairs," Reuters, February 7, 2011, available at www.reuters.com/article/2011/02/07/us-usa-immigration-fastfood-idUSTRE71664T20110207.

46. Sasha Aslanian, "1,200 Janitors Fired in 'Quiet' Immigration Raid," Minnesota Public Radio, November 9, 2009, available at http://minnesota.publicradio.org/display/web/2009/11/09/immigrants-fired/.

47. Perez, Letter to Mr. Bill Montgomery.

48. "U.S. Replaces Noisy Immigration Raids at Place of Employment with 'Silent Audits.'"

49. Jason Ryan, Matthew Jaffe, and Devin Dwyer, "Obama 'Scheming' on Immigrant Amnesty? Memo Draws Republican Fire," ABC News, July 30, 2010. See also Julia Preston, "Students Spared amid an Increase in Deportations," *New York Times,* August 8, 2010.

50. John Morton, "Exercising Prosecutorial Discretion Consistent with the Civil Immigration Enforcement Priorities of the Agency for the Apprehension, Detention, and Removal of Aliens," Memorandum for All Field Office Directors, All Special Agents in Charge, All Chief Counsel, Immigration and Customs Enforcement, Department of Homeland Security, Policy Number: 10075.1, June 17, 2011, available at www.ice.gov/doclib/secure-communities/pdf/prosecutorial-discretion-memo.pdf.

51. Ibid.

52. CNN Wire, "Administration Begins to Pare Down Immigration Cases," *In America,* November 17, 2011, available at http://inamerica.blogs.cnn.com/2011/11/17/administration-begins-discretionary-review-of-immigration-cases/.

53. Julianne Hing, "ICE Announces Minor Deportation Policy Shift for Secure Communities," *COLORLINES News for Action,* May 3, 2012.

54. Julia Preston and John H. Cushman, "Obama to Permit Young Migrants to Remain in the U.S.," *New York Times,* June 15, 2012.

55. John Sandweg, "Facilitating Parental Interests in the Course of Civil Immigration Enforcement Activities," Department of Homeland Security, Policy Number: 11064.1, August, 23 2013, available at www.ice.gov/doclib/detention-reform/pdf/parental_interest_directive_signed.pdf.

56. Elizabeth Llorente, "New Obama Directive Aims to Stop Detention of Undocumented Parents with Minor Children," Fox News Latino, August 26, 2013, available at http://latino.foxnews.com/latino/politics/2013/08/26/new-obama-directive-urges-discretion-for-undocumented-parents-minors/.

57. U.S. Citizenship and Immigration Services, "Executive Actions on Immigration," November 21, 2014, available at www.uscis.gov/immigrationaction.

58. Ibid.

59. Arizona has long been a focal point in immigration politics, having regularly introduced and passed state statutes restricting immigrants (documented and undocumented) and passing citizen-sponsored initiatives for the same purpose. Arizona is also a center of nativist activity, such as the Minutemen Project, and Maricopa County Sheriff Joe Arpaio has become infamous in the past decade for his hard line against Latinas/os and immigrants. See Gebe Martinez, "Hot Spot for Illegal Immigration," *Politico,* April 17, 2008.

60. Senate Bill 1070, State of Arizona, Senate, Forty-Ninth Legislature, Second Regular Session, 2010, available at www.azleg.gov/DocumentsForBill.asp?Bill_Number=1070. See also House Bill 2162, State of Arizona, House of Representatives, Forty-ninth Legislature, Second Regular Session, 2010, available at www.azleg.gov/DocumentsForBill .asp?Bill_Number=2162; and Ann Morse, "Arizona's Immigration Enforcement Laws: An Overview of SB 1070 and HB 2162," National Conference of State Legislatures, July 7, 2010, available at www.ncsl.org/?tabid=20263.

61. Russell Pearce, "Arizona or San Francisco: Which Path on Immigration?" *Human Events* 66, no. 18 (2010): 1–10.

62. Nathan Thornburgh, "The Battle for Arizona," *Time* 175, no. 23 (2010): 38–43.

63. Senator Melvin, Testimony Regarding Senate Bill 1070, Arizona State Senate, Forty-Ninth Legislature, Second Regular Session, Final Reading, April 19, 2010, available at http://azleg.granicus.com/MediaPlayer.php?view_id=13&clip_id=7519.

64. See, for example, Senator Gould, Testimony Regarding Senate Bill 1070, Arizona State Senate, Forty-Ninth Legislature, Second Regular Session, Final Reading, April 19, 2010, available at http://azleg.granicus.com/MediaPlayer.php?view_id=13&clip_id=7519.

65. While the language of homeland security and terrorism was largely absent from the debates in Arizona and other states, it did not disappear altogether. Comments from those on the far right still invoked similar themes. In the floor debate on SB 1070, Senator Russell Pearce provided the following equation:

Did you know, had law enforcement enforced immigration laws we would have averted 9/11? The terrorist attacks on September 11, 2001, underscored for all Americans the link between immigration law, enforcement, and terrorism. Four of the five leaders of the 9/11 attack were in violation of immigration laws, and had contact with law enforcement prior to that. (Pearce, Testimony Regarding Senate Bill 1070)

Similarly, J. D. Hayworth, who battled Republican Senator John McCain in a fierce primary election, argued for the removal of all unauthorized immigrants, suggesting that failure to do so could lead to another 9/11-style attack (see Thornburg, "The Battle for Arizona"). Both played to the same dynamics documented in earlier chapters in the book; however, both were regarded as extreme elements, even among their own party. Thus, while the language of terrorism may still exist, it no longer reflects the dominant discourse on immigration.

66. CNN Wire Staff, "Arizona's Brewer: Most Illegal Immigrants Are 'Drug Mules,'" CNN, June 27, 2010, available at www.cnn.com/2010/US/06/25/arizona.immigrants .drugs/.

67. By 2014, the discourse on Latina/o immigrants had shifted notably at both the federal and state levels. In particular, while the Obama administration elevated and emphasized its security discourse, extending the use of masculinist logic to ground its immigrant agenda, it decoupled these efforts from the racialization of immigrants as terrorist threats. Increasingly, the language of securitization focused on the need to protect against drug smugglers and the escalation of violent drug cartels and away from conflations of individual border crossers as potential terrorist threats. In this context, racialization of immigrants continued, albeit with different outcomes. In some instances, as with many of the legislation and policy changes proffered by the White House, immigrants were described as victims of nativism, border violence, and economic instability in their home countries. Among opponents of immigration reform, immigrants were commonly depicted as threatening foreign criminals. In both instances, the process of equating immigrants with terrorism abated; however, this provided little comfort given the continued targeting of immigrants in new policies outlined above and in restrictive state legislation.

68. Tim Gaynor, "Migrants Sell Up and Flee Arizona Ahead of Crackdown," Yahoo-News.com, July 25, 2010.

69. See Mae M. Ngai, "Birthright Citizenship and the Alien Citizen," *Fordham Law Review* 75, no. 5 (2007): 2521–2530, available at http://ir.lawnet.fordham.edu/flr/vol75/ iss5/10; and Priscilla Huang, "Anchor Babies, Over-breeders and the Population Bomb: The Reemergence of Nativism and Population Control in Anti-immigration Policies," *Harvard Law and Policy Review* 2 (2008): 385–406.

70. Samuel P. Huntington, "The Hispanic Challenge," *Foreign Policy,* October 28, 2009, available at www.foreignpolicy.com/articles/2004/03/01/the_hispanic_challenge. See also Samuel P. Huntington, *Who Are We? The Challenges to America's National Identity* (New York: Simon and Schuster, 2004).

71. Shankar Vedantam, "Several States Want Court Ruling on Birthright Citizenship," *Washington Post,* January 6, 2011.

72. Bob Dane, "Dictionary's 'Anchor Baby' Decision Is Definition of Foolish," FoxNews.com, December 9, 2011, available at www.foxnews.com/opinion/2011/12/09/ dictionarys-anchor-baby-decision-is-definition-foolish/.

73. Adam Liptak, "Blocking Parts of Arizona Law, Justices Allow Its Centerpiece," *New York Times,* June 25, 2012; and *Arizona et al. v. United States,* Supreme Court Opinion, October Term 2011, No. 11-182, June 25, 2012. The Supreme Court's ruling in the challenge to SB 1070 differed from a ruling it issued on May 26, 2011, upholding the 2007 Legal Arizona Workers Act, thus allowing the state to suspend the licenses of businesses that "intentionally or knowingly" violated work-eligibility requirements. The law, which required businesses in Arizona to use the federal database E-Verify to check the

documentation of current and prospective employees, reflected the same expansion of state authority on immigration matters as was present in SB 1070. Moreover, in recommending judicial review of the law, the Obama administration sided politically with the U.S. Chamber of Commerce and a variety of civil rights and immigrants' rights organizations in their challenge to Arizona. See Bill Mears, "High Court Backs Arizona Immigration Law That Punishes Businesses," CNN, May 26, 2011, available at www.cnn.com/2011/US/05/26/scotus.arizona.law/index.html.

74. Before the Supreme Court's decision, the Arizona law had already been curtailed when U.S. District Court Judge Susan Bolton issued a preliminary injunction in July 2010 blocking four provisions, including the most controversial section upheld by the Supreme Court. In April 2011, the 9th Circuit Court of Appeals upheld the injunction, upon which the state of Arizona petitioned the Supreme Court to hear the case, while the Obama administration encouraged the justices to reject the appeal. James Vicini, "U.S Supreme Court to Decide Arizona Immigration Law," Reuters, December 12, 2011; and Jacques Billeaud and Paul Davenport, "Judge Hears Arguments on Arizona Immigration Law," Associated Press, July 22, 2010, available at www.news.findlaw.com/ap/other/1110/07-22-2010/20100722033504_01.html.

75. The proliferation of state-level activity on immigration legislation even spawned efforts among lower-level city councils, county supervisors, townships, and municipal governments to enact immigration restriction. For example, Freemont, Nebraska, and Riverside, New Jersey, passed ordinances barring unauthorized immigrants from renting property in those cities, while the county supervisors of Prince William County, Virginia, authorized local law enforcement to stop and arrest persons if they had reasonable suspicion they were in the country without proper authorization. Immigration Policy Center, *A Question and Answer Guide to State Immigration Laws: What You Need to Know If Your State Is Considering Anti-immigrant Legislation* (Washington, DC: American Immigration Council, 2012), 14.

76. Morse, "Arizona's Immigration Enforcement Laws."

77. Immigration Policy Center, *A Question and Answer Guide to State Immigration Laws*, 4.

78. Ibid.

79. Ibid.

80. Paloma Esquivel, "Judge Permanently Bars Provisions of Indiana Immigration Law," *Los Angeles Times*, March 30, 2013; and Daniel C. Vock, "With Little Choice, Alabama Backs Down on Immigration Law," *Stateline*, Pew Charitable Trusts, October 30, 2013, available at www.pewstates.org. Among the states replicating SB 1070, Georgia went the furthest with passage of HB 87, the "Illegal Immigration Reform and Enforcement Act of 2011." HB 87 authorized police to demand "papers" demonstrating citizenship or immigration status during traffic stops, criminalized knowingly transporting or harboring an unauthorized immigrant during the course of another crime, and restricted undocumented immigrant access to state facilities and services. While a district court permanently blocked the provisions for harboring or transporting an undocumented immigrant, it let stand the more controversial aspects that allowed local police to ask about the immigration status of certain suspects and to detain them if there was evidence they were unauthorized. See Kimberly Bennett, "Federal Judge Dismisses Georgia Immigration Law Challenge," Jurist, July 21, 2013, available at www.jurist.org.

81. Kimberly Hefling, "More States Grant In-state Tuition to Immigrants," Associated Press, February 2, 2014.

82. Cindy Carcamo, "States Back Off from Enacting Immigration Laws," *Los Angeles Times*, October 12, 2013.

83. Elise Foley and Roque Planas, "Trust Act Signed in California to Limit Deportation Program," *Huffington Post*, October 5, 2013, available at www.huffingtonpost.com/2013/10/05/trust-act-signed_n_4050168.html.

84. Morse, "Arizona's Immigration Enforcement Laws."

85. David Waldenstein, "Arizona Immigration Law Criticized by Mets' Barajas," *New York Times*, May 2, 2010. See also Gene Cherry, "Players Voice Opposition to Arizona Immigration Law," Reuters, July 13, 2010, available at www.reuters.com/article/2010/07/13/idINIndia-50099220100713.

86. CNN Wire Staff, "10 Nations Join Mexican Opposition to Arizona Law, Politician Says," CNN, July 21, 2010, available at www.cnn.com/2010/WORLD/americas/07/21/mexico.arizona.immigration.law/.

87. Specifically, Latinas/os from Mexico, Central and South America, and the Caribbean constitute approximately 46 percent of the total foreign-born population in the United States. Seth Motel and Eileen Patten, *Statistical Portrait of the Foreign-Born Population in the United States, 2011*, Table 5, Pew Research Hispanic Trends Project, January 29, 2013.

88. Under the Obama administration, more than 2 million immigrants have been deported. Barnett, "U.S. Deportations Reach Historic Levels."

Bibliography

Acosta, Teresa Palomo. "In Re Ricardo Rodriguez." In *Handbook of Texas Online*. Texas State Historical Association. June 15, 2010. Available at www.tshaonline.org/hand book/online/articles/pqitw.

Acuña, Rodolfo. *Occupied America: A History of Chicanos*. 3rd ed. New York: Harper-Collins, 1987.

Adams, Chris. "INS to Put in Federal Criminal Databases the Names of People Ordered Deported." *Wall Street Journal*. December 6, 2001.

American Civil Liberties Union. "Documents Obtained by ACLU Show Sexual Abuse of Immigration Detainees Is Widespread National Problem." ACLU.org. October 19, 2011.Available at www.aclu.org/immigrants-rights-prisoners-rights-prisoners-rights/documents-obtained-aclu-show-sexual-abuse.

———. "Sexual Abuse in Immigration Detention—Raquel's Story." ACLU.org. October 16, 2011. Available at www.aclu.org/immigrants-rights/sexual-abuse-immigration-detention-raquels-story.

Anthias, Floya, and Nira Yuval-Davis. "Contextualising Feminism: Gender, Ethnic and Class Divisions." *Feminist Review* 15 (November 1983): 62–75.

———. *Racialized Boundaries: Race, Nation, Gender, Colour and Class and the Anti-racist Struggle*. London: Routledge, 1992.

Anzaldúa, Gloria. *Borderlands/La Frontera: The New Mestiza*. San Francisco: Spinsters/Aunt Lute Press, 1987.

Ashcroft, John. "John Walker Lindh Press Conference." Department of Justice Conference Center. January 15, 2002.

Aslanian, Sasha. "1,200 Janitors Fired in 'Quiet' Immigration Raid." Minnesota Public Radio. November 9, 2009. Available at http://minnesota.publicradio.org/display/web/2009/11/09/immigrants-fired/.

Ávalos, Jorge Ramos. "Mensaje a Obama: No Nos Falles." January 19, 2009. Available at www.univision.com.

Baertlein, Lisa, Mary Milliken, and Ed Stoddard. "U.S. Fast Food Caught in Immigration Crosshairs." Reuters. February 7, 2011. Available at www.reuters.com/arti cle/2011/02/07/us-usa-immigration-fastfood-idUSTRE71664T20110207.

Balderrama, Francisco, and Raymond Rodriguez. *Decade of Betrayal: Mexican Repatriation in the 1930s.* Albuquerque: University of New Mexico Press, 1995.

Barnett, Jim. "U.S. Deportations Reach Historic Levels." CNN. October 18, 2011. Available at www.CNN.com.

Bennett, Brian. "Deportations from U.S. Drop for First Time in Obama's Tenure." *Los Angeles Times.* December 19, 2013.

Bennett, Kimberly. "Federal Judge Dismisses Georgia Immigration Law Challenge." Jurist. July 21, 2013. Available at www.jurist.org.

Bernstein, Nina. "Immigrant Workers Caught in Net Cast for Gangs." *New York Times.* November 25, 2007.

Billeaud, Jacques, and Paul Davenport. "Judge Hears Arguments on Arizona Immigration Law." Associated Press. July 22, 2010. Available at www.news.findlaw.com/ap/ other/1110/07-22-2010/20100722033504_01.html.

Billeaud, Jacques, and Amanda Lee Myers. "Arizona Files Appeal as Sheriff Launches New Sweep." *Denver Post.* July 29, 2010.

Blea, Irene. *La Chicana and the Intersection of Race, Class, and Gender.* New York: Praeger, 1992.

Blumner, Robyn E. "Ashcroft's Power to Detain without Charges Continues without Oversight." *St. Petersburg Times.* May 5, 2002.

Bodnar, John. *The Transplanted: A History of Immigrants in Urban America.* Bloomington: Indiana University Press, 1985.

Bogden, Daniel G. *Joint Law Enforcement Investigation Promotes Airport Security: Workers at Reno-Tahoe Airport Face Federal Charges.* U.S. Attorney, District of Nevada, U.S. Department of Justice. February 2002. Available at www.usdoj.gov/usao/nv/ home/pressrelease/february2002/tarmac222.htm.

Borjas, George. *Heaven's Door: Immigration Policy and the American Economy.* Princeton, NJ: Princeton University Press, 2001.

———, ed. *Mexican Immigration to the U.S.* Chicago: University of Chicago Press, 2007.

Bridis, Ted. "US Lifts FBI Criminal Database Checks." Associated Press. March 25, 2002.

Brotherton, David C., and Philip Kretsedemas, eds. *Keeping Out the Other: A Critical Introduction to Immigration Enforcement Today.* New York: Columbia University Press, 2008.

Bush, Laura. "The Taliban's War against Women." Radio Address to the Nation, Crawford, Texas. November 17, 2001. Available at www.state.gov/g/drl/rls/rm/2001/6206 .htm.

Butler, Judith. *Gender Trouble: Feminism and the Subversion of Identity.* New York: Routledge, 1990.

Caban, Pedro A. *Constructing a Colonial People: Puerto Rico and the United States, 1898–1932.* Boulder, CO: Westview Press, 2009.

Cabranes, Jose. *Citizenship and the American Empire.* New Haven, CT: Yale University Press, 1979.

Capps, Randy, Rosa Maria Castaneda, Ajay Chaudry, and Robert Santos. *Paying the Price: The Impact of Immigration Raids on America's Children.* Washington, DC: Urban Institute, 2007.

Carby, Hazel. "A Stranger and Bitter Crop: The Spectacle of Torture." *openDemocracy.*

October 10, 2004. Available at www.opendemocracy.net/media-abu_ghraib/arti cle_2149.jsp.

Carcamo, Cindy. "States Back Off from Enacting Immigration Laws." *Los Angeles Times.* October 12, 2013.

Chan, Sucheng. *Asian Americans: An Interpretive History.* Boston: Twayne, 1991.

Chang, Nancy. *Silencing Political Dissent: How Post–September 11 Anti-terrorism Measures Threaten Our Civil Liberties.* Washington, DC: Center for Constitutional Rights, 2002.

Charlip, Julie. "Sanger Sweep Stirs Questions on Civil Rights Violations." *Fresno Bee.* October 14, 1984.

Chavez, Leo. *The Latino Threat: Constructing Immigrants, Citizens, and the Nation.* Stanford, CA: Stanford University Press, 2008.

Cheney, Richard. "Interview of the Vice President by CBS's *60 Minutes II.*" The White House. November 14, 2001. Available at www.whitehouse.gov/vicepresident/news-speeches/speeches/vp20011114.html.

Cherry, Gene. "Players Voice Opposition to Arizona Immigration Law." Reuters. July 13, 2010. Available at www.reuters.com/article/2010/07/13/idININdia-50099220100713.

Cloherty, Jack, and Jason Ryan. "FBI Spied on PETA, Greenpeace, Anti-war Activists." ABC News. September 20, 2010. Available at http://abcnews.go.com/News/Blotter/fbi-spied-peta-greenpeace-anti-war-activists/story?id=11682844.

CNN Wire. "Administration Begins to Pare Down Immigration Cases." *In America.* November 17, 2011. Available at http://inamerica.blogs.cnn.com/2011/11/17/admin istration-begins-discretionary-review-of-immigration-cases/.

CNN Wire Staff. "Arizona's Brewer: Most Illegal Immigrants Are 'Drug Mules.'" CNN. June 27, 2010. Available at www.cnn.com/2010/US/06/25/arizona.immigrants .drugs/.

———. "10 Nations Join Mexican Opposition to Arizona Law, Politician Says." CNN. July 21, 2010. Available at www.cnn.com/2010/WORLD/americas/07/21/mexico.arizona .immigration.law/.

Cole, David. *Enemy Aliens: Double Standards and Constitutional Freedoms in the War on Terrorism.* New York: New Press, 2003.

Collins, Patricia Hill. *Black Feminist Thought: Knowledge, Empowerment, and Consciousness.* New York: Routledge, 2000.

Cordes, Nancy. "New Airport Screening Bares All." *CBS Evening News.* May 23, 2009. Available at www.cbsnews.com/stories/2009/05/23/eveningnews/main5036146 .shtml.

Córdova, Teresa, Norma Cantú, Gilberto Cárdenas, Juan García, and Christine Sierra, eds. *Chicana Voices: Intersections of Class, Race, and Gender.* Austin: University of Texas, Austin, Center for Mexican American Studies Publications, 1986.

Crenshaw, Kimberlé. "Mapping the Margins: Intersectionality, Identity Politics, and Violence against Women of Color." *Stanford Law Review* 43, no. 6 (1991): 1241–1299.

Crenshaw, Kimberlé, Neil Gotanda, Gary Peller, and Kendall Thomas, eds. *Critical Race Theory: The Key Writings That Formed the Movement.* New York: New Press, 1995.

Dane, Bob. "Dictionary's 'Anchor Baby' Decision Is Definition of Foolish." FoxNews. com. December 9, 2011. Available at www.foxnews.com/opinion/2011/12/09/dic tionarys-anchor-baby-decision-is-definition-foolish/.

Daniels, Roger. *Coming to America: A History of Immigration and Ethnicity in American Life.* 2nd ed. New York: Harper Perennial, 2002.

———. *Guarding the Golden Door: American Immigration Policy and Immigrants since 1882*.New York: Hill and Wang, 2004.

———. *Prisoners without Trial: Japanese Americans in World War II*. New York: Hill and Wang, 1993.

Daniels, Rogers, and Otis L. Graham. *Debating American Immigration, 1882–Present*. Lanham, MD: Rowman and Littlefield, 2001.

Davico, Ana. "Protesters Disrupt Owens Luncheon[;] Three Supporters of Mexican Civil Rights Placed Under Arrest." *Rocky Mountain News*. September 17, 1999.

"Declaration of Michael Mobbs." Special Advisor to the Undersecretary of Defense for Policy. Unclassified Memo. August 27, 2002. Available at http://news.findlaw.com/hdocs/docs/padilla/padillabush82702mobbs.pdf.

De Genova, Nicholas. "The Deportation Regime: Sovereignty, Space, and the Freedom of Movement." In *The Deportation Regime*, edited by Nicholas de Genova and Nathalie Peutz, 33–62. Durham, NC: Duke University Press, 2010.

De León, Arnoldo. *In Re Ricardo Rodríguez: An Attempt at Chicano Disenfranchisement in San Antonio, 1896–1897*. San Antonio, TX: Caravel Press, 1979.

Delgado, Richard, and Jean Stefanic. *Critical Race Theory: An Introduction*. 2nd ed. New York: New York University Press, 2011.

Department of Homeland Security. "Department Responsibilities: Enforcing Our Immigration Laws." July 14, 2010. Available at www.dhs.gov/xabout/gc_1240610592951.shtm.

———."Fact Sheet: Section 287 (g) Immigration and Nationality Act." August 16, 2006.

———."Fact Sheet: Secure Border Initiative." November 2, 2005. Available at www.dhs.gov/xnews/releases/press_release_0794.shtm.

———. "Fact Sheet: Southwest Border Next Steps." June 23, 2010. Available at www.dhs.gov/ynews/releases/pr_1277310093825.shtm.

———. "Readout of Secretary Napolitano's Remarks on Border Security and Law Enforcement at the Center for Strategic and International Studies." June 23, 2010. Available at www.dhs.gov/ynews/releases/pr_1277311620062.shtm.

———. "Remarks by Secretary of Homeland Security Michael Chertoff, Immigration and Customs Enforcement Assistant Secretary Julie Myers, and Federal Trade Commission Chairman Deborah Platt Majoras at a Press Conference on Operation Wagon Train." December 13, 2006. Available at www.dhs.gov/xnews/releases/pr_1166047951514.shtm.

Dhamoon, Rita. 2009. *Identity/Difference Politics: How Difference Is Produced, and Why It Matters*. Vancouver, BC: University of British Columbia Press, 2009.

Dilanian, Ken. "Tough Enforcement against Illegal Immigrants Is Decried." *Los Angeles Times*. July 12, 2010.

"Dozens Use Fake IDs to Work at Chicago Airport." Agence France Presse. November 8, 2007.

Dreby, Joanna. *How Today's Immigration Enforcement Policies Impact Children, Families, and Communities: A View from the Ground*. Center for American Progress. August 2012.

Dwyer, Devin. "Immigrant Students Seeking Executive Order Disappointed after White House Meeting." ABC News. June 15, 2010.

———. "President Obama Prods Republicans in Speech on Comprehensive Immigration Reform." ABC News. July 1, 2010. Available at http://abcnews.go.com/Politics/obama-renews-push-comprehensive-immigration-reform/story?id=11062758.

Ellermann, Antje. *States against Immigrants: Deportation in Germany and the United States*. New York: Cambridge University Press, 2009.

Elshtain, Jean Bethke. *Women and War*. Chicago: University of Chicago Press, 1987.

Emirbayer, Mustafa, and Anne Mische. "What Is Agency?" *American Journal of Sociology* 103, no. 4 (1998): 962–1023.

Esquivel, Paloma. "Judge Permanently Bars Provisions of Indiana Immigration Law." *Los Angeles Times*. March 30, 2013.

Finley, Bruce. "Migrant Cases Burden System." Denver Post.com. October 2, 2006.

———. "Road to U.S. Citizenship Slow, Crowded, under Construction." Denver Post. com. January 13, 2008.

Flanders, Laura. "Beyond the Burqa: The Rights Women Need in Afghanistan Are Basic Human Rights." Common Dreams. December 13, 2001. Available at www.common dreams.org/cgi-bin/print.cgi?file=/views01/1214-03.htm.

Foley, Elise, and Roque Planas. "Trust Act Signed in California to Limit Deportation Program." *Huffington Post*. October 5, 2013. Available at www.huffingtonpost .com/2013/10/05/trust-act-signed_n_4050168.html.

Foucault, Michel. *Discipline and Punish: The Birth of the Prison*. New York: Vintage, 1979.

———. "Governmentality." In *The Foucault Effect: Studies in Governmentality*, edited by Graham Burchell, Colin Gordon, and Peter Miller, 87–104. Chicago: University of Chicago Press, 1991.

Fuller, Janet Rausa, and Robert C. Herguth, "Feds Charge 25 in Airport Probe." *Chicago Sun-Times*, News Special Edition. December 11, 2002.

Galarza, Ernesto. *Strangers in Our Fields*. Washington, DC: Report of the Fund for the Republic, 1956.

Garcia, Alma. *The Mexican Americans*. Westport, CT: Greenwood Press, 2002.

Garcia, Arnoldo. *When Collaboration Is a Dirty Word*. Oakland, CA: National Network for Immigrant and Refugee Rights, 2003.

Garcia, Michelle. "N.Y. Using Terrorism Law to Prosecute Street Gang: Critics Say Post 9/11 Legislation Is Being Applied Too Broadly." *Washington Post*. February 1, 2005.

Garcia Bedolla, Lisa. *Latino Politics*. Cambridge, UK: Polity Press, 2009.

Garcia y Griego, Manuel. 1983. "The Importation of Mexican Contract Laborers to the United States, 1942–1964." In *The Border That Joins: Mexican Migrants and U.S. Responsibility*, edited by Peter G. Brown and Henry Shue, 49–98. Totowa, NJ: Rowman and Littlefield, 1983.

Gaynor, Tim. "Migrants Sell Up and Flee Arizona Ahead of Crackdown." YahooNews. com. July 25, 2010.

Gilroy, Paul. *Postcolonial Melancholia*. New York: Columbia University Press, 2006.

Givens, Terri E., Gary P. Freeman, and David L. Leal, eds. *Immigration Policy and Security: U.S., European, and Commonwealth Perspectives*. New York: Routledge, 2009.

Golash-Boza, Tanya Maria. *Immigration Nation: Raids, Detentions, and Deportations in Post-9/11 America*. Boulder, CO: Paradigm Press, 2011.

Gonzales, Alfonso. *Reform without Justice: Latino Migrant Politics and the Homeland Security State*. New York: Oxford University Press, 2013.

Gorman, Anna. "Detained Immigrants Can Now be Located Online." *Los Angeles Times*. July 24, 2010.

Government Accountability Office. *Immigration Enforcement: Better Controls Needed over Program Authorizing State and Local Enforcement of Federal Immigration Laws*. GAO-09-109. Washington, DC. January 2009.

Greenwald, Glenn. "NSA Collecting Phone Records of Millions of Verizon Customers Daily." *The Guardian*. June 5, 2013. Available at www.theguardian.com/world/2013/jun/06/nsa-phone-records-verizon-court-order.

Guerin-Gonzales, Camile. *Mexican Workers and American Dreams: Immigration, Repatriation, and California Farm Labor, 1900–1939*.New Brunswick, NJ: Rutgers University Press, 1994.

Gutiérrez, David Gregory, ed. *Between Two Worlds: Mexican Immigrants in the United States*. Wilmington, DE: Scholarly Resources, 1996.

———. *Walls and Mirrors: Mexican Americans, Mexican Immigrants, and the Politics of Ethnicity*. Berkeley: University of California Press, 1995.

Hancock, Ange-Marie. *The Politics of Disgust: The Public Identity of the Welfare Queen*. New York: New York University Press, 2004.

———. "When Multiplication Doesn't Equal Quick Addition: Examining Intersectionality as a Research Paradigm." *Perspectives on Politics* 5, no. 1 (2007): 63–79.

Handlin, Oscar. *The Uprooted: The Epic Story of the Great Migrations That Made the American People*. 2nd ed. Boston: Little, Brown, 1973.

Harding, Sandra. *The Science Question in Feminism*. New York: Cornell University Press, 1986.

———. *Whose Science? Whose Knowledge: Thinking from Women's Lives*. New York: Cornell University Press, 1991.

Harvey, Neil. *The Chiapas Rebellion: The Struggle for Land and Democracy*. Durham, NC: Duke University Press, 1998.

Hawkesworth, Mary. "Congressional Enactments of Race-Gender: Toward a Theory of Raced-Gendered Institutions." *American Political Science Review* 97, no. 4 (2003): 529–550.

———. *Feminist Inquiry: From Political Conviction to Methodological Innovation*. New Brunswick, NJ: Rutgers University Press, 2006.

Hedges, Michael. "Hundreds of Airport Workers Picked Up in Crackdown." *Houston Chronicle*, Section A. April 24, 2002.

Hefling, Kimberly. 2014. "More States Grant In-state Tuition to Immigrants." Associated Press. February 2, 2014.

Hersh, Seymour M. "Annals of National Security: Torture at Abu Ghraib." *New Yorker*. May 10, 2004.

Higham, John. *Strangers in the Land, Patterns of American Nativism (1860–1925)*. New Brunswick, NJ: Rutgers University Press, 1963.

Hing, Bill Ong. *Defining America through Immigration Policy*. Philadelphia: Temple University Press, 2004.

Hing, Julianne. "ICE Announces Minor Deportation Policy Shift for Secure Communities." *COLORLINES News for Action*. May 3, 2012.

"Homeland Security Cuts Ties with Arizona Sheriff." Associated Press. December 15, 2011.

Honig, Bonnie. *Democracy and the Foreigner*. Princeton, NJ: Princeton University Press, 2003.

Hoover, Tim. "Ritter Weighs Civil Rights v. Enforcement System That Flags Jailed Illegal Immigrants." *Denver Post*. August 1, 2010.

Hsu, Spencer S. "Immigration Raid Jars a Small Town." *Washington Post*. May 18, 2008. Available at www.washingtonpost.com/wp-dyn/content/article/2008/05/17/AR2008051702474.html.

———. "Little New in Obama's Immigration Policy." *Washington Post.* May 20, 2009.

Huang, Priscilla. "Anchor Babies, Over-breeders and the Population Bomb: The Reemergence of Nativism and Population Control in Anti-immigration Policies." *Harvard Law and Policy Review* 2 (2008): 385–406.

Hunt, Krista, and Kim Rygiel, eds. "(En)gendered War Stories and Camouflaged Politics." In *(En)gendering the War on Terror: War Stories and Camouflaged Politics,* 1–26. Burlington, VT: Ashgate, 2006.

Huntington, Samuel P. "The Hispanic Challenge." *Foreign Policy.* October 28, 2009. Available at http://foreignpolicy.com/2009/10/28/the-hispanic-challenge/.

———. *Who Are We? The Challenges to America's National Identity.* New York: Simon and Schuster, 2004.

Huysmans, Jef. *The Politics of Insecurity: Fear, Migration, and Asylum in the EU.* London: Routledge, 2006.

"ICE Arrests 60 Illegals Working in Sensitive Areas." *Washington Times.* May 21, 2005.

"ID Thieves Targeted in Immigration Raids: Feds Raid Swift Meat-Packing Plants at Six Locations across Country." Associated Press. December 12, 2006. Available at www.msnbc.msn.com/id/16169899/.

"Illegal Immigrants Nabbed in California Raid." Associated Press. September 22, 2004.

Immigration and Human Rights Policy Clinic. *The Policies and Politics of Local Immigration Enforcement Laws: 287(g) Program in North Carolina.* Chapel Hill: University of North Carolina, February 2009.

Immigration Policy Center. *A Question and Answer Guide to State Immigration Laws: What You Need to Know If Your State Is Considering Anti-immigrant Legislation.* Washington, DC: American Immigration Council, 2012.

Inda, Jonathan Xavier. *Targeting Immigrants: Government, Technology and Ethics.* Oxford, UK: Blackwell, 2006.

Ingold, John. "Police Locate More 'Spy Files' in Search Connected with Suit[;] Chief Unhappy They Weren't Found Earlier." *Denver Post.* September 17, 2002.

———. "Webb Orders Spy-File Review Police Misinterpreted Policy, Mayor Says." *Denver Post.* March 14, 2002.

Irons, Peter. *Justice at War: The Story of the Japanese-American Internment Cases.* Berkeley: University of California Press, 1993.

Johnson, Kevin. *The "Huddled Masses" Myth: Immigration and Civil Rights.* Philadelphia: Temple University Press, 2003.

"Jones Reacts to Arrest of Illegal Aliens Working at Seymour Johnson Air Force Base." Congressional Press Releases. July 7, 2005.

Kandel, William. "Immigration Provisions of the Violence Against Women Act (VAWA)." Congressional Research Services. May 15, 2012. Available at www.fas.org/sgp/crs/misc/R42477.pdf.

Kanstroom, Dan. *Deportation Nation: Outsiders in American History.* Cambridge, MA: Harvard University Press, 2007.

Kohi, Aarti, Peter Markowitz, and Lisa Chavez. *Secure Communities by the Numbers: An Analysis of Demographics and Due Process. A Report from the Chief Earl Warren Institute on Law and Social Policy.* October 2011. Available at http://www.law.berkeley.edu/files/Secure_Communities_by_the_Numbers.pdf.

Leinwand, Donna. "Immigration Raid Linked to ID Theft, Chertoff Says." *USA Today.* December 13, 2006. Available at www.usatoday.com/news/nation/2006-12-13-immigration_x.htm.

Lima, Roberto, and Bassina Farbenblum. "Freedom of Information Act Request/Expedited Processing Request." Seton Hall School of Law, Center for Social Justice. December 13, 2007.

Liptak, Adam. "Blocking Parts of Arizona Law, Justices Allow Its Centerpiece." *New York Times.* June 25, 2012.

Llorente, Elizabeth. "New Obama Directive Aims to Stop Detention of Undocumented Parents with Minor Children." Fox News Latino. August 26, 2013. Available at http://latino.foxnews.com/latino/politics/2013/08/26/new-obama-directive-urges-discretion-for-undocumented-parents-minors/.

"Local Officials Adopt New, Harder Tactics on Illegal Immigrants." *New York Times.* June 9, 2008.

Lodhia, Sharmila. "Constructing an Imperfect Citizen-Subject: Globalization, National 'Security,' and Violence against South Asian Women." *WSQ: Women's Studies Quarterly* 38, nos. 1–2 (2010): 168–182.

Lombardo, Kristen. "American Nightmare." *Boston Globe,* City Weekly Section. May 5, 2002.

Lopez, Ian Haney. *White by Law: The Legal Construction of Race in America.* New York: New York University Press, 2006.

Lopez, Mark Hugo. *The Hispanic Vote in 2008.* Washington, DC: Pew Hispanic Center, 2008.

Lopez, Mark Hugo, and Susan Minushkin. *2008 National Survey of Latinos: Hispanics See Their Situation in the U.S. Deteriorating; Oppose Key Immigration Enforcement Measures.* Washington, DC: Pew Hispanic Center, September 2008.

Mahmood, Saba. "Feminist Theory, Embodiment, and the Docile Agent: Some Reflections on the Egyptian Islamic Revival." *Cultural Anthropology* 16, no. 2 (2001): 202–236.

Martinez, Gebe. 2008. "Hot Spot for Illegal Immigration." *Politico.* April 17, 2008.

Massey, Douglas S., Jorge Durand, and Nolan J. Malone. *Beyond Smoke and Mirrors: Mexican Immigration in an Era of Economic Integration.* New York: Russell Sage Foundation, 2003.

Mears, Bill. "High Court Backs Arizona Immigration Law That Punishes Businesses." CNN. May 26, 2011. Available at www.cnn.com/2011/US/05/26/scotus.arizona.law/index.html.

Mendelson, Margot, Shayna Strom, and Michael Wishni. *Collateral Damage: An Examination of ICE's Fugitive Operations Program.* A Report of the Migration Policy Institute. Washington, DC: Migration Policy Institute, 2009.

Minushkin, Susan, and Mark Hugo Lopez. *The Hispanic Vote in the 2008 Democratic Presidential Primaries.* Washington, DC: Pew Hispanic Center, 2008.

Moraga, Cherrie. *Loving in the War Years: Lo Que Nunca Paso Por Sus Labios.* Boston: South End Press, 1983.

Moraga, Cherrie, and Gloria Anzaldúa, eds. *This Bridge Called My Back: A Collection of Writings by Radical Women of Color.* Watertown, MA: Persephone Press, 1981.

Morse, Ann. "Arizona's Immigration Enforcement Laws: An Overview of SB 1070 and HB 2162." National Conference of State Legislatures. July 7, 2010. Available at www.ncsl.org/?tabid=20263.

———. "E-Verify: Frequently Asked Questions." Immigrant Policy Project. National Conference of State Legislatures. February 4, 2010. Available at www.ncsl.org/default.aspx?tabid=13127.

Morton, John. "Exercising Prosecutorial Discretion Consistent with the Civil Immigration Enforcement Priorities of the Agency for the Apprehension, Detention, and Removal of Aliens." Memorandum for All Field Office Directors, All Special Agents in Charge, All Chief Counsel. Immigration and Customs Enforcement. Department of Homeland Security. Policy Number: 10075.1. June 17, 2011. Available at www.ice.gov/doclib/secure-communities/pdf/prosecutorial-discretion-memo.pdf.

Motel, Seth, and Eileen Patten. *Statistical Portrait of the Foreign-Born Population in the United States, 2011.* Table 5. Pew Research Hispanic Trends Project. January 29, 2013.

Murillo, Mario. *Islands of Resistance: Puerto Rico, Vieques, and U.S. Policy.* New York: Seven Stories Press, 2011.

Myers, Julie, Assistant Secretary, U.S. Department of Homeland Security. Letter to Ms. Christina DeConcini, Directory of Policy, National Immigration Forum. July 6, 2007.

National Hispanic Leadership Agenda. *How the Latino Community's Agenda on Immigration Enforcement and Reform Has Suffered since 9/11.* Washington, DC. 2004.

National Immigrant Justice Center. "Fact Sheet: Children Detained by the Department of Homeland Security in Adult Detention Facilities." May 2013.

National Network of Immigrant and Refugee Rights. "Increased Security Scrutiny Keeps Refugee Families Apart." Fall/Winter 2003.

Nevins, Joseph. *Operation Gatekeeper and Beyond: The War on "Illegals" and the Remaking of the U.S.-Mexico Boundary.* 2nd ed. New York: Routledge, 2010.

Newton, Lina. "'It Is Not a Question of Being Anti-immigration': Categories of Deservedness in Immigration Policymaking." In *Deserving and Entitled: Social Constructions and Public Policy,* edited by Anne Schneider and Helen Ingram, 139–171. New York: State University of New York Press, 2005.

Ngai, Mae M. "Birthright Citizenship and the Alien Citizen." *Fordham Law Review* 75, no. 5 (2007): 2521–2530. Available at http://ir.lawnet.fordham.edu/cgi/viewcontent.cgi?article=4263&context=flr.

———. *Impossible Subjects: Illegal Aliens and the Making of Modern America.* Princeton, NJ: Princeton University Press, 2004.

Norlen, Nick. "Immigration Raid Tactics Alarm Princeton Advocates." *Princeton Packet.* January 25, 2008.

Obama, Barack. "Address to the National Council of La Raza." NCLR Annual Conference. San Diego, CA. July 12, 2008.

———. "Remarks by the President at Cinco de Mayo Reception." White House, Office of the Press Secretary. May 5, 2010. Available at www.whitehouse.gov/the-press-office/remarks-president-cinco-de-mayo-reception.

———. "Remarks by the President on Comprehensive Immigration Reform, Del Sol High School, Las Vegas, Nevada." White House, Office of the Press Secretary. January 29, 2013.

———. "Remarks of President Barack Obama—As Prepared for Delivery, State of the Union Address." White House, Office of the Press Secretary. February 12, 2013.

———. "Transcript: Obama's Immigration Speech." *Washington Post.* November 20, 2014. Available at www.washingtonpost.com/politics/transcript-obamas-immigration-speech/2014/11/20/14ba8042-7117-11e4-893f-86bd390a3340_story.html.

———. "Transcript: Obama's Victory Speech." November 7, 2012. *Political Ticker. . . .* Available at http://politicalticker.blogs.cnn.com/2012/11/07/transcript-obamas-victory-speech/.

Office of Public Affairs, U.S. Department of Homeland Security. "Fact Sheet: Section 287(g) Immigration and Nationality Act, U.S. Immigration and Customs Enforcement," August 16, 2006.

Okihiro, Gary. *Whispered Silences: Japanese Americans and World War II.* Seattle: University of Washington Press, 1996.

Ong, Aihwa. *Buddha Is Hiding: Refugees, Citizenship, the New America.* Berkeley: University of California Press, 2003.

Pearce, Russell. "Arizona or San Francisco: Which Path on Immigration?" *Human Events* 66, no. 18 (2010): 1–10.

Peele, Thomas, and Daniel J. Willis. "Surveillance: Civil Rights Groups Seek End to Collection of Government Reports on 'Suspicious Activity' by Americans." San Jose Mercury News.com. September 20, 2013.

Perez, Thomas E., Assistant Attorney General, U.S. Department of Justice, Civil Rights Division. Letter to Mr. Bill Montgomery, County Attorney, Maricopa County, Re: United States' Investigation of the Maricopa County Sheriff's Office. December 15, 2011.

Peterson, Jonathan. "Response to Terror: INS Fugitives to Be Listed on FBI Database." *Los Angeles Times.* December 6, 2001.

Peterson, Susan Rae. "Coercion and Rape: The State as a Male Protection Racket." In *Feminism and Philosophy,* edited by Mary Vetterling-Braggin, Frederick A. Elliston, and Jane English, 360–371. New Jersey: Littlefield Adams, 1977.

Peterson, V. Spike. "Thinking Through Intersectionality and War." *Race, Gender and Class* 14, nos. 3–4 (2007): 10–27.

Pew Hispanic Center. *National Survey of Latinos: As Illegal Immigration Issue Heats Up, Hispanics Feel a Chill.* Washington, DC: Pew Hispanic Center, 2007.

Pohlman, H. L. *Terrorism and the Constitution: The Post-9/11 Cases.* Boulder, CO: Rowman and Littlefield, 2008.

Portes, Alejandro, and Robert L. Bach. *Latin Journey: Cuban and Mexican Immigrants in the United States.* Berkeley: University of California Press, 1985.

Portes, Alejandro, and Ruben Rumbaut. *Immigrant America.* Berkeley: University of California Press, 1990.

Preston, Julia. "Obama to Push Immigration Bill as One Priority." *New York Times.* April 9, 2009.

———. "Students Spared amid an Increase in Deportations." *New York Times.* August 8, 2010.

Preston, Julia, and John H. Cushman. "Obama to Permit Young Migrants to Remain in the U.S." *New York Times.* June 15, 2012.

Puar, Jaspir K. "Abu Ghraib: Arguing against Exceptionalism." *Feminist Studies* 30, no. 2 (2004): 522–534.

Reisler, Mark. "Always the Laborer, Never the Citizen: Anglo Perceptions of the Mexican Immigrant during the 1920s." *Pacific Historical Review* 45, no. 2 (1976): 231–254.

Rocco, Raymond. *Transforming Citizenship: Democracy, Membership and Belonging in Latino Communities.* East Lansing: Michigan State University Press, 2014.

Rodriguez, Clara. "A Summary of Puerto Rican Migration to the United States." In *Challenging Fronteras: Structuring Latina and Latino Lives in the U.S.,* edited by Mary Romero, Pierrette Hondagneu-Sotelo, and Vilma Ortiz, 101–113. New York: Routledge, 1997.

Rovira, Guillermo. *Mujeres de Maiz: La Voz de Las Indıgenas de Chiapas y la Rebelion Zapatista*. Mexico City, Mexico: Virus, 1996.

Rubin, Alissa J. "Afghans Detail Detention in 'Black Jail' at U.S. Base." *New York Times*. November 28, 2009. Available at www.nytimes.com/2009/11/29/world/asia/29bagram.html?_r=1&hpw.

Ruiz, Rosanna. "Airport Sweep Nets 143 Arrests: Workers Charged with False IDs." *Houston Chronicle*, Section A. September 10, 2002.

———."Airport Sweep Outpaces Other Cities' Efforts: Houston Nets Most Indictments." *Houston Chronicle*, Section A. September 11, 2002.

Ryan, Jason, Matthew Jaffe, and Devin Dwyer. "Obama 'Scheming' on Immigrant Amnesty? Memo Draws Republican Fire." ABC News. July 30, 2010.

Saito, Natsu. 2001. "Symbolism under Siege: Japanese American Redress and the 'Racing' of Arab Americans as 'Terrorists.'" *Asian Law Journal* 8 (2001): 11–26.

Samora, Julian. *Los Mojados: The Wetback Story*. Notre Dame, IN: University of Notre Dame Press, 1971.

Sampaio, Anna. "Latinas and Electoral Politics: Expanding Participation and Power in State and National Elections." In *Gender and Elections: Shaping the Future of American Politics*, edited by Susan J. Carroll and Richard Fox, 146–166. 3rd ed. New York: Cambridge University Press, 2014.

———. "Transforming Chicana/o and Latina/o Politics: Globalization, and the Formation of Transnational Resistance in the U.S. and Chiapas." In *Transnational Latino/a Communities: Politics, Process, and Cultures*, edited by Carlos Vélez-Ibáñez and Anna Sampaio, 47–71. Boulder, CO: Rowman and Littlefield, 2002.

———. "Transnational Feminisms in a New Global Matrix: *Hermanas en La Lucha*." *International Feminist Journal of Politics* 6, no. 2 (2004): 181–206.

Sandoval, Chela. "U.S. Third World Feminism: The Theory and Method of Oppositional Consciousness in the Postmodern World." *Genders* 10 (1991): 1–24.

Sandweg, John, Acting Director, U.S. Immigration and Customs Enforcement. "Facilitating Parental Interests in the Course of Civil Immigration Enforcement Activities." Department of Homeland Security. Policy Number: 11064.1. August, 23 2013. Available at www.ice.gov/doclib/detention-reform/pdf/parental_interest_directive_signed.pdf.

Savage, Charlie, Edward Wyatt, and Peter Baker. "U.S. Confirms That It Gathers Online Data Overseas." *New York Times*. June 6, 2013. Available at www.nytimes.com/2013/06/07/us/nsa-verizon-calls.html?emc=etal.

Schneider, Anne L., and Helen M. Ingram. *Policy Design for Democracy*. Lawrence: University Press of Kansas, 1997.

———. "Social Construction of Target Population: Implications for Politics and Policy." *American Political Science Review* 87, no. 2 (1993): 334–347.

Scott, Joan. "Gender: A Useful Category for Historical Analysis." *American Historical Review* 91 (1986): 1053–1075.

"Secretary Seeks Review of Immigration Raid." *New York Times*. February 26, 2009.

Senator Gould. Testimony Regarding Senate Bill 1070. Arizona State Senate. 49th Legislature, Second Regular Session. Final Reading. April 19, 2010. Available at http://azleg.granicus.com/MediaPlayer.php?view_id=13&clip_id=7519.

Senator Melvin. Testimony Regarding Senate Bill 1070. Arizona State Senate. 49th Legislature, Second Regular Session. Final Reading. April 19, 2010. Available at http://azleg.granicus.com/MediaPlayer.php?view_id=13&clip_id=7519.

Senator Pearce. Testimony Regarding Senate Bill 1070. Arizona State Senate. 49th Legislature, Second Regular Session. Final Reading. April 19, 2010. Available at http:// azleg.granicus.com/MediaPlayer.php?view_id=13&clip_id=7519.

Sheridan, Mary Beth. "INS Seeks Law Enforcement Aid in Crackdown Move: Targets 300,000 Foreign Nationals in U.S. Despite Deportation Orders." *Washington Post.* December 6, 2001.

Shulman, Robin. "Immigration Raid Rips Families." *Washington Post.* March 18, 2007. Available at www.washingtonpost.com/wp-dyn/content/article/2007/03/17/ AR2007031701113.html.

Sklair, Leslie. *Assembling for Development: The* Maquila *Industry in Mexico and the United States.* San Diego: Center for U.S. Mexican Studies, 1993.

Smith, Amy. "Operation Tarmac: Overkill?" *Austin Chronicle.* March 14, 2003.

Standart, Sister Mary Collete. "The Sonoran Migration to California, 1848–1856: A Study in Prejudice." *Southern California Quarterly* 57 (Fall 1976): 333–357.

Stiehm, Judith. "The Protected, the Protector, the Defender." *Women's Studies International Forum* 5, no. 3 (1982): 367–376.

Street, Paul. "Background Check: Operation Tarmac and the Many Faces of Terror." *Z Magazine.* January 11, 2003. Available at www.zmag.org/sustainers/content/2003-01/11street.cfm.

Suárez-Orozco, M. "Latin American Immigration to the United States." In *The United States and Latin America: The New Agenda,* edited by V. Bulmer-Thomas and J. Dunkerly, 227–244. Cambridge, MA: Harvard University Press, 1999.

Suthers, John, "Over 100 Workers at DIA Indicted for Falsifying Security Applications—All Had Access to Restricted Areas." Press Release. United States Attorney's Office, Colorado. September 17, 2002. Available at www.usdoj.gov/usao/ co/091702Frame1Source1.htm.

Takaki, Ronald. *Strangers from a Different Shore: A History of Asian Americans.* New York: Little, Brown, 1989.

Talhelm, Jennifer. "Raids in Six States May Be Largest Ever." Associated Press. December 13, 2006.

Tebo, Margaret Graham. "The Closing Door: U.S. Policies Leave Immigrants Separate and Unequal." *American Bar Association Journal* 8, no. 9 (2002): 43–47.

Thornburgh, Nathan. "The Battle for Arizona." *Time* 175, no. 23 (2010): 38–43.

Tiano, Susan. *Patriarchy on the Line: Labor, Gender, and Ideology in the Mexican Maquila Industry.* Philadelphia: Temple University Press, 1994.

U.S. Citizenship and Immigration Services. "Executive Actions on Immigration." November 21, 2014. Available at www.uscis.gov/immigrationaction.

U.S. Customs and Border Protection. "CBP Statistics as of Fiscal Year 2009." February 16, 2010.

———. "Secure Borders, Safe Travel, Legal Trade: U.S. Customs and Border Protection Fiscal Year 2009–2014 Strategic Plan." July 2009.

U.S. Department of Justice, Office of the Inspector General. "The September 11 Detainees: A Review of the Treatment of Aliens Held on Immigration Charges in Connection with the Investigation of the September 11 Attacks." Washington, DC. April 2003.

U.S. Department of Labor, Annual Report of the Commissioner-General of Immigration. Washington, DC. 1924.

U.S. Department of State. "Report on the Taliban's War against Women: Executive Summary." Washington, DC. November 17, 2001. Available at www.state.gov/g/drl/rls/6183.htm.

"U.S. Ends Job 'Safety' Immigration Raids." Associated Press. March 29, 2006.

U.S. General Accounting Office. "Report to Congressional Committees-Aviation Security: Computer-Assisted Passenger Prescreening System Faces Significant Implementation Challenges." GAO-04-385.February 2004.

U.S. Immigration and Customs Enforcement. "Fact Sheet: Worksite Enforcement Overview." April 30, 2009. Available at www.ice.gov/news/library/factsheets/worksite.htm.

———. "FY 2012 ICE Immigration Removals." December 18, 2013. Available at www.ice.gov/removal-statistics/2012statistics.htm.

———. "FY 2013 ICE Immigration Removals, ERO Annual Report." December 18, 2013. Available at www.ice.gov/doclib/about/offices/ero/pdf/2013-ice-immigration-removals.pdf.

———. "ICE Multifaceted Strategy Leads to Record Enforcement Results." October 23, 2008.

———. "ICE Strategic Plan FY 2010–2014." 2010.

"U.S. Replaces Noisy Immigration Raids at Place of Employment with 'Silent Audits.'" *Business of Homeland Security.* July 12, 2010.

Vedantam, Shankar. "Several States Want Court Ruling on Birthright Citizenship." *Washington Post.* January 6, 2011.

Vicini, James. 2011. "U.S. Supreme Court to Decide Arizona Immigration Law." Reuters. December 12, 2011.

Vock, Daniel C. "With Little Choice, Alabama Backs Down on Immigration Law." *Stateline.* Pew Charitable Trusts. October 30, 2013. Available at www.pewstates.org.

Wald, Matthew. "Officials Arrest 104 Airport Workers in Washington Area." *New York Times.* April 24, 2002.

Waldenstein, David. "Arizona Immigration Law Criticized by Mets' Barajas." *New York Times.* May 2, 2010.

Walker, Alice. *In Search of Our Mothers' Gardens: Womanist Prose.* Orlando, FL: Harcourt Brace Jovanovich, 1983.

Walker, Marilyn, and Frank Lindh. "Interview with Amy Goodman." *Democracy Now.* July 31, 2009. Available at www.democracynow.org/2009/7/31/exclusive_john_walker_lindhs_parents_discuss.

Webb, John K. "Use of the Social Security Fraud Statute in the Battle against Terrorism 42 U.S.C. §408 (a)(7)(A)(C)." *United States Attorney's Bulletin* 50, no. 3 (2002).

Wessler, Seth Freed. *The Perilous Intersection of Immigration: Enforcement and the Child Welfare System.* Applied Research Center. 2011. Available at http://arc.org/shatteredfamilies.

Womack, John, Jr. *Rebellion in Chiapas: An Historical Reader.* New York: New Press, 1999.

Young, Iris Marion. "The Logic of Masculinist Protection: Reflections on the Current Security State." *Signs: Journal of Women in Culture and Society* 29 (2003): 1–25.

Yuval-Davis, Nira. *The Politics of Belonging: Intersectional Contestations.* London: Sage, 2011.

Index

Anna Sampaio, Associate Professor of Ethnic Studies and Political Science and Director of Ethnic Studies at Santa Clara University, is the co-editor (with Carlos Vélez-Ibáñez) of *Transnational Latina/o Communities: Politics, Processes, Cultures.*